# Reimagining Schools

In the **World Library of Educationalists**, international experts themselves compile career-long collections of what they judge to be their finest pieces – extracts from books, key articles, salient research findings, major theoretical, and practical contributions – so the world can read them in a single manageable volume. Readers will be able to follow themes and strands of the topic and see how their work contributes to the development of the field.

Elliot W. Eisner has spent the last 40 years researching, thinking and writing about some of the key and enduring issues in Arts Education, Curriculum Studies, and Qualitative Research. He has contributed over 20 books and 500 articles to the field.

In *Reimagining Schools*, Elliot Eisner brings together 21 of his key writings in one place. Starting with a specially written Introduction, which gives an overview of his career and contextualises his selection, the chapters cover a wide range of issues, including:

- children and art
- the uses of educational connoisseurship
- aesthetic modes of knowing
- absolutism and relativism in curriculum theory
- education reform and the ecology of schooling
- the future of education research.

This is a must-have book for anyone wishing to know more about the development of Arts Education, Curriculum Studies, and Qualitative Research over the last four decades, and about Elliot Eisner's contribution to these exciting fields.

**Elliot W. Eisner** is Lee Jacks Professor of Education and Professor of Art at Stanford University.

Contributors to the series include: Richard Aldrich, Stephen J. Ball, John Elliott, Elliot W. Eisner, Howard Gardner, John K. Gilbert, Ivor F. Goodson, David Labaree, John White, E. C. Wragg.

# World Library of Educationalists series

Other books in the series:

**Lessons from History of Education**
The selected works of Richard Aldrich
*Richard Aldrich*

**Education Policy and Social Class**
The selected works of Stephen J. Ball
*Stephen J. Ball*

**Reimagining Schools**
The selected works of Elliot W. Eisner
*Elliot W. Eisner*

**Reflecting Where the Action Is**
The selected works of John Elliott
*John Elliott*

**Development and Education of the Mind**
The selected works of Howard Gardner
*Howard Gardner*

**Constructing Worlds through Science Education**
The selected works of John K. Gilbert
*John K. Gilbert*

**Learning, Curriculum and Life Politics**
The selected works of Ivor F. Goodson
*Ivor F. Goodson*

**The Curriculum and the Child**
The selected works of John White
*John White*

**The Art and Science of Teaching and Learning**
The selected works of Ted Wragg
*E. C. Wragg*

# Reimagining Schools

The selected works of Elliot W. Eisner

## Elliot W. Eisner

 Routledge
Taylor & Francis Group

LONDON AND NEW YORK

First published 2005
by Routledge
2 Park Square, Milton Park, Abingdon, Oxon OX14 4RN

Simultaneously published in the USA and Canada
by Routledge
270 Madison Ave, New York, NY 10016

*Routledge is an imprint of the Taylor & Francis Group*

© 2005 Elliot W. Eisner

Typeset in Sabon by
Newgen Imaging Systems (P) Ltd, Chennai, India
Printed and bound in Great Britain by
MPG Books Ltd, Bodmin

*British Library Cataloguing in Publication Data*
A catalogue record for this book is available
from the British Library

*Library of Congress Cataloging in Publication Data*
A catalog record for this book has been requested

ISBN 0–415–36644–5 (hbk)
ISBN 0–415–36645–3 (pbk)

# CONTENTS

# ACKNOWLEDGMENTS

The following articles have been reproduced with the kind permission of the respective journals

"Can educational research inform educational practice?" *Phi Delta Kappan*, 1984, 65(7): 447–452.

"Children's creativity in art: a study of types." *American Educational Research Journal*, 1965, 2(3): 125–136.

"Educational connoisseurship and criticism: their form and functions in educational evaluation." *Journal of Aesthetic Education*, 1976, 135–150.

"Educational objectives: help or hindrance?" *The School Review*, 1967, 75(3): 250–260.

"Educational reform and the ecology of schooling." *Teachers College Record*, 1992, 93(4): 610–627.

"Forms of understanding and the future of educational research." *Educational Research*, 1993, 22(7): 5–11.

"From episteme to phronesis to artistry in the study and improvement of teaching." *Teaching and Teacher Education*, 2002, 18: 375–385.

"On the differences between scientific and artistic approaches to qualitative research." *Educational Researcher*, 1981, 10(4): 5–9.

"On the uses of educational connoisseurship and criticism for evaluating classroom life." *Teachers College Record*, 1977, 78(3): 345–358.

"Slippery moves and blind alleys: my travels with absolutism and relativism in Curriculum Theory." *Curriculum Inquiry*, 1989, 19(1): 59–65.

"Standards for American schools: help or hindrance?" *Phi Delta Kappan*, 1995, 76(10): 758–764.

"The celebration of thinking." *Educational Horizons*, 1987, 66(1): 1–4.

"The misunderstood role of the arts in human development." *Phi Delta Kappan*, 1992, 73(8): 591–595.

"The primacy of experience and the politics of method." *Educational Researcher*, 1988, 17(5): 15–20.

"The promise and perils of alternative forms of data representation." *Educational Researcher*, 1997, 26(6): 4–10.

"The role of the arts in cognition and curriculum." *Journal of Art & Design Education*, 1986, 5(1 and 2): 57–67.

"What can education learn from the arts about the practice of education?" *Journal of Curriculum and Supervision*, 2002, 18(1): 4–16.

"What do children learn when they paint." *Art Education*, 1978, 21(3): 6–10.

"What does it mean to say a school is doing well?" *Phi Delta Kappan*, 2001, 82(5): 367–372.

**The following chapters have been reproduced with the kind permission of the respective publishers**

"Aesthetic modes of knowing," 84th Yearbook of the National Society for the Study of Education, *Learning and Teaching the Ways of Knowing*, Chicago, IL: University of Chicago Press, 1985, pp. 23–36.

"Instructional and expressive educational objectives: their formulation and use in curriculum," W. James Popham, E. Eisner, H. Sullivan, and W. Bruneau (eds), *Instructional Objectives*, Chicago, IL: McNally & Co., 1969 (Monograph Series on Curriculum Evaluation), pp. 1–18.

# INTRODUCTION
## My journey as a writer in the field of education

The opportunity that the editors of this collection of volumes have afforded me is rarely available to most who write in a field. I wish to start my comments concerning the evolution of my work by expressing my gratitude to the publishers for making the opportunity and the entire series possible.

Anyone who knows my background will also know that I started out life as a painter. I mention art and its place in my life because it is central to my work in education. I tend to look at problems and opportunities with an eye towards their aesthetic qualities. I also, though long ago, had a major interest in understanding children's creativity, an interest that is reflected in the first paper in this volume. "Children's creativity in art: a study of types," was a distillation from my doctoral dissertation at the University of Chicago. Subsequently it was published in the *American Educational Research Journal* and, to my surprise and delight, received the Palmer O. Johnson Memorial Award for what was considered the best article published in volume 2 of that Journal in 1965.

Forty years is a long time to work in any field, but if my interests and views were transient, they would have relatively little significance. On the contrary, my interest in the arts and to a lesser degree in creativity and my orientation to knowledge as the symbolic representation of human understanding were all shaped by my experience as a painter, first as a child in elementary school and later following university studies in the field of design. "Children's creativity in art: a study of types," was an effort to bring together my work and interests in both art and in creativity. As I said, to my delight, it fared well in halls populated largely by social scientists.

"Educational objectives: help or hindrance?" was published a couple of years later and has, since its publication in the *School Review* been reprinted in eighteen books of readings. The piece is short, to the point and, again, I was delighted and surprised to have such interest applied to my work.

The position taken in "Educational objectives: help or hindrance?" reflects a deep-seated *dis*interest in approaches to teaching that were predicated on the view that the teacher's job was to get all of the children to the same destination at about the same point in time. That certainly was not, in my view, what artistry in education was about. Artistry courts surprise, it plays at the edge of possibility, it trades in ambiguities, it addresses dilemmas, and it provides a certain kind of delight, if one can take some risks. Heterogeneity, or better yet, diversity of outcome, is, in general, a much more important form of educational realization than an image of teaching that displays an army of students marching in step to the same place.

I suspect the interest in "Educational objectives: help or hindrance?" was due to the fact that it was expressing values that were widely shared but not made public. Despite a covert attraction to the possibilities of what might be called romanticism in education there is also an attractiveness to a position that embraces rigor, precision, and predictability. There is a certain sense of strength in embracing a practice that is guided by as hard a science as one can get. "Educational objectives: help or hindrance?" however, adumbrated another vision and, as I said, there were a large number of "takers." The view expressed in that article was expanded and refined in the distinctions I made later between instructional objectives, problem solving objectives, and expressive outcomes. Instructional objectives, I argued, seeks to realize goals whose form and content are already known. What one seeks when teaching is at its best *in this form of practice* is the creation of an isomorphic relationship between what is intended and what is realized. In problem-solving objectives, the end may be known such as the construction of a house that has five bedrooms, one kitchen, a dining room, and a living room, but the particular form it will take has not. The specifications can be general, but applicable to prospective solutions. Thus in problem-solving objectives, the aim is clear, but the method and form of its solution is not; there are many ways to design five bedroom houses. It is precisely the kind of problems that designers, both industrial and graphic, deal with every day in their work.

Expressive outcomes, (originally called expressive objectives until I realized the mistake) are efforts to describe what the actual outcomes have been and, as we know, the actual outcomes both exceed and fall short of our intentions. Students learn both more and less than what teachers hope for. So, expressive outcomes are determined after the fact by looking backward to identify the consequences of the activities and pedagogies that were employed. In looking back at side effects, one might discover that they are the main effect. Expressive outcomes seek not predictability, but visibility. They help us see the consequences of our own actions. Those consequences, once understood, can provide a useful platform for subsequent pedagogical efforts.

A subsequent conceptual move for me pertains to the concepts of connoisseurship and criticism. Both concepts and the approach to the study of classrooms and, frankly to virtually anything, are rooted in the arts. In the field of the visual arts, connoisseurs are people for whom small differences are large differences. Questions of authenticity, value, merit, and meaning and significance are a part of what connoisseurs are supposed to discern. Critics, however, are people who are able, through their writing or speaking, to reeducate the perception of the work at hand. Indeed, John Dewey describes the aim of criticism as the reeducation of the perception of the work of art. Connoisseurs can know in private, critics, however, must transform what they have experienced into language capable of influencing the perception of the work by others. That general model, so powerful in the arts, I argued, could be applied to the study of teaching. Surely teaching at its best is an art form. Classrooms are places in which dramas are enacted. Why not use concepts from the arts as a basic framework for revealing qualities of classroom life?

The idea of using expressive narratives to facilitate the perceptions of others as they try to understand classrooms is a counter-intuitive activity when it comes to educational research and even educational evaluation. Questions of subjectivity, reliability, validity, and all the standard conceptual paraphernalia of positivist social science come into play. Nevertheless, the people who embraced my view of objectives also found attractive my view of connoisseurship and criticism and its potential role in the improvement of education.

I must say the ramifications of these two concepts yielded more than I expected. The specific terms of "connoisseurship" and "criticism," are not necessarily used, but the general spirit of the effort is shared and growing more widespread. For example, interest in narrative and in the aesthetic shaping of language, not for ornamental reasons but for epistemological ones, is not at all uncommon. The paradigm for practice is no longer dominated by a rigorous effort at quantification, although efforts are made at the moment to return the field of educational research to those methodological ideals. There is growing interest in what is called qualitative research, or qualitative inquiry, in arts based research, in post-modern efforts to exploit the capacities of language and other symbol systems to reveal what language, treated literally or even logically, and especially quantitatively, cannot address.

In 1978, I wrote a paper titled "What do children learn when they paint?" The significance of this particular piece pertains to my realization that engagement in painting is about a lot more than engagement in painting. There are various skills developed, attitudes cultivated, concepts embraced, realizations fostered that come from the process of painting, particularly in the context of working with other students. The point here being that if someone wants to understand the educational consequences of art, or science, or history, one needs to understand the context and the demands made by tasks in those fields. Those demands influence what students have the opportunity to learn. As Dewey puts it, "It is one of the greatest of educational fallacies to assume the student learns only what he is being taught at the time." Thus, understanding what children learn when they paint means paying attention to a lot more than painting. Their social interaction in an art room also matters. A simple observation, but I think a very important one.

My developing interests in epistemological issues seemed to me to be potentially very important since I believe how we conceive of knowing, whether in a school or in a university research center, has profound effects on what we believe is credible. Does art provide knowledge? Can a work of art be "wrong?" If art provides knowledge, what kind does it provide? Do the arts have anything to teach about the world within which they reside?

Questions such as these intrigue me and the differences between scientific forms of inquiry and artistic forms of inquiry seem to me to be extraordinarily important in making policy decisions regarding what schools should teach and how they should assess what has taken place when they do so. My paper, "On the differences between artistic and scientific approaches to qualitative research," was designed to explore the similarities and differences between the arts and science as modes of inquiry. Although I would write the paper differently today, the topic and gist of the paper forecast an interest in epistemology that would continue to develop over the years. This interest is reflected in my paper, "The role of the arts in cognition and curriculum."

Marrying the arts and cognition has not been all that common. We tend to think about the arts as trafficking in the emotions, while the sciences deal with matters of cognition. I reject such a dichotomy and regard any practice done well as potentially artistic in character. Thus, the practice of science – when practiced well – is an art form. So is painting. Exploring the differences and similarities between the arts and the sciences is one way to become grounded with respect to what it means to be knowledgeable.

The question that often torments me is whether we can tolerate an approach to human understanding that cannot be demonstrated to be in error. But, at the same time, whether the concept of error with respect to the content of an image is an appropriate criterion to apply is itself a debatable issue. How then do we discriminate between art forms that inform and art forms that mislead? These are some of the questions that attract my attention.

Another aspect of my work, which warrants mention is my interest in what is known as "the curriculum field." I am deeply interested in how we decide what to teach and how to reform schools so that they genuinely educate. So much of what we do in the name of reform is little more than trying to "tinker towards utopia," as my colleagues David Tyack and Larry Cuban (1995) would put it. My background in the arts has taught me to try to pay attention to configurations, to the ways in which components relate to each other and how it is that they influence each other. Those considerations apply to the reform of schools as well. Curriculum, when I was making decisions about what to focus upon in my doctoral studies, appeared to me to reflect the broadest of the fields or specializations that were offered at that time. Educational ethnography was not a viable alternative and the terms qualitative research seemed to be oxymoronic in character, if they were used at all.

The dominant paradigm into which I was socialized as a doctoral student at the University of Chicago was strongly conceptual, but operationally positivistic. The experiment was the gold standard.

One might say that my work in education has attempted to reconceptualize the ways in which we think about teaching, school structure, educational aims, pedagogical practices, and educational evaluation. They are all related and I wanted to show how. In addition, I was interested in looking at educational ideas in a fresh way. For example, the distinction that I drew between teaching and instruction, the former having a softer, warmer, more personal character than the term instruction, was, I think, important to point out. Instruction one might receive in the army or the church, but teaching has a more maternal character to it. The terms "individualized instruction" might be replaced by the terms "personalized teaching." Language matters and in some of my work I tried to show just why it does.

In a way, from the perspective that personal history provides, I was interested in problematizing ideas that seemed to me to be inhospitable to the kind of educational life that I hoped individuals would lead. I was less interested in achievement, than in the promotion of inquiry. I was more interested in the journey than in the destination. I felt more strongly about apt metaphor than precise measurement. I was more interested in searching than in finding, more interested in being than in becoming. Put another way, my views of education, which have shaped my language and the concepts that I pay attention to, was a kind of – and still is a kind of – romanticism, or at least a view that is touched, some would say tainted by, romanticism. I am far less interested in making the world more tidy than in making it more interesting.

For a period of time, during the 1960s and 1970s, there was a strong mix of both a romantic orientation to educational practice and a tough minded view centered on accountability and the measurement paraphernalia that went with that notion. For many, the concept that got at the heart of how we could improve schools was accountability. If we only made people accountable, then they would be held responsible for their results and with responsibility comes effectiveness, and with effectiveness, our whole society can be improved.

I regard such aspirations as naïve. People need to be accountable, but not solely in terms of measured outcomes. The outcomes of education are far wider and it is critical that we look not only at the intended outcomes, but at both the collateral damage and the virtues that we might be achieving, unbeknownst to us. My work has, I think, provided some degree of voice to people who resonate with what I have written and who find in it a substance that they feel reflects their own views as well. Authors not only provide their own voice, they also provide voice to readers who are unable to articulate what they would have said had they been able to write.

In my paper, "The primacy of experience and the politics of method," I tried to get at a root idea, namely, that decisions about method are not simply decisions about method, they are also political decisions that have to do with who is competent and who is not, who is powerful and who is weak, who is skilled and who is unskilled, who does work that is relevant and who does not. When new methods get legitimized, the range of relevant competencies expands. For those who are already riding high in the field, there can be some degree of threat from efforts to expand or redefine what counts as useful research and what functions as meaningful evaluation. While I don't think of myself as a radical, I suspect I move more to the left in the methodological spectrum than to the right.

My epistemological interests emerged in a particularly vivid way in my Presidential Address to the American Educational Research Association. The article titled, "Forms of understanding and the future of educational research," was, in fact, my Presidential Address. In it I used multimedia material to empirically illustrate what I was claiming, namely, that the kind of understanding we secure is not indifferent to the forms we have selected to make such understanding possible. The meanings, for example, secured through poetry are not identical with the meanings capable of being expressed through prose, or through literal language, or through number. Dance gives us a world different from poetry and the visual arts and video and film do other things as well. I was trying, in that paper and in the address that preceded it, to present something of an invitation to those in the audience and in the field at large to consider other ways of thinking about both the perception of the educational world they care about, and the way in which that world is revealed. The tools, I argued, that we know how to use have an enormous impact on what it is that we are able to see and to say. Forms of representation both reveal and conceal aspects of the world and therefore had not only implications for understanding, they had implications for the politics of the field itself.

The implications of the views I was addressing get articulated in a debate between Howard Gardner and me regarding the question, "Should a novel count as a dissertation in education?" Gardner and I, friends of longstanding, differ on the central issue. Gardner believes that the role of the doctoral program is to train competent journeymen. I believe that the key role of the doctoral preparation is to prepare students to think imaginatively about the ways in which the educational world can be studied and improved. These debates received much attention in the American Educational Research Association, and represent, I think, the kind of debate that the field needs more of. The debates were reflective, but not hostile.

Another area in the theoretical landscape in education within which I have written pertains to the relationship of standards to curriculum planning and to assessment. As almost everyone knows, there is a strong push in the United States towards formulation of standards as a mechanism for guiding the creation of curriculum and for assessing the consequences of the curriculum after it has been taught. The general idea is to develop a level of specificity that makes the empirical identification of consequences possible. The approach has a strong rational orientation and is, I believe, superficially attractive.

If one consults the history of American education from the turn of the twentieth century onwards, it is possible to find periods during that history in which standards or what was called objectives were the rage. There is an appeal to the idea that if one could only specify expectations and do so at a level of specificity that makes their empirical identification possible, educational practice would be significantly improved. The accountability movement, also strong in the United States, reflects such a belief. The need to measure outcomes is a condition that accountable systems need to meet.

Yet, precision and predictability in teaching is not teaching's strong hallmark. Teachers are, among other things, opportunists who exploit possibilities that they could not predict, at least artful teachers do. The notion that a sound education consists of meeting hundreds of relatively specific standards is an image of teaching that is as unrealistic as it is problematic. If one is trying to organize an assembly line, the appropriateness of quality control standards is undoubtable. Classrooms, however, are not assembly lines, at least they shouldn't be. To think about educational practice as a procedure designed to enable students to appropriate hundreds of discrete standards is simply a misconception of what the practice of education is about. The educational process ought to court surprise, push at the edges and not be afraid to take risks. The development and implementation of a routinized set of procedures that yield predictable outcomes is significantly problematic, at least for most of what we teach and it is certainly problematic for our loftiest educational aspirations. My writing on this issue problematizes widespread, politically driven assumptions about what the practice of education is about.

The problem for educators is to provide alternatives that will satisfy the public. If high-level specification and the measurement of such specifications are wrong headed in their orientation to practice, what constitutes an alternative? My paper titled, "What does it mean to say a school is doing well?" represents an effort to suggest alternatives that educators might consider. These alternatives admittedly complicate educational life rather than simplify it. But some things need to be appropriately complicated, lest we over simplify what it is that we are trying to do and accomplish.

The most recent evolution of my thinking pertains to the question, "What can education learn from the arts about the practice of education?" With this question, I try to turn the tables. The current educational policy push in the United States is highly mechanistic and based on the assumption that subject fields such as the arts are mushy and that their improvement requires becoming "rigorous," a widely used term for both evaluation and educational research. The position that I have taken is that the arts need not come to look like the way some people believe academic fields should function, but rather academic fields would do quite well to try to look more like the arts when the arts are well taught. Put another way, I am trying to develop the view that artistry could serve as a regulative ideal for the ways in which we think about the means and ends of education. The arts should not look more like the academic fields; academic fields in practice and conception would do well to look more like the arts. My paper, "What can education learn from the arts about the practice of education?" is intended to articulate the grounds for such a view.

This tour of my work should give the reader a fair sense of how it has evolved over the years. It has changed, but it has also stayed the same in very significant ways. It has been – and is – rooted in the arts and the lessons they have to teach to both individuals who work with them and to policy makers who need to make decisions about how schools should operate. The field of education will always have problems to deal with. Thank heavens! They make inquiry possible and through inquiry, one can feel the tingle of a mind at work. Not a bad aspiration, not only for us who work in education but for our students as well.

## Reference

Tyack, David and Cuban, Larry. *Tinkering Toward Utopia*. Cambridge, MA: Harvard University Press, 1995.

Elliot W. Eisner
Stanford University
September 2004

# CHAPTER 1

# CHILDREN'S CREATIVITY IN ART
## A study of types

*American Educational Research Journal*, 1965, 2(3): 125–136

## Introduction

Through research, the conception of creativity has undergone an important change. Once considered an elusive, almost mystical gift belonging to a special few, creativity is now being seen as a capacity common to all – one that should be effectively developed by the school. Once considered a rare type of behavior limited to the arts, creativity is now viewed as penetrating, to some degree, almost all kinds of human activity. Even educators who are usually chary of accepting new responsibilities for an already overloaded curriculum are fascinated by the idea of teaching for the development of creativity.

Art education has long been concerned with the development of creativity. Unlocking the creative impulse has been a major function of the teacher of art. Although he may sometimes have confused mere impulsivity with serious creative art, his concern with creativity has been real and sincere. Viktor Lowenfeld (1939, 1957), Herbert Read (1945), and Henry Shaefer-Simmern (1948) are only a few of those who have contributed to both the theory and the practice of developing children's creativity in the arts. The recent flow of creativity research by psychologists is beginning to persuade those working in other academic fields that education for creativity is not solely the responsibility of those working in the arts. Thus, research based largely on scientific grounds is providing new and important directions in American education.

## Approaches to the study of creativity

Guilford, whose work has been particularly influential, has postulated a set of factors and factorized tests that are theoretically relevant to understanding the structure of the human intellect (Guilford *et al.*, 1952). He sees creativity as a complex of unitary abilities that are displayed singly or in combination in the creative act. His factor-analysis methods have provided a major approach to the study of creativity, and his tests have been widely used by workers in this area.

A second approach, taken by Blatt and Stein (1957) and others, has been to study individuals known to have high creative ability (as evidenced through patents, discoveries, publications, inventions, and the like) in the hope of finding common personality traits.

A third approach has been the identification of process characteristics through examination of the completed product. This method, developed by Beittel and Burkhart (1963), has been especially valuable in the field of art education, where the product's characteristics are indicative of the methods and modes of action employed by the artist. The constructs *spontaneous, divergent,* and *academic* have proved useful for analyzing the artistic process, and significant personality correlates have been found for individuals displaying these process-strategies.

The research reported here presents a fourth approach to the study of creativity. It represents an effort to formulate and test a typology of creative behavior in the visual arts.

## Types of creativity in the visual arts

The treatment of *types* of creativity as distinct from that of creativity in general may have advantages. First, kinds of behavior that are now excluded from the conception of creativity in general may be brought into a wider view of creativity. Second, if art works are analyzed with an eye to the different sorts of "creativeness" that they exhibit, it may be possible to arrive at defensible views about the creative competencies of different individuals and, with this knowledge, encourage these competencies more efficiently.

The conception of types of creativity is based upon the various qualities and characteristics that have historically been considered creative in the visual arts. Analyses of children's art works, as well as those of adults, show that their qualities can be classified into a system of types. Some artists make their creative contribution through the treatment of form; others through their selection of subject matter; some in the novel treatment of the conventional; others in the creation of the utterly new. Some children develop unique ways of combining media; others formulate new methods of expression; still others are able to bring aesthetic order to conventional visual elements. Creativity in art does not seem to be a simple unitary trait. Like art itself, creativity has many faces.

The purpose of the present study was to see whether the types of creativity found in the art products of sixth-grade pupils could be systematically identified and, if so, to determine the relationships existing among these types.[1]

Four types of creativity and two loci constitute the typology. The types are (1) *Boundary Pushing,* (2) *Inventing,* (3) *Boundary Breaking,* and (4) *Aesthetic Organizing.* They are described *in general* in the four sections that follow. The loci are (1) content and (2) form. Content is defined as an attempt at representation and is evidenced by the presence of conventional signs. Form is defined as the presence of formal qualities. Thus, every visual art product contains formal qualities but may or may not contain conventional signs.

### Boundary Pushing

In every culture, objects are embedded within various mental fields. These fields are bounded in such a way as to enable members of the culture to place an object in some meaningful context, usually that in which the object is normally found. These fields also act as a sort of psychic economy, a slicing up of the world so that objects within it can be meaningfully and efficiently classified. In addition, they provide the culture with a common set of object-field expectations that act to discourage bizarre actions by individuals within that culture. The fields specify and encourage acceptable, stereotyped, and restricted behavior on the part of individuals who act within the limits of the fields. Some individuals, however, are able to extend these limits. The process of extending or redefining the limits of common objects is called *Boundary Pushing.*

In the area of technology, *Boundary Pushing* was demonstrated by the individual who first thought of installing electric shaver outlets in automobiles, thus extending the usual limits of both the automobile and the shaver. It was also demonstrated by the person who first thought of using rubber for the blades of electric fans and by the individual who first used nylon for the wheels of roller skates. In the classroom, *Boundary Pushing* is displayed by the child who uses numerals to create designs or pictures or who uses an inked eraser as a rubber stamp. *Boundary Pushing* is displayed in the recognition that plywood can be molded into a chair, that a cellophane strip can be used to open a package of cigarettes, and that a key can open a can of coffee. Thus, *Boundary Pushing* is the ability to attain the possible by extending the given.

## Inventing

*Inventing* is the process of employing the known to create an essentially new object or class of objects. The inventor does not merely extend the usual limits of the conventional; he creates a new object by restructuring the known. Edison, to use a classic case, exemplifies the inventor, for his activities were directed not merely toward the novel implementation of known materials or objects but rather toward their combination and reconstruction. His contributions differ markedly from those produced by *Boundary Pushing*. The terminus of *Inventing* is the creation of a new product that may itself be creatively employed, thus being the subject of *Boundary Pushing*. Gutenberg, Bell, and Marconi are only a few of those who have displayed inventive behavior; and our recognition of their contributions, combined with our general reluctance to call them scientists, is indicative of the distinction we make at the common-sense level regarding the ways in which creativity is displayed.

## Boundary Breaking

*Boundary Breaking* is defined as the rejection or reversal of accepted assumptions, thus making the "given" problematic. This type of behavior is probably characterized by the highest level of cognition. In *Boundary Breaking*, the individual sees gaps and limitations in current theories and proceeds to develop new premises, which contain their own limits. Copernicus, for example, displayed *Boundary Breaking* in his conceptual (if not theological) rejection of the theory that the earth was the center of the universe. His hypothesis that the earth moves around the sun (and not vice versa) led him to develop a theory that, as far as we know, is valid for the astronomical system. His rejection of the knowledge of the period – theories and beliefs that were limiting – allowed him to contribute significantly to man's understanding of the universe. In the present era, Einstein's notion of simultaneity allowed him to develop new concepts useful for understanding nature through his theory of relativity. His questioning of currently accepted beliefs regarding relationships in time and space led him to propose a theory from which certain natural phenomena can be more accurately predicted.

Another example of *Boundary Breaking* is found in the work of Binet. "Binet's approach was the direct opposite of that of his predecessors. Instead of trying to find a single index of intelligence, he went to the other extreme and deliberately searched for a multiplicity of indexes" (Stephens, 1951, p. 181). By making the "given" problematic and by reversing the approach taken by others, Binet set the pattern for over fifty years of intelligence testing.

Two kinds of behavior characteristically displayed by *Boundary Breakers* – insight and imagination – may function in the following ways. Insight may help the *Boundary Breaker* grasp relationships among seemingly discrete events. It may also enable him to recognize incongruities or gaps in accepted explanations or descriptions. As he recognizes these gaps, his imagination may come into play and enable him to generate images or ideas (or both) useful for closing the gaps. Through the production of these images and ideas, he is able to reorganize or even reject the accepted in order to formulate a more comprehensive view of the relationships among the elements that gave impetus to the initial insight. Insight into gaps in contemporary theory or actions and visions of the possible are probably insufficient to satisfy the *Boundary Breaker*; he must be able to establish an order and structure between the gaps he has "seen" and the ideas he has generated.

### Aesthetic Organizing

*Aesthetic Organizing* is characterized by the presence in objects of a high degree of coherence and harmony. The individual who displays this type of creativity confers order and unity upon matters; his overriding concern is in the aesthetic organization of qualitative components. Decisions about the placement of objects are made through what may be called a qualitative creativity.

Individuals who are able to organize components aesthetically probably obtain a great deal of pleasure from so doing. This inclination toward aesthetic order also seems to be displayed in the way in which forms are *perceived*. Barron (1958) has reported that both creative artists and creative scientists show more preference for designs that are highly complex, asymmetrical, and seemingly disorganized than do less creative individuals. In this sense, the *Aesthetic Organizer* may be an aesthetic see-er as well; that is, he may obtain his aesthetic pleasures by seeing through disorder to identify orderly elements. Some artists and writers report that they are controlled by these urges and drives and admit to following their lead consciously, rather than having and adhering to carefully preconceived plans of execution.

It should be noted that a major difference exists between *Aesthetic Organizing* and the other three types of creativity. In *Boundary Breaking, Inventing*, and *Boundary Pushing*, novelty is a defining characteristic. Either a new use for an object or a new object itself is created. In *Aesthetic Organizing*, this is not necessarily the case; neither a new use nor a new object may have been created. The object upon which creativity was exercised, however, displays a high degree of coherence. Its parts hang together harmoniously. For most artists the aesthetic organization of form is a prime concern, but in children (and they are the subjects of the present study) high aesthetic organizing ability is relatively rare. The preadolescent who is able to organize form to a high degree of coherence and harmony is often said to be gifted; in this study this particular kind of giftedness is considered one type of creativity.

### Subjects and instruments

Once the classes constituting the typology were formulated, the problem shifted to the empirical question: could this typology be used to identify types of creative characteristics displayed in children's art products?

In order to answer this question, specific criteria were deduced from each general description of a type. These criteria stated the characteristics that would be present in an art product if the subject had displayed a particular type of creativity. For example, a subject who engaged in *Aesthetic Organizing* would produce a work with satisfying formal qualities. Its parts would hang together and it would be unified; balance between figure and ground would be achieved. A subject who engaged in *Boundary Pushing* would produce a work in which either form or content was used in a novel way; his treatment of these aspects of the art product would be original.

Eighty-five sixth-grade pupils – 46 boys and 39 girls – in a mid-western private school were the subjects. Their IQs ranged from 93 to 180, with a median of 128. Where IQ measures other than the Stanford-Binet had been used, scores were converted to Stanford-Binet equivalents.

The subjects were asked to produce two kinds of art works. One was a piece of sculpture made from one-quarter pound of oil-base clay, a handful of colored toothpicks, and a paper plate to be used as a base. To insure privacy, each *S* worked in an enclosed booth. The instructions were as follows:

> In the booth before you, you will find a paper plate, some colored toothpicks, and some oil-base clay. You may build anything you wish out of the clay and toothpicks. The paper plate is to be used as a base so that whatever you make can be moved easily. You will have 45 minutes to complete your work. You may begin.

The second product consisted of a set of nine drawings made in an $8''$-by-$11\frac{1}{2}''$ booklet. On each page, the *S*s found an abstract line, which was to be used as the starting point or stimulus for their drawing. Each page had a border line $1\frac{1}{2}''$ from the edge. The *S*s had two minutes to work on each page and were given a signal by the test administrator when the two minutes had elapsed. The instructions were as follows:

> On each page of this booklet you will find some simple lines. You are to use your pencil to change each of the lines in any way you wish. You will have two minutes to work on each page so you will have to work rapidly. Wait for the signal before you begin. Once you complete one page, don't turn to the next page until you are told to do so. You may begin.

## Procedure and treatment of data

Three judges were selected to identify the various types of creativity that each art product might display. Each one had had over five years of art-teaching experience with children as well as considerable experience as a practicing visual artist. The judges met daily for two weeks to discuss the criteria and to practice using them in judging the creative characteristics of works similar to those produced in the study. At the end of this time, the judges believed that they adequately understood the criteria and their application and proceeded to the actual evaluation.

The art products of the *S*s were arranged in two large rooms. The judges, using a nine-point scale, independently evaluated each product for each type of creativity – one type at a time. As soon as a judge completed one evaluation, he handed in his score sheet and received one for another type; he then selected a different point in the display to begin his next evaluation. This procedure, the purpose of which was to reduce halo effect, was used throughout the judging.

To determine interjudge agreement, the data were treated as follows:

1 For each evaluation[2] the 85 raw scores assigned by each judge were transformed into normalized standard scores. The 14 normalized standard scores from each judge's evaluations were summed for each subject. This procedure yielded three over-all creativity scores for each subject. These three sets of 85

summed scores (one set for each judge) were intercorrelated to determine how well the judges agreed in over-all assessment of creativity.

2   An analogous procedure was followed for *each medium* separately, thus providing individual measures of how well the judges agreed in evaluating structures and how well they agreed in evaluating drawings.

3   The raw scores assigned to the products by each judge in each type and locus of creativity were intercorrelated.

Obtaining measures on these three bases – ranging from over-all assessment of creativity to successively more specific assessments – made it possible to locate the points at which interjudge agreement diminished.

On the first basis, over-all assessment of creativity, interjudge agreement was rather high; the coefficients were 0.82, 0.78, and 0.72. When the two media were taken separately, the amount of interjudge agreement dropped slightly; the coefficients for structures were 0.74, 0.65, and 0.61; for drawings, 0.80, 0.79, and 0.71. Finally, when *each type and locus in each medium* was taken individually, the coefficients ranged from 0.90 to 0.10, with a median of 0.59. These data are shown in Table 1.1.

Once it was decided that the interjudge agreement was high enough to warrant using the data, it became feasible to investigate the relationships existing among the types and between each type and other variables. The following questions guided the investigation:

1   What relationships exist among the scores in the various types of creativity within and between media?

2   When the boys and the girls are grouped separately, are the relationships among the types different in the two groups?

*Table 1.1* Interjudge correlations computed from raw scores

| Type and locus of creativity | Judges | | |
|---|---|---|---|
| | A vs. B (N = 85) | A vs. C (N = 85) | B vs. C (N = 85) |
| Boundary Pushing – content, structures | 0.80[a] | 0.70 | 0.90 |
| Boundary Breaking – form, structures | 0.88 | 0.72 | 0.75 |
| Boundary Pushing – form, drawings | 0.74 | 0.58 | 0.68 |
| Aesthetic Organizing – form, drawings | 0.55 | 0.60 | 0.76 |
| Inventing – content, drawings | 0.52 | 0.73 | 0.60 |
| Aesthetic Organizing – form, structures | 0.58 | 0.56 | 0.68 |
| Inventing – form, structures | 0.52 | 0.62 | 0.61 |
| Inventing – form, drawings | 0.55 | 0.56 | 0.65 |
| Boundary Pushing – form, structures | 0.53 | 0.53 | 0.63 |
| Inventing – content, structures | 0.51 | 0.47 | 0.54 |
| Boundary Pushing – content, drawings | 0.39 | 0.60 | 0.49 |
| Boundary Breaking – form, drawings | 0.33 | 0.38 | 0.68 |
| Boundary Breaking – content, drawings | 0.10 | 0.81 | 0.42 |
| Boundary Breaking – content, structures | 0.27 | 0.27 | 0.76 |
| Median | 0.53 | 0.59 | 0.66 |

Note
a The smallest product-moment correlation coefficient based upon 85 cases that is significantly different from zero at the 0.01 level is 0.25 (one-tailed test).

3    When the subjects above the median in intelligence and those below the median are grouped separately, are the relationships among the types different in the two groups?

4    What are the correlations between the scores in each of the types and the Stanford-Binet IQs?

As mentioned earlier – to make the ratings by the three judges comparable, each set of 85 raw scores was transformed into a set of normalized standard scores. The three corresponding standard scores (one from each judge) of each subject were summed; this provided a *single* score on each type (and locus) of creativity in each medium for each child. The intercorrelations of these summed scores and their correlations with Binet IQs are presented in Table 1.2.

The first conclusion to be drawn from the data in Table 1.2 is that the relationship between creative performance in one medium and creative performance in the other was low. The median coefficient among the 49 *r*'s between media was 0.11. This finding is consonant with the situation among professional artists. Aside from a few outstanding exceptions, such as Degas, Michelangelo, Picasso, and Moore, most artists display high-level creativity in one or, at best, two media. When they do function creatively in more than one medium, it is most often in media of the same kind – collage and drawing or sculpture and has relief. The apparent specificity of creative behavior in the visual arts is probably a function of the status of certain skills that are necessary in working in two rather than in three dimensions (or vice versa) or in working in color rather than in black and white (or vice versa). The type of demands a particular medium makes upon an individual probably affects the extent to which he can employ those cognitive abilities that exemplify or make possible creative thinking. A person unable to perceive depth might be able to function in a highly creative way in the production of mosaics but surely would be severely handicapped in the production of sculpture. Since the *S*s in the present study had had about the same amount of experience in the two media they used, the character of these media and the different kinds of abilities that they elicit may account for the low correlations between them.

Although the relationships indicated by these correlations tend to be slight, seven significant relationships did emerge. Six of these seven occur between types having the same locus. For example, *Boundary Pushing* in content in structures is significantly correlated with *Boundary Pushing* in content in drawings, also *Inventing* in content in structures with *Boundary Pushing* in content in drawings, etc. These relationships may be due to the mental set that each *S* brought to his work. Those *S*s who obtained high creativity scores in the locus of *form* may have sought the stimulation of emerging formal qualities rather than the successful imposition of a preconceived idea or symbol upon the medium. Instead of attempting to master the medium, they may have preferred to treat it as a partner, taking their cues from the unexpected forms that flowed from their actions.

The second conclusion from the correlation table is that the relationships among types of creativity in drawing were higher than those in structures. The fact, that the scores in drawing were based on *nine* work samples whereas there was only one structure, may partially account for this difference.

The third conclusion is that scores on *Boundary Breaking* in form and content for structures were more highly correlated than were the other types of creativity in form and content. In addition, scores on this type of creativity were least highly correlated with scores in the other types.

The fourth finding from the table isolates a particular type of creative behavior: *Boundary Breaking*, in both form and content, emerged as the most independent

Table 1.2 Correlations among types and loci of creativity and between types and IQ (N = 85)

| Type and locus of creativity | Form, structures | | | | Content, structures | | | Form, drawings | | | | Content, drawings | | |
|---|---|---|---|---|---|---|---|---|---|---|---|---|---|---|
| | BP | I | BB | AO | BP | I | BB | BP | I | BB | AO | BP | I | BB |
| IQ | -0.02 | 0.05 | -0.04 | -0.01 | 0.21 | 0.18 | -0.09 | 0.05 | 0.16 | 0.03 | 0.07 | 0.15 | 0.01 | -0.15 |
| Form, structures BP | | 0.40 | -0.05 | 0.76 | 0.33 | 0.32 | -0.03 | 0.25 | 0.19 | 0.17 | 0.25 | 0.13 | 0.27 | 0.20 |
| I | | | -0.30 | 0.39 | 0.02 | 0.20 | -0.38 | 0.13 | 0.09 | 0.04 | 0.05 | 0.13 | 0.09 | 0.04 |
| BB | | | | 0.08 | -0.00 | -0.05 | 0.64 | 0.11 | 0.16 | 0.01 | 0.18 | -0.04 | -0.04 | 0.05 |
| AO | | | | | 0.34 | 0.29 | 0.10 | 0.27 | 0.14 | -0.03 | 0.25 | 0.07 | 0.17 | 0.04 |
| Content, structures BP | | | | | | 0.83 | 0.22 | 0.09 | 0.06 | 0.11 | 0.18 | 0.28 | 0.18 | -0.05 |
| I | | | | | | | 0.05 | 0.06 | 0.07 | 0.11 | 0.16 | 0.29 | 0.21 | -0.06 |
| BB | | | | | | | | -0.04 | -0.03 | -0.02 | 0.11 | -0.01 | -0.09 | -0.06 |
| Form, drawings BP | | | | | | | | | 0.77 | 0.26 | 0.73 | 0.52 | 0.45 | 0.39 |
| I | | | | | | | | | | 0.39 | 0.76 | 0.60 | 0.52 | 0.45 |
| BB | | | | | | | | | | | 0.26 | 0.33 | 0.39 | 0.50 |
| AO | | | | | | | | | | | | 0.56 | 0.55 | 0.35 |
| Content, drawings BP | | | | | | | | | | | | | 0.75 | 0.36 |
| I | | | | | | | | | | | | | | 0.57 |
| BB | | | | | | | | | | | | | | |

Notes
BP = Boundary Pushing; I = Inventing; BB = Boundary Breaking; AO = Aesthetic Organizing.

of the four types. This may be explained by the nature of *Boundary Breaking*; to engage in this type of creativity, an individual must reject or reverse (or both) the premises upon which the problem rests. Persons able to escape the limits of deeply embedded cultural expectations are rare, and since *Boundary Breaking* is the most dramatic kind of successful escape from such expectations, its rarity (and, therefore, its relatively infrequent occurrence with other types of creativity) is not surprising.

One child who engaged in *Boundary Breaking* in structures used the paper plate, which was intended only as a base, as an integral part of his structure and, in addition, combined torn pieces of cardboard as a functional element. Another child used the colored toothpicks not as a structural element in the clay but as a burden carried by the clay donkey that he built. In drawings, one child carefully punched holes in the several pages so that his drawings had a relief quality. These subjects rejected or reversed the premises on which the problem was built in order to develop novel solutions.

To find out whether different relationships existed among the types of creativity for each sex, the intercorrelations were computed separately for boys and for girls. In 19 of the 91 pairs of coefficients, significance was attained by only one of the coefficients in the pair. However, no pattern could be discerned in these 19 pairs.

The intercorrelations were also computed separately for those *S*s above the median IQ and for those below it. All of the 19 significant relationships, found were in the matrix based on the scores of *S*s in the high-IQ group. In other words, consistency in level of creative performance across media occurred more frequently among high-IQ than among low-IQ subjects.

As has been found in other studies, the relationships between creativity scores and the kind of cognition assessed by Stanford-Binet IQs were small. In no case did a significant relationship appear between the scores on any type of creativity and IQ.

## Summary

Creativity was differentiated according to type and according to the locus (i.e. form or content) at which it was displayed within an art product. The typology was then used to evaluate two art products made by each of 85 sixth-grade pupils. One product was a nine-page booklet of drawings, and the other was a three-dimensional structure of clay and toothpicks. Each product was rated independently by three artistically experienced judges, using a nine-point scale. The degree of interjudge agreement was sufficiently high to warrant investigating the relationships among the ratings.

The relationships between creative performance in one medium and creative performance in the other were low, the median coefficient being 0.11. However, when significant (0.25 or higher) coefficients between two types did occur, they were between types having the same locus. That is, creativity in form in one medium was most likely to be related to creativity in form in the other medium; creativity in content in one medium was most likely to be related to creativity in content in the other medium.

One type of creativity, *Boundary Breaking*, occurred much less frequently than the other types. Whereas *Boundary Pushing*, *Inventing*, and *Aesthetic Organizing* were displayed in some degree by almost all subjects, *Boundary Breaking* was not. The difficulty in achieving this type of creative behavior may account for its rarity.

When correlations were computed for the boys and the girls separately, no differences in the pattern of relationships among the types of creativity were found. However, when the sample was divided in half at the median IQ, those subjects in the upper half were more consistent in their creative performance across media than those in the lower half. No significant relationships emerged between IQ and any of the types of creativity.

## Notes

1   The study also investigated the relationship between each type of creativity and psychological health. These findings are reported elsewhere.
2   The types and loci on which the 14 evaluations were based are listed in Table 1.1. For obvious reasons, only the locus *form* was used in conjunction with *Aesthetic Organizing*.

## References

Barron, Frank. "The psychology of imagination." *Scientific American* 199: 150–66; September 1958.

Beittel, Kenneth R. and Burkhart, Robert C. "Strategies of spontaneous, divergent, and academic art students." *Studies in Art Education* 5: 20–41; Fall 1963.

Blatt, Sidney J. and Stein, Morris I. "Some personality, value, and cognitive characteristics of the creative person." Paper presented to the American Psychological Association, September 1957.

Guilford, Joy P., Wilson, R. C., and Christensen, P. R. *A Factor-Analytic Study of Creative Thinking: II. Administration of Tests and Analysis of Results*. Reports from the Psychological Laboratory, No. 8. Los Angeles, CA: University of Southern California, 1952. 24 pp.

Lowenfeld, Viktor. *The Nature of Creative Activity*. New York: Harcourt, Brace and Co., 1939. 272 pp.

Lowenfeld, Viktor. *Creative and Mental Growth*. Third edition. New York: Macmillan Co., 1957. 541 pp.

Read, Herbert E. *Education Through Art*. New York: Pantheon Books, 1945. 320 pp.

Schaefer-Simmern, Henry. *The Unfolding of Artistic Activity*. Berkeley, CA: University of California Press, 1948. 201 pp.

Stephens, John M. *Educational Psychology: The Study of Educational Growth*. New York: Henry Holt and Co., 1951. 692 pp.

# CHAPTER 2

# EDUCATIONAL OBJECTIVES
## Help or hindrance?

*The School Review*, 1967, 75(3): 250–260

If one were to rank the various beliefs or assumptions in the field of curriculum that are thought most secure, the belief in the need for clarity and specificity in stating educational objectives would surely rank among the highest. Educational objectives, it is argued, need to be clearly specified for at least three reasons: first, because they provide the goals toward which the curriculum is aimed; second, because once clearly stated they facilitate the selection and organization of content; third, because when specified in both behavioral and content terms they make it possible to evaluate the outcomes of the curriculum.

It is difficult to argue with a rational approach to curriculum development – who would choose irrationality? And, if one is to build curriculum in a rational way, the clarity of premise, end or starting point, would appear paramount. But I want to argue in this paper that educational objectives clearly and specifically stated can hamper as well as help the ends of instruction and that an unexamined belief in curriculum as in other domains of human activity can easily become dogma which in fact may hinder the very functions the concept was originally designed to serve.[1]

When and where did beliefs concerning the importance of educational objectives in curriculum development emerge? Who has formulated and argued their importance? What effect has this belief had upon curriculum construction? If we examine the past briefly for data necessary for answering these questions, it appears that the belief in the usefulness of clear and specific educational objectives emerged around the turn of the century with the birth of the scientific movement in education.

Before this movement gained strength, faculty psychologists viewed the brain as consisting of a variety of intellectual faculties. These faculties, they held, could be strengthened if exercised in appropriate ways with particular subject matters. Once strengthened, the faculties could be used in any area of human activity to which they were applicable. Thus, if the important faculties could be identified and if methods of strengthening them developed, the school could concentrate on this task and expect general intellectual excellence as a result.

This general theoretical view of mind had been accepted for several decades by the time Thorndike, Judd, and later Watson began, through their work, to chip away the foundations upon which it rested. Thorndike's work especially demonstrated the specificity of transfer. He argued theoretically that transfer of learning occurred if and only if elements in one situation were identical with elements in the other. His empirical work supported his theoretical views, and the enormous stature he enjoyed in education as well as in psychology influenced educators to approach curriculum development in ways consonant with his views. One of those who was caught up in the scientific movement in education was Franklin Bobbitt, often thought of as the father of curriculum theory. In 1918 Bobbitt published a signal work titled simply, *The Curriculum*.[2] In it he argued that educational theory is not so difficult to construct as commonly held and that curriculum theory is logically derivable from educational theory. Bobbitt wrote in 1918:

> The central theory is simple. Human life, however varied, consists in its performance of specific activities. Education that prepares for life is one that prepares definitely and adequately for these specific activities. However numerous and diverse they may be for any social class, they can be discovered. This requires that one go out into the world of affairs and discover the particulars of which these affairs consist. These will show the abilities, habits, appreciations, and forms of knowledge that men need. These will be the objectives of the curriculum. They will be numerous, definite, and particularized. The curriculum will then be that series of experiences which childhood and youth must have by way of attaining those objectives.[3]

In *The Curriculum*, Bobbitt approached curriculum development scientifically and theoretically: study life carefully to identify needed skills, divide these skills into specific units, organize these units into experiences, and provide these experiences to children. Six years later, in his second book, *How To Make a Curriculum*,[4] Bobbitt operationalized his theoretical assertions and demonstrated how curriculum components – especially educational objectives – were to be formulated. In this book Bobbitt listed nine areas in which educational objectives are to be specified. In these nine areas he listed 160 major educational objectives which run the gamut from "Ability to use language in all ways required for proper and effective participation in community life" to "Ability to entertain one's friends, and to respond to entertainment by one's friends."[5]

Bobbitt was not alone in his belief in the importance of formulating objectives clearly and specifically. Pendleton, for example, listed 1,581 social objectives for English, Guiler listed more than 300 for arithmetic in grades 1–6, and Billings prescribed 888 generalizations which were important for the social studies.

If Thorndike was right, if transfer was limited, it seemed reasonable to encourage the teacher to teach for particular outcomes and to construct curriculums only after specific objectives had been identified.

In retrospect it is not difficult to understand why this movement in curriculum collapsed under its own weight by the early 1930s. Teachers could not manage fifty highly specified objects, let alone hundreds. And, in addition, the new view of the child, not as a complex machine but as a growing organism who ought to participate in planning his own educational program, did not mesh well with the theoretical views held earlier.[6]

But, as we all know, the Progressive movement too began its decline in the 1940s, and by the mid-1950s, as a formal organization at least, it was dead.

By the late 1940s and during the 1950s, curriculum specialists again began to remind us of the importance of specific educational objectives and began to lay down guidelines for their formulation. Rationales for constructing curriculums developed by Ralph Tyler[7] and Virgil Herrick[8] again placed great importance on the specificity of objectives. George Barton[9] identified philosophic domains, which could be used to select objectives. Benjamin Bloom and his colleagues[10] operationalized theoretical assertions by building a taxonomy of educational objectives in the cognitive domain; and in 1964, Krathwohl, Bloom, and Masia[11] did the same for the affective domain. Many able people for many years have spent a great deal of time and effort in identifying methods and providing prescriptions for the formulation of educational objectives, so much so that the statement "Educational objectives should be stated in behavioral terms" has been elevated – or lowered – to almost slogan status in curriculum circles. Yet, despite these efforts, teachers seem not to take educational objectives seriously – at least as they are prescribed from above. And when teachers plan curriculum guides, their efforts first to identify over-all educational aims, then specify school objectives, then identify educational objectives for specific subject matters, appear to be more like exercises to be gone through than serious efforts to build tools for curriculum planning. If educational objectives were really useful tools, teachers, I submit, would use them. If they do not, perhaps it is not because there is something wrong with the teachers but because there might be something wrong with the theory.

As I view the situation, there are several limitations to theory in curriculum regarding the functions educational objectives are to perform. These limitations I would like to identify.

Educational objectives are typically derived from curriculum theory, which assumes that it is possible to predict with a fair degree of accuracy what the outcomes of instruction will be. In a general way this is possible. If you set about to teach a student algebra, there is no reason to assume he will learn to construct sonnets instead. Yet, the outcomes of instruction are far more numerous and complex for educational objectives to encompass. The amount, type, and quality of learning that occurs in a classroom, especially when there is interaction among students, are only in small part predictable. The changes in pace, tempo, and goals that experienced teachers employ when necessary and appropriate for maintaining classroom organization are dynamic rather than mechanistic in character. Elementary school teachers, for example, are often sensitive to the changing interests of the children they teach, and frequently attempt to capitalize on these interests, "milking them" as it were for what is educationally valuable.[12] The teacher uses the moment in a situation that is better described as kaleidoscopic than stable. In the very process of teaching and discussing, unexpected opportunities emerge for making a valuable point, for demonstrating an interesting idea, and for teaching a significant concept. The first point I wish to make, therefore, is that the dynamic and complex process of instruction yields outcomes far too numerous to be specified in behavioral and content terms in advance.

A second limitation of theory concerning educational objectives is its failure to recognize the constraints various subject matters place upon objectives. The point here is brief. In some subject areas, such as mathematics, languages, and the sciences, it is possible to specify with great precision the particular operation or behavior the student is to perform after instruction. In other subject areas, especially the arts, such specification is frequently not possible, and when possible may not be desirable. In a class in mathematics or spelling, uniformity in response is desirable, at least insofar as it indicates that students are able to perform a particular operation adequately, that is, in accordance with accepted procedures. Effective instruction in such areas enables students to function with minimum error in these fields. In the arts and in subject matters where, for example, novel or creative responses are desired, the particular behaviors to be developed cannot easily be identified. Here curriculum and instruction should yield behaviors and products, which are unpredictable. The end achieved ought to be something of a surprise to both teacher and pupil. While it could be argued that one might formulate an educational objective which specified novelty, originality, or creativeness as the desired outcome, the particular referents for these terms cannot be specified in advance; one must judge after the fact whether the product produced or the behavior displayed belongs in the "novel" class. This is a much different procedure than is determining whether or not a particular word has been spelled correctly or a specific performance, that is, jumping a 3-foot hurdle, has been attained. Thus, the second point is that theory concerning educational objectives has not taken into account the particular relationship that holds between the subject matter being taught and the degree to which educational objectives can be predicted and specified. This, I suppose, is in part due to the fact that few curriculum specialists have high degrees of intimacy with a wide variety of subject matters and thus are unable to alter their general theoretical views to suit the demands that particular subject matters make.

The third point I wish to make deals with the belief that objectives stated in behavioral and content terms can be used as criteria by which to measure the outcomes of curriculum and instruction. Educational objectives provide, it is argued, the standard against which achievement is to be measured. Both taxonomies are built upon this assumption since their primary function is to demonstrate how objectives can be used to frame test items appropriate for evaluation. The assumption that objectives can be used as standards by which to measure achievement fails, I think, to distinguish adequately between the application of a standard and the making of a judgment. Not all – perhaps not even most – outcomes of curriculum and instruction are amenable to measurement. The application of a standard requires that some arbitrary and socially defined quantity be designated by which other qualities can be compared. By virtue of socially defined rules of grammar, syntax, and logic, for example, it is possible to quantitatively compare and measure error in discursive or mathematical statement. Some fields of activity, especially those which are qualitative in character, have no comparable rules and hence are less amenable to quantitative assessment. It is here that evaluation must be made, not primarily by applying a socially defined standard, but by making a human qualitative judgment. One can specify, for example, that a student shall be expected to know how to extract a square root correctly and in an unambiguous way, through the application of a standard, determine whether this end has been achieved. But it is only in a metaphoric sense that one can measure the extent to which a student has been able to produce an aesthetic object or an expressive narrative. Here standards are unapplicable; here judgment is required. The making of a judgment in distinction to the application of a standard implies that valued qualities are not merely socially defined and arbitrary in character. The judgment by which a critic determines the value of a poem, novel, or play is not achieved merely by applying standards already known to the particular product being judged; it requires that the critic – or teacher – view the product with respect to the unique properties it displays and then, in relation to his experience and sensibilities, judge its value in terms which are incapable of being reduced to quantity or rule.

This point was aptly discussed by John Dewey in his chapter on "Perception and criticism" in *Art as Experience*.[13] Dewey was concerned with the problem of identifying the means and ends of criticism and has this to say about its proper function:

> The function of criticism is the reeducation of perception of works of art; it is an auxiliary process, a difficult process, of learning to see and hear. The conception that its business is to appraise, to judge in the legal and moral

sense, arrests the perception of those who are influenced by the criticism that assumes this task.[14]

Of the distinction that Dewey makes between the application of a standard and the making of a critical judgment, he writes:

> There are three characteristics of a standard. It is a particular physical thing existing under specifiable conditions; it is *not* a value. The yard is a yard-stick, and the meter is a bar deposited in Paris. In the second place, standards are measures of things, of lengths, weights, capacities. The things measured are not values, although it is of great social value to be able to measure them, since the properties of things in the way of size, volume, weight, are important for commercial exchange. Finally, as standards of measure, standards define things with respect to *quantity*. To be able to measure quantities is a great aid to further judgments, but it is not a mode of judgment. The standard, being an external and public thing, is applied *physically*. The yard-stick is physically laid down upon things to determine their length.[15]

And I would add that what is most educationally valuable is the development of that mode of curiosity, inventiveness, and insight that is capable of being described only in metaphoric or poetic terms. Indeed, the image of the educated man that has been held in highest esteem for the longest period of time in Western civilization is one which is not amenable to standard measurement. Thus, the third point I wish to make is that curriculum theory which views educational objectives as standards by which to measure educational achievement overlooks those modes of achievement incapable of measurement.

The final point I wish to make deals with the function of educational objectives in curriculum construction.

The rational approach to curriculum development not only emphasizes the importance of specificity in the formulation of educational objectives but also implies when not stated explicitly that educational objectives be stated prior to the formulation of curriculum activities. At first view, this seems to be a reasonable way to proceed with curriculum construction: one should know where he is headed before embarking on a trip. Yet, while the procedure of first identifying objectives before proceeding to identify activities is logically defensible, it is not necessarily the most psychologically efficient way to proceed. One can, and teachers often do, identify activities that seem useful, appropriate, or rich in educational opportunities, and from a consideration of what can be done in class, identify the objectives or possible consequences of using these activities. MacDonald argues this point cogently when he writes:

> Let us look, for example, at the problem of objectives. Objectives are viewed as directives in the rational approach. They are identified prior to the instruction or action and used to provide a basis for a screen for appropriate activities.
>
> There is another view, however, which has both scholarly and experiential referents. This view would state that our objectives are only known to us in any complete sense after the completion of our act of instruction. No matter what we thought we were attempting to do, we can only know what we wanted to accomplish after the fact. Objectives by this rationale are heuristic devices which provide initiating consequences which become altered in the flow of instruction.

In the final analysis, it could be argued, the teacher in actuality asks a fundamentally different question from "What am I trying to accomplish?" The teacher asks "What am I going to do?" and out of the doing comes accomplishment.[16]

Theory in curriculum has not adequately distinguished between logical adequacy in determining the relationship of means to ends when examining the curriculum as a *product* and the psychological processes that may usefully be employed in building curriculums. The method of forming creative insights in curriculum development, as in the sciences and arts, is as yet not logically pre-scribable. The ways in which curriculums can be usefully and efficiently developed constitute an empirical problem; imposing logical requirements upon the process because they are desirable for assessing the product is, to my mind, an error. Thus, the final point I wish to make is that educational objectives need not precede the selection and organization of content. The means through which imaginative cur-riculums can be built is as open-ended as the means through which scientific and artistic inventions occur. Curriculum theory needs to allow for a variety of processes to be employed in the construction of curriculums.

I have argued in this paper that curriculum theory as it pertains to educa-tional objectives has had four significant limitations. First, it has not sufficiently emphasized the extent to which the prediction of educational outcomes cannot be made with accuracy. Second, it has not discussed the ways in which the subject matter affects precision in stating educational objectives. Third, it has con-fused the use of educational objectives as a standard for measurement when in some areas it can be used only as a criterion for judgment. Fourth, it has not distinguished between the logical requirement of relating means to ends in the curriculum as a product and the psychological conditions useful for constructing curriculums.

If the arguments I have formulated about the limitations of curriculum the-ory concerning educational objectives have merit, one might ask: what are their educational consequences? First, it seems to me that they suggest that in large measure the construction of curriculums and the judgment of its consequences are artful tasks. The methods of curriculum development are, in principle if not in practice, no different from the making of art – be it the art of painting or the art of science. The identification of the factors in the potentially useful educational activity and the organization or construction of sequence in curriculum are in principle amenable to an infinite number of combinations. The variable teacher, student, class group, require artful blending for the educationally valuable to result.

Second, I am impressed with Dewey's view of the functions of criticism – to heighten one's perception of the art object – and believe it has implications for cur-riculum theory. If the child is viewed as an art product and the teacher as a critic, one task of the teacher would be to reveal the qualities of the child to himself and to others. In addition, the teacher as critic would appraise the changes occurring in the child. But because the teacher's task includes more than criticism, he would also be responsible, in part, for the improvement of the work of art. In short, in both the construction of educational means (the curriculum) and the appraisal of its consequences, the teacher would become an artist, for criticism itself when car-ried to its height is an art. This, it seems to me, is a dimension to which curriculum theory will someday have to speak.

# Notes

1   This is a slightly expanded version of a paper presented at the fiftieth annual meeting of the American Educational Research Association, Chicago, IL, February, 1966.
2   Franklin Bobbitt, *The Curriculum* (Boston, MA: Houghton Mifflin Co., 1918).
3   Ibid., p. 42.
4   Franklin Bobbitt, *How to Make a Curriculum* (Boston, MA: Houghton Mifflin Co., 1924).
5   Ibid., pp. 11–29.
6   For a good example of this view of the child and curriculum development, see *The Changing Curriculum, Tenth Yearbook*, Department of Supervisors and Directors of Instruction, National Education Association and Society for Curriculum Study (New York: Appleton-Century Crofts Co., 1937).
7   Ralph W. Tyler, *Basic Principles of Curriculum and Instruction* (Chicago, IL: University of Chicago, IL Press, 1951).
8   Virgil E. Herrick, "The concept of curriculum design." *Toward Improved Curriculum Theory*, Virgil E. Herrick and Ralph W. Tyler (eds) (Supplementary Educational Monographs, No. 71 (Chicago, IL: University of Chicago Press, 1950)), pp. 37–50.
9   George E. Barton, Jr, "Educational objectives: improvement of curriculum theory about Their Determination." ibid., pp. 26–35.
10  Benjamin S. Bloom and David R. Krathwohl (eds), "Taxonomy of educational objectives: the classification of educational goals, by a committee of college and university examiners." *Handbook I: The Cognitive Domain* (New York: Longmans, Green, 1956).
11  David R. Krathwohl, Benjamin S. Bloom, and Bertram Masia (eds), "Taxonomy of educational objectives." *Handbook II: The Affective Domain* (New York: David McKay, Inc., 1964).
12  For an excellent paper describing educational objectives as they are viewed and used by elementary school teachers, see Philip W. Jackson and Elizabeth Belford, "Educational objectives and the joys of teaching." *School Review*, LXXIII (1965), 267–291.
13  John Dewey, *Art as Experience* (New York: Minton, Balch & Co., 1934).
14  Ibid., p. 324.
15  Ibid., p. 307.
16  James B. MacDonald, "Myths about instruction." *Educational Leadership*, XXII, No. 7 (May, 1965), 613–614.

# CHAPTER 3

# INSTRUCTIONAL AND EXPRESSIVE EDUCATIONAL OBJECTIVES
## Their formulation and use in curriculum

W. James Popham, E. Eisner, H. Sullivan and W. Bruneau (eds), *Instructional Objectives*, Chicago, IL: McNally & Co., 1969 (Monograph Series on Curriculum Evaluation), pp. 1–18

The concept of educational objectives holds a central position in the literature of curriculum, yet the way in which educational objectives should be formulated – if at all – continues to be the subject of professional debate. This chapter will examine the concept "educational objectives," its evolution in educational literature and the research which has been undertaken to appraise its usefulness. A primary function of the chapter is to distinguish between two types of objectives – instructional and expressive. This distinction might prove useful for ameliorating the arguments of those holding contrasting views on their usefulness in curriculum theory and instruction.

There is little need to document the fact that educational literature has devoted much attention to the character and the methods through which educational objectives are to be formulated. Bloom *et al.* (1956), Gagné (1967), Krathwohl, Bloom and Masia (1964), Mager (1962), Tyler (1950), and others have worked diligently at the task of clarifying, classifying, and specifying the manner in which objectives are to be formulated and the characteristics they are to have once developed. Through the efforts of these writers a number of characteristics necessary for having a useful statement of objectives have been identified. For one, it is argued that educational objectives should describe pupil behavior, not teacher behavior; that is, they should describe how pupils are to perform after having had edu-cational experiences. Second, objectives should describe both the behavior to be displayed and the content in which the behavior is to occur. Thus, not just critical thinking is to be identified but critical thinking in history or mathematics or biology. Third, objectives should be stated at a level of specificity that makes it possible to recognize the behavior should it be displayed, thus avoiding the pitfalls of making inferences to nonempirical phenomena such as mental events. (The reader should note that the example of critical thinking just offered would not pass muster.)

These and other rules or principles have been offered to the wouldbe curriculum maker to facilitate his labors in the field of education. For once having formulated objectives that meet such criteria, a number of subsequent functions are facilitated. First, a clear statement of educational objectives gives direction to curriculum planning. Second, they provide criteria for selecting content and organizing curriculum activities. Third, they provide cues for formulating evaluation procedures inasmuch as evaluation should proceed from specifications set forth by objectives.

Tyler, in describing the importance of educational objectives in his rationale for curriculum development, states,

> By defining these desired educational results [educational objectives] as clearly as possible the curriculum-maker has the most useful set of criteria for selecting

content, for suggesting learning activities, for deciding on the kind of teaching procedures to follow, in fact to carry on all the further steps in curriculum planning. We are devoting much time to the setting up and formulations of objectives because they are the most critical criteria for guiding all the other activities of the curriculum-maker.

(Tyler, 1950, p. 40)

And Gagné writing in the first AERA monograph of the Curriculum Evaluation Series goes beyond Tyler in emphasizing the importance of educational objectives by reducing content to objectives. He writes:

Possibly the most fundamental reason of all for the central importance of defining educational objectives is that such definition makes possible the basic distinction between content and method. It is the defining of objectives that brings an essential clarity into the area of curriculum design and enables both educational planners and researchers to bring their practical knowledge to bear on the matter. As an example of the kind of clarification which results by defining content as "descriptions of the expected capabilities of students," the following may be noted. Once objectives have been defined, there is no step in curriculum design that can legitimately be entitled "selecting content."

(Gagné, 1967, pp. 21–22)

Here we have two distinguished students of education emphasizing the importance of educational objectives. Each of these statements, as well as the statements of other thoughtful citizens of the educational community, affirms belief in the importance of educational objectives as a boon to teaching, curriculum making, and educational planning.

And yet, and yet... if we reflect on our own teaching or observe the teaching behavior of others, if we compare the courses of the "haves" and "have nots" of educational objectives, we are, I believe, hard pressed to identify the power they are believed to have by their advocates. Why is it that teachers do not eagerly use tools that would make their lives easier? Perhaps because they are ignorant of how objectives should be specified... perhaps. But why should those who know how objectives are to be specified disregard them in their own course work? Perhaps because they have acquired "bad" professional habits... perhaps. Is it possible that the power and utility assigned to objectives in theoretical treatises are somewhat exaggerated when tested in the context of the classroom? Is it possible that the assumptions on which prescriptions about objectives are based are somewhat oversimplified? Is it also possible that the prescription of a set of procedures for the formulation of objectives and the identification of appropriate criteria for their adequacy implicitly contain an educational *Weltanschauung* that is not shared by a substantial proportion of those who are responsible for curriculum planning and teaching in America's schools?

The formulation of educational means is never a neutral act. The tools employed and the metaphors used to describe education lead to actions which are not without consequences with respect to value. Many of the metaphors used to describe the importance and function of educational objectives have been associated with conceptions of education which I believe are alien to the educational values held by many of those who teach. These metaphors are not new; they have been with educators for some time, and it will be fruitful, I believe, to compare some of the arguments and metaphors used today with conceptions of education developed within the past fifty years.

It seems to me that three metaphors can be used to characterize dominant views about the nature of education – at least as it has been conceived and carried on in American schools. These metaphors are *industrial*, *behavioristic*, and *biological*.

The industrial metaphor was perhaps most influential in education during the first and second decades of this century, a period in which the efficiency movement emerged. This movement, described brilliantly by Callahan (1962), adopted and adapted industrial methods – especially time and motion study – to improve the educational process and make it more efficient. Under pressure from local boards of education and the muckraking magazines of the early twentieth century, school administrators tried to protect their positions and to reduce their vulnerability to public criticism by employing methods developed by Francis Taylor in industry in order to improve the efficiency of the school. If the school could be managed scientifically, if the procedures which had been employed so successfully in the production of steel could be used in schooling, education might become more efficient and school administrators would have a mantle to protect themselves from the barrage of criticism that befell them during these times. With the adoption of scientific methods they would have evidence that they were not running a "loose shop."

To bring about this metamorphosis in the schools certain tasks had to be accomplished. First and foremost, quantitative and qualitative standards had to be formulated for judging the educational product. Second, time and motion studies had to be made to identify the most efficient means. Third, nothing that could be routinized and prescribed was to be left to the judgment of the worker since his decisions might lead to inefficiency and error. Fourth, the quality of the product was to be judged not by the workers in the school but by the consumers of the product – in this case, society. Fifth, the tasks were to be divided into manageable units so that they could be taught and evaluated at every step along the production line. With these prescriptions for practice, prescriptions taken from industrial management, emerged metaphors through which education was viewed. These metaphors, like the means, were industrial in character. The school was seen as a *plant*. The *superintendent* directed the operation of the plant. The teachers were engaged in a job of *engineering*, and the pupils were the *raw material* to be processed in the plant according to the demands of the *consumers*. Furthermore, the product was to be judged at regular intervals along the production line using *quality control standards* which were to be quantified to reduce the likelihood of error. *Product specifications* were to be prescribed before the raw material was processed. In this way efficiency, measured with respect to cost primarily, could be determined.

The industrial metaphor once having been imposed on schools had several tragic consequences. Callahan identified these:

> The tragedy itself was fourfold: that educational questions were subordinated to business considerations; that administrators were produced who were not, in any true sense, educators; that a scientific label was put on some very unscientific and dubious methods and practices; and that an anti-intellectual climate, already prevalent, was strengthened. As the business-industrial values and procedures spread into the thinking and acting of educators, countless educational decisions were made on economic or on noneducational grounds.
>
> (Callahan, 1962, pp. 246–247)

Before comparing the educational assumptions embedded in the industrial metaphor with some of the assumptions and positions regarding educational objectives argued in the literature today, I should like to pass on to the second metaphor through which education has been viewed.

The behavioristic metaphor had its birth with efforts to construct a science of education and psychology. At the same time that school administrators were embracing the principles of scientific management in an effort to make schools more efficient, Thorndike, Watson, Judd, and Bobbitt were trying to construct and employ scientific methods useful for the study and conduct of education. One part of the task, if it was to be accomplished at all, was to relinquish the heritage of a psychology that did not lend itself to scientific verification. Intra-psychic events, thoughts, and mental states couched in romantic language saturated with surplus meaning had to give way to careful, quantifiable descriptions of human behavior. The poetic and insightful language of a William James had to give way to the objective precision of a John Watson, if psychology was to become a science. By defining psychology as "That division of natural science which takes human activity and conduct as its subject matter" (Watson, 1919), Watson was able to attend to the observable event in order to accomplish two scientific goals: "To predict human activity with reasonable certainty" and to formulate "laws and principles whereby men's actions can be controlled by organized society" (1919). Thorndike, although more broadly ranging in his interest in and his concept of psychology, shared Watson's quest for precision in science and wrote of three stages in the description of human nature.

The first and most primitive stage is the postulation of mythical potencies. Conceptualizations of human nature through reified concepts could lead to little. Thorndike wrote: "Science of this sort could prophesy very little of the behavior of any given man in any given situation" (1921).

A second and somewhat more advanced stage of description according to Thorndike consists:

> of more or less clearly described states of affairs to which man responds by more or less clearly described thoughts, movements, emotions or other responses…We thus seek in this second stage of thought [about human nature] not a potency that vaguely produces large groups of consequences but bonds that unite particular responses or relations to particular situations or stimuli. Science of this sort leads to many successful prophesies of what a man will think or do in a given case, but these prophesies are crude and subject to variability and qualification.
>
> (Thorndike, 1921)

What Thorndike sought was a precise, exact, objective science of human behavior, one without spiritual or metaphysical bogey-men.

> In the third stage, behavior will be defined in terms of events in the world which any impartial observer can identify and, with the proper facilities, verify…. Science of this sort, by giving perfect identifiability and fuller knowledge, leads to completer and finer prophecy and control of human nature.
>
> (Thorndike, 1921)

The significance of these views about the nature of science of psychology and education cannot in my opinion be overemphasized. If what education is after is a change in behavior – something that you can bring about and then observe – there is little use talking about the development of fugitive forms of nonempirical thought. If educational objectives are to be meaningful, they must be anchored in sense data and the type of data with which education is concerned is that of human behavior.

When one combines these assumptions with the research of Thorndike and Woodworth on the transfer of training (1901), research which wrecked the understructure of faculty psychology and which clearly demarcated the limits of transfer, it is easy to understand how curriculum writers could heed Thorndike's admonitions and prepare hundreds of specific, behaviorally defined objectives for the curriculum (Billings, 1929). If transfer is indeed limited, as Thorndike was thought to have demonstrated, it made little sense to prepare general statements of objectives referring to phenomena beyond the realm of observation. The formulation of educational objectives was to be stated in specific behavioral terms.

A third metaphor that can be used to characterize educational thought and practice during the twentieth century is biological in character. The birth of the child study movement in the 1880s, the development of egalitarian liberalism, but especially the ideas of Darwin, all had implications for conceiving the means and ends of education. With the advent of John Dewey, educationists had a powerful spokesman whose conception of man was biological. According to Dewey, man is an organism who lives not only in but through an environment. For Dewey and for those who followed his lead the child was not simply a matter to be molded but an individual who brings with him needs, potentialities, and experiences with which to transact with the environment. What was important educationally for Dewey was for the child to obtain increasing, intelligent control in planning his own education. To do this, to become a master of his own educational journey, required a teacher sympathetic to the child's background and talents. Educational experience was to be differentiated to suit the characteristics of a changing child; the cultivation of idiosyncracy was a dominant concern of those who held a biological view. Dewey writes:

> A truly scientific education can never develop so long as children are treated in the lump, merely as a class. Each child has a strong individuality, and any science must take stock of all the facts in its material. Every pupil must have a chance to show what he truly is, so that the teacher can find out what he needs to make him a complete human being. Only as a teacher becomes acquainted with each one of her pupils can she hope to understand childhood, and it is only as she understands it that she can hope to evolve any scheme of education which will approach either the scientific or the artistic standard. As long as educators do not know their individual facts they can never know whether their hypotheses are of value. But how are they to know their material if they impose themselves upon it to such an extent that each portion is made to act just like every other portion? If the pupils are marched into line, information presented to them which they are then expected to give back in uniform fashion, nothing will ever be found out about any of them. But if every pupil has an opportunity to express himself, to show what are his particular qualities, the teacher will have material on which to base her plans of instruction.
>
> (Dewey and Dewey, 1915, pp. 137–138)

The concept of education implied by the biological metaphor is one concerned neither with molding behavior through extrinsic rewards, nor with formulating uniform, quantifiable and objective standards through which to appraise achievement. Those who viewed (and view) education through the biological metaphor were (and are) much more concerned with the attainment of lofty goals, with helping children realize their unique potential, with the development of a sense of self-respect and intellectual and emotional autonomy which can be used throughout their lives. Educational practice in this view is an artful, emerging affair, one that requires teachers who are sensitive students of children and who follow as well as lead the children in the development of intelligence (Harap, 1937).

The reason for identifying these strains in past educational thought is because I believe they are still with us. Indeed, I believe it is the differences in the metaphoric conception of education that, in part, accounts for the debates and differences regarding the use and the import of educational objectives. If education is conceived of as shaping behavior, then it is possible, indeed appropriate, to think of teachers as behavioral engineers. If the process of education is designed exclusively to enable children to acquire behaviors whose forms are known in advance, then it is possible to develop product specifications, to use quality control standards, and to identify terminal behaviors which students are to possess after having been processed properly. In this view the task of the teacher is to use scientifically developed materials which reduce error and thus make his task as a behavioral engineer more efficient. If the child is not interested in doing the task we set for him, the teacher's problem is not to find out what he is interested in but to motivate him. By establishing the appropriate reinforcement schedule we can mold the child in the image identified previously. In this view, it is not crucial to distinguish between the process of education and the process of training. The process of education enables individuals to behave intelligently through the exercise of judgment in situations that demand reflection, appraisal, and choice among alternative courses of action. The process of training develops specific types of behavioral responses to specific stimuli or situations.

If, however, education is viewed as a form of experience that has something to do with the quality of an individual's life, if it involves helping him learn to make authentic choices, choices that are a result of his own reflection and which depend upon the exercise of free will, then the problem of educational objectives takes a different turn.

What I am arguing is that the problem of determining how educational objectives should be stated or used is not simply a question of technique but a question of value. The differences between individuals regarding the nature and the use of educational objectives spring from differences in their conceptions of education; under the rug of technique lies an image of man.

Compare for example the following two statements related to educational objectives:

> The behavioral technologist equates "knowledge" and "understanding" with behavior. He argues that there need not be any concern as to whether knowledge is basically behavior or not. The significant consideration is that the only tangible evidence of "knowledge" is behavioral evidence.
>
> To sum up, then, the behavioral technologist approaches a problem by going through the following basic steps:
>
> 1   He specifies the behavior which the student is to acquire. (Behavior may be considered as evidence of knowledge.)
> 2   He specifies the relevant characteristics of the student, including the student's present level of knowledge.
> 3   He performs a behavioral analysis of the material to be taught. This involves "atomizing" the knowledge to be imparted according to learning theory principles. The knowledge is broken down into concepts, discriminations, generalizations, and chains.
> 4   He constructs a teaching system or program by which the behavior may be built into the student's repertoire.
> 5   He tests the teaching system on sample students and revises it according to the results, until the desired result is obtained reliably in student after student.
>
> (Mechner, 1965, pp. 443–444)

Now consider the following:

> The artist in the classroom is neither prevalent, nor, in fact particularly valued. He balks at established curricula, which makes administrators nervous and parents fearful, and oftentimes confuses children. He is constantly told that the school is for the students, and not a place for the teacher to push his pet

fancies. When small avid groups of students congregate around him, he is reminded that school is for *all* the students, not just the few who see some perverse value in his unique conversations.

So we begin with the fact that most teachers see themselves as professionals. In their training, they want to be shown how to become professional; they want to learn how to purvey the wisdom of the culture in a reasonably standard and explicit way. In short, they want to know how to do their job....

In these terms, the problem of teaching is construed less as the need for more creative artists to teach, but rather as the need for general scientific solutions to meet educational problems. We look not for unique personalities to provide a leavening for the flat culture; we create teams of increasingly specialized professionals to administer full-tested teaching "systems." The ultimate educational context then is not the free-flowing human dialogue; it is the student in the booth strapped up with a variety of teaching-learning devices monitored by a professional teacher. The implicit image is the operating room or the blood-cleansing kidney machine.

(Oliver, 1967, p. 111)

What we have here are not merely two views related to the problem of stating educational objectives, but two radically different conceptions of the nature of education. The former conceives of education as the shaping of behavior; the latter as an emergent process guided through art.

Thus far I have indicated that the task of defining educational objectives rests upon a conception of value in education. In addition, I have indicated that the prescriptions offered for formulating educational objectives are related to the three metaphors through which education has been and is conceived: the industrial, the behavioristic, and the biological. These competing orientations, I am arguing, are implicit in the recommendations made by students of education as they go about the task of illuminating and improving the process of education by clarifying and prescribing the manner in which educational objectives are to be formulated and used.

As long as individuals in the educational field aspire toward different educational goals there can be no single set of research findings that will satisfy an individual who holds educational values different from those toward which the research was directed. While we can properly ask, for example, whether a clear statement of objectives on the part of the teacher facilitates curriculum planning, teaching, or student learning, and while, in principle, we can secure data to answer such questions, the significance of the answer depends not merely on the adequacy and precision of the research undertaken but on the goals toward which the educational program was directed. If education is seen as the practice of an art in which children have an opportunity to work as young apprentices with someone who himself is inquiring into a problem for which he has no answer, the relevance of concepts like terminal behavior, educational product, and deployment to learning stations, as well as research bearing upon them is likely to be considered beside the point educationally.

What of the research on educational objectives? What in fact has been found concerning the utility of educational objectives when specified according to criteria identified in the opening pages of this chapter?

A number of questions can be asked about educational objectives that are in principle amenable to empirical study. We can attempt to determine how in fact they are formulated by various groups such as curriculum developers, administrators and teachers, and it is possible to compare the methods used in their formulation to the recommendations of experts. We can determine the extent to which teachers have educational objectives and whether they meet the criteria for adequacy described by

Tyler, Bloom, Gagné, and others. We can compare the curriculum planning behavior of those who have precise educational objectives with the planning of those who do not have precise educational objectives. We can determine the effect of clearly stated objectives on the process of instruction, and, perhaps most important, we can determine the relationship between clearly formulated educational objectives and student learning. Do teachers who know what they want students to be able to do as measured by the teachers' ability to state their objectives precisely (using criteria set forth by Mager, for example) have a greater effect on particular types of learning than teachers who do not? In short, we can ask questions about: (1) the relationship between the way educational objectives are formulated and their quality; (2) the extent to which teachers have educational objectives; (3) the effect of educational objectives on curriculum planning; (4) the effect of educational objectives on instruction; and (5) the usefulness of educational objectives in facilitating learning.

Although such questions are complex they are important objects for empirical attention. When one looks for research on these questions, one soon finds that for the most part they have been neglected. There are some exceptions however. Margaret Ammons' study (1964) of the process and the product in curriculum development is one. In that study, Ammons set about to achieve three goals: to discover whether school systems used any systematic way of formulating educational objectives, to determine the relationship between the process used in formulating objectives and their quality, and to identify the extent to which factors thought to influence teacher appraisal of educational objectives do in fact influence such appraisal. Using a questionnaire on objectives Ammons selected a sample of school systems from a pool of 359 systems where it was possible to study the responses of board members, administrators, and teachers. At the end of her study Ammons states:

The writer believes that this study has made the following contributions:

1   the discovery that some systems do not have objectives, as this term is defined here, to guide their educational programs;
2   the discovery that the school systems which participated in this study do not follow a process recommended by authorities to develop their educational objectives;
3   the discovery that teachers in this study appear to base their instructional programs on what they customarily have done rather than on the system's educational objectives;
4   the discovery that while no significant relation exists between process and product using the data collected for this study, there is enough relation to suggest further research before the process is discarded;
5   the possibility of using empirical tests to evaluate curriculum theories;
6   areas for further research have been identified.

(Ammons, 1964, pp. 451–457)

Gagné (1965) discusses the importance of educational objectives in the development of instructional systems. He refers to French's work in training apprentice Air Force mechanics and to Briggs and Bernards' work also in Air Force maintenance training as providing evidence on the effectiveness of instructional objectives. Evidence on the effectiveness of high level specification of objectives in educational settings is considerably more tenuous.

Although Nerbovig (1956) found that intermediate grade teachers who had participated in the formulation of objectives and who had longer experience as teachers used objectives more frequently in planning their curriculums, Ammons' findings contradict Nerbovig's.

In an interesting effort to create an instructional objectives preference list, Popham and Baker (1965) asked students to rate on a five-point scale instructional objectives arranged according to usefulness. One class of statements was both behaviorally stated and important, a second class behaviorally stated and unimportant, a third nonbehaviorally stated and important, and a fourth nonbehaviorally stated and not important. When the subjects' (in this case student teachers) lesson plans were surreptitiously observed with respect to the use of behaviorally defined objectives and correlated with the subjects' preferences as revealed in their ranking of objectives, $r = 0.25$ ($p < 0.05$). Although reported only as a note in the *Journal of Educational Measurement* the research by Popham and Baker appears promising; it suggests the type of inquiry needed to clarify the function of educational objectives in educational settings.

In view of the admonitions in curriculum literature to state objectives in behavioral terms, it is surprising to find such a paucity of empirical studies available. Most of the studies that have been undertaken were done in training systems in industry or in the military services. One would think – and hope – that there would be some differences between industrial and military training and education. In the *Review of Educational Research* John Goodlad (1960) wrote, "There appear to be no studies establishing an actual relationship between increased clarification of educational objectives and improved discrimination in the selection of classroom learning opportunities for students." With respect to quantitative empirical research in school settings the situation appears not to have changed much in the past eight years.

From the published studies of educational objectives one can conclude that:

1   a very limited amount of empirical data is available on the subject;
2   a narrow range of questions have been asked;
3   most of the discussion on the usefulness of educational objectives has been based primarily upon rational analysis.

Now I have no bone to pick with the rational analysis of educational issues if empirical data are unavailable for unobtainable. Indeed, in a previous paper (1967a) I explicated some of the problems concerning high-level specification of educational objectives and such explication was a result of analysis rather than a result of conclusions based upon quantitative data. In that paper I identified a number of limitations in theory about high-level specification of objectives. Without elaborating them here, they were as follows:

1   they tend to overestimate the degree to which it is possible to predict educational outcomes;
2   they tend to treat all subject-matters alike regarding the degree of specificity possible in stating educational objectives;
3   they tend to confuse the application of a standard and the making of a judgment regarding the appraisal of educational outcomes;
4   they have tended to imply that the formulation of objectives should be a first step in curriculum development and hence have confused the logical with the psychological in educational planning.

In a subsequent paper (1967b), I argued further that those who have advocated high-level specification of objectives have not differentiated between establishing a direction and formulating an objective. I argued that much in school practice which is educational is a consequence of establishing directions rather than formulating objectives.

I see even more problems now. For one, if we follow Gagné's suggestions (1967) regarding the identity of content and objective, we would select or use no content which had no objective and therefore have objectives for each unit of content we selected. What would this mean in the classroom? If the suggestion is followed strictly, the teacher would have to formulate behaviorally defined objectives for each unit of content for each educational program for which she was responsible and in the elementary school she may teach as many as fourteen subject-areas.

Let us assume that a teacher has one unit of content to be learned by a group of thirty children for each seven subject areas a day. Let us assume further that she has her class divided in thirds in order to differentiate content for students with differing abilities. This would mean that the teacher would have to formulate objectives for seven units of content, times five days a week, times three groups of students, times four weeks a month, times ten months a school year. She would therefore have to have 4,200 behaviorally defined objectives for a school year. A six-year school employing such a curriculum rationale would have to have 25,200 behaviorally defined educational objectives.

Aside from the question of the sheer feasibility of such a scheme, what those who object to such an approach are concerned with, I think, is that even if the scheme could be implemented, it would alter the type of relationship between the teacher and the student which they value. If a teacher focuses primarily on the attainment of clearly specified objectives, she is not likely to focus on other aspects of the educational encounter, for although clearly specified objectives provide windows, they also create walls. Those who are not enthusiastic about high-level specification of objectives are not eager, I believe, to look through the windows of those who conceive of education as behavioral engineering.

Can such differences in orientation to education be resolved when it comes to the issue of how, if at all, educational objectives should be formulated? The remainder of this chapter will elucidate a conception of educational objectives which might make this resolution possible.

As an institution responsible for the transmission of culture, the school is concerned with enabling students to acquire those intellectual codes and skills which will make it possible for them to profit from the contributions of those who have gone before. To accomplish this task an array of socially defined skills must be learned – reading, writing, and arithmetic are some examples of coding systems that are basic to further inquiry into human culture.

While school programs attempt to enable children to acquire these skills, to learn to employ the tools necessary for using cultural products, schools are also concerned with enabling children to make a contribution to that culture by providing opportunities for the individual to construe his own interpretation to the material he encounters or constructs. A simple repetition of the past is the surest path to cultural rigor mortis.

Given these dual concerns – helping children to become skilled in the use of cultural tools already available and helping them to modify and expand these tools so that the culture remains viable – it seems to me appropriate to differentiate between two types of educational objectives which can be formulated in curriculum planning. The first type is familiar to most readers and is called an *instructional objective*; the second I have called an *expressive objective*.

Instructional objectives are objectives which specify unambiguously the particular behavior (skill, item of knowledge, and so forth) the student is to acquire after having completed one or more learning activities. These objectives fit the scheme or criteria identified earlier. They are usually drawn from cultural products such as the disciplines and are laid out in intervals of time appropriate for the children who are to acquire them.

Instructional objectives are used in a predictive model of curriculum development. A predictive model is one in which objectives are formulated and activities selected which are predicted to be useful in enabling children to attain the specific behavior embodied in the objective. In this model, evaluation is aimed at determining the extent to which the objective has been achieved. If the objective has not been achieved, various courses of action may follow. The objective may be changed. The instructional method may be altered. The content of the curriculum may be revised.

With an instructional objective the teacher as well as the children (if they are told what the objective is) are likely to focus upon the attainment of a specific array of behaviors. The teacher in the instructional context knows what to look for as an indicator of achievement since the objective unambiguously defines the behavior. Insofar as the children are at similar stages of development and insofar as the curriculum and the instruction are effective, the outcomes of the learning activity will be homogeneous in character. The effective curriculum, when it is aimed at instructional objectives, will develop forms of behavior whose characteristics are known beforehand and, as likely as not, will be common across students – if not at the identical point in time, at some point during the school program.

The use of instructional objectives has a variety of educational ramifications. In preparing reading material in the social studies, for example, study questions at the beginning of a chapter can be used as cues to guide the student's attention to certain concepts or generalizations which the teacher intends to help the student learn. In the development of certain motor skills the teacher may provide examples of such skills and thus show the student what he is supposed to be able to do upon terminating the program. With the use of instructional objectives clarity of terminal behavior is crucial since it serves as a standard against which to appraise the effectiveness of the curriculum. *In an effective curriculum using instructional objectives the terminal behavior of the student and the objectives are isomorphic.*

Expressive objectives differ considerably from instructional objectives. An expressive objective does not specify the behavior the student is to acquire after having engaged in one or more learning activities. An expressive objective describes an educational encounter: it identifies a situation in which children are to work, a problem with which they are to cope, a task in which they are to engage; but it does not specify what from that encounter, situation, problem, or task they are to learn. An expressive objective provides both the teacher and the student with an invitation to explore, defer, or focus on issues that are of peculiar interest or import to the inquirer. An expressive objective is evocative rather than prescriptive.

The expressive objective is intended to serve as a theme around which skills and understandings learned earlier can be brought to bear, but through which those skills and understandings can be expanded, elaborated, and made idiosyncratic. With an expressive objective what is desired is not homogeneity of response among students but diversity. In the expressive context the teacher hopes to provide a situation in which meanings become personalized and in which children produce products, both theoretical and qualitative, that are as diverse as themselves. Con-sequently the evaluative task in this situation is not one of applying a common standard to the products produced but one of reflecting upon what has been produced in order to reveal its uniqueness and significance. In the expressive context, the product is likely to be as much of a surprise to the maker as it is for the teacher who encounters it.

Statements of expressive objectives might read:

1   to interpret the meaning of *Paradise Lost*;
2   to examine and appraise the significance of *The Old Man and the Sea*;

3   to develop a three-dimensional form through the use of wire and wood;
4   to visit the zoo and discuss what was of interest there.

What should be noted about such objectives is that they do not specify what the student is to be able to do after he engages in an educational activity; rather they identify the type of encounter he is to have. From this encounter both teacher and student acquire data useful for evaluation. In this context the mode of evaluation is similar to aesthetic criticism; that is, the critic appraises a product, examines its qualities and import, but does not direct the artist toward the painting of a specific type of picture. The critic's subject-matter is the work done – he does not prescribe a blueprint of its construction.

Now I happen to believe that expressive objectives are the type that teachers most frequently use. Given the range and the diversity of children it is more useful to identify potentially fruitful encounters than to specify instructional objectives.

Although I believe that the use of expressive objectives is generally more common than the use of instructional objectives, in certain subject areas curriculum specialists have tended to emphasize one rather than the other. In mathematics, for example, much greater attention historically has been given to the instructional objective than in the visual arts where the dominant emphasis has been on the expressive (Eisner, 1965).

I believe that the most sophisticated modes of intellectual work – those, for example, undertaken in the studio, the research laboratory, and the graduate seminar – most frequently employ expressive rather than instructional objectives. In the doctoral seminar, for example, a theme will be identified around which both teacher and students can interact in an effort to cope more adequately with the problems related to the theme. In such situations educational outcomes are appraised after they emerge; specific learnings are seldom formulated in terms of instructional objectives. The dialogue unfolds and is followed as well as led. In such situations the skills and understandings developed are used as instruments for inquiring more deeply into the significant or puzzling. Occasionally such problems require the invention of new intellectual tools, thus inducing the creative act and the creative contribution. Once devised or fashioned these new tools become candidates for instructional attention.

Since these two types of objectives – instructional and expressive – require different kinds of curriculum activities and evaluation procedures, they each must occupy a distinctive place in curriculum theory and development. Instructional objectives embody the codes and the skills that culture has to provide and which make inquiry possible. Expressive objectives designate those circumstances in which the codes and the skills acquired in instructional contexts can be used and elaborated; through their expansion and reconstruction culture remains vital. Both types of objectives and the learning activities they imply constitute, to modify Whitehead's phrase, "the rhythm of curriculum." That is, instructional objectives emphasize the acquisition of the known; while expressive objectives its elaboration, modification, and, at times, the production of the utterly new.

Curriculum can be developed with an eye toward the alternating of such objectives. We can, I believe, study curriculum to determine the extent to which instructional and expressive educational objectives are employed, and we can raise questions about the types of relationships between them which are most productive for various types of students, for various types of learning, and for various subject matters.

In this chapter I have argued that the problem of formulating educational objectives is not simply a question of technique but is related directly to one's conception of education. The manner in which educational objectives are couched is, at base, a value decision. Second, I have tried to provide evidence of the differences among these values by examining the metaphors used by those who have contributed to the literature of the field. Third, I have cited empirical research aimed at examining the usefulness of educational objectives. Fourth, I have distinguished between two types of educational objectives – instructional and expressive – and indicated how they function in curriculum planning. The formulation and use of these objectives have implications for the selection of learning activities and for evaluation. The consequences of their use seem to me to be appropriate subject-matter for research.

## Acknowledgment

I wish to express my gratitude to Professors Robert Bridgham, D. Bob Gowin, and Alan Peshkin for their helpful comments on an earlier draft of this paper.

## References

Ammons, Margaret. An empirical study of progress and product in curriculum development. *Journal of Educational Research*, 1964, 27(9), 451–457.

Billings, N. *A determination of generalizations basic to the social studies curriculum.* Baltimore, MD: Warwick & York, 1929.

Bloom, B. S., Engelhart, M. D., Faust, E. J., Hill, W. H., and Krathwohl, D. R. *Taxonomy of educational objectives: Handbook I, the cognitive domain.* New York: Longmans, Green (David McKay), 1956.

Callahan, R. E. *Education and the cult of efficiency.* Chicago, IL: University of Chicago Press, 1962.

Dewey, J. and Dewey, Evelyn. *Schools of to-morrow.* New York, Dutton, 1915.

Eisner, E. W. Curriculum ideas in time of crisis. *Art Education*, 1965, 18(7).

Gagné, R. The analysis of instructional objectives for the design of instruction. In R. Glaser (ed.), *Teaching machines and programmed learning, II: Data and directions.* Washington, WA: Department of Audio Visual Instruction, N.E.A., 1965, pp. 21–65.

Gagné, R. Curriculum research and the promotion of learning. In R. Tyler, R. Gagné, and M. Scriven (eds), *Perspectives of curriculum evaluation*, AERA Monograph 1. Chicago, IL: Rand McNally, 1967.

Goodlad, J. I. Curriculum: The state of the field. *Review of Educational Research*, 1960, 20(3), 192.

Harap, H. (ed.) *The changing curriculum.* New York: Appleton-Century, 1937.

Krathwohl, D. R., Bloom, B. S., and Masia, B. B. *Taxonomy of educational objectives: Handbook II, the affective domain.* New York: David McKay, 1964.

Mager, R. F. *Preparing objectives for programmed instruction.* Palo Alto, CA: Fearon, 1962.

Mechner, F. Science education and behavioral technology. In R. Glaser (ed.), *Teaching machines and programmed learning, II: Data and directions.* Washington, WA: Department of Audio Visual Instruction, N.E.A., 1965, pp. 443–444.

Nerbovig, Marcella H. Teachers' perceptions of the function of objectives. Doctoral thesis, University of Wisconsin, 1956. Dissertation Abstracts, 1956, 16(12), 2406–2407.

Oliver, D. The education industries. *Harvard Educational Review*, 1967, 37(1), 111.

Popham, W. J. and Baker, Eva L. The instructional objectives preference test. *Journal of Educational Measurement*, UCLA, 1965, 2, 186.

Thorndike, E. L. *Educational psychology, Vol. I. The original nature of man.* New York: Teachers College, Columbia University, 1921, pp. 11–12.

Thorndike, E. L. and Woodworth, R. S. The influence of improvement in one mental function upon the efficiency of other functions. *Psychological Review*, 1901 (May).

Tyler, R. *Basic principles of curriculum and instruction.* Chicago, IL: University of Chicago Press, 1950.

Watson, J. B. *Psychology from the standpoint of a behaviorist.* Philadelphia, PA: Lippincott, 1919, pp. 1–2.

# CHAPTER 4

# EDUCATIONAL CONNOISSEURSHIP AND CRITICISM

## Their form and functions in educational evaluation

*Journal of Aesthetic Education*, 1976, 135–150

The major thesis of this paper is that the forms used in conventional approaches to educational evaluation have a set of profound consequences on the conduct and character of schooling in the United States. Unless those forms can be expanded so that they attend to qualities of educational life relevant to the arts, it is not likely that the arts will secure a meaningful place in American schools. To understand why we evaluate the way that we do, it is important to examine the sources through which evaluation became a kind of field within American education. If we examine the past we will find that since the turn of the century, since the early work of Edward L. Thorndike, there has been a strong aspiration among psychologists to create a science of education which would provide educational practitioners – administrators as well as teachers – with the kind of knowledge that would permit prediction through control of the process and consequences of schooling. Laws that would do for educational practitioners what the work of Einstein, Maxwell, and Bohr have done for physicists were the object of the educational scientist's dream. This yearning for prediction through control was, of course, reflected in the desire to make schools more efficient and presumably more effective. Educational research was to discover the laws of learning that would replace intuition and artistry with knowledge and prescribed method. The hunt was on for the one best method to teach the various fields of study that constituted the curriculum. This aspiration to discover the laws of learning was allied with the efficiency movement in education that sought to install scientific management procedures in schools through time-and-motion study of teaching practice.[1] It reflected then, as it does today, the need to discover the principles and practices that would give us efficient and effective schools.

This desire was, of course, based upon a particular view of the world and of man's position within it. That view was scientific in character. The task of educational research was to treat educational practice as a nomothetic activity, one controlled by laws rather than an ideographic activity, one which was guided by the unique characteristics of the particular situation. Describing the philosophic differences between the nomothetic and the ideographic George Henrik von Wright writes:

> All these thinkers [Droysen, Dilthey, Simmel, Max Weber, Windelband, Rickert, Croce, and Collingwood] reject the methodological monism of positivism and refuse to view the pattern set by the exact natural sciences as the sole and supreme ideal for a rational understanding of reality. Many of them

emphasize a contrast between those sciences which, like physics or chemistry or physiology, aim at generalizations about reproducible and predictable phenomena, and those which, like history, want to grasp the individual and unique features of their objects. Windelband coined the label "nomothetic" for sciences which search for laws, and "ideographic" for the descriptive study of individuality.[2]

As for evaluation practices, they were to be objective, that is, they were to describe in quantitative, empirical terms whether or not the goals of the curriculum were achieved.

If I dwell upon these matters of the past it is because I believe they are crucial for understanding what we do today and why. Arts education might not be possible except in the skimpiest form in institutions that are controlled by unexamined assumptions which create a climate, establish a tone, foster a set of priorities that are inhospitable to the kind of life that work in the arts might yield. Although scientific and technological approaches to the methods of schooling have made some important contributions, I believe they have had at least four major deleterious consequences. Let me identify these.

First, because scientific assumptions and scientifically oriented inquiry aim at the search for laws or law-like generalizations, such inquiry tends to treat qualities of particular situations as instrumentalities. The uniqueness of the particular is considered "noise" in the search for general tendencies and main effects. This, in turn, leads to the oversimplification of the particular through a process of reduction aimed at the characterization of complexity by a single set of scores. Quality becomes converted to quantity and then summed and averaged as a way of standing for the particular quality from which the quantities were initially derived. For the evaluation of educational practice and its consequences, the single numerical test score is used to symbolize a universe of particulars, in spite of the fact that the number symbol itself possesses no inherent quality that expresses the quality of the particular it is intended to represent.

The distinction between symbols that possess in their form the expressive content to which they are related and those symbols which through associative learning we relate to certain ideas is an extremely important one. The art symbol exemplifies the former while the word or number exemplifies the latter. Scientific activity yields propositions so that truth can be determined in relation to its instrumental value, a value dependent upon its predictive or explanatory accuracy. Artistic activity creates symbolic forms which themselves present directly an idea, image, or feeling which resides within rather than outside of the symbol.

Second, the technological orientation to practice tends to encourage a primary focus on the achievement of some future state and in the process tends to undermine the significance of the present. Take, as an example, the concern in recent years with the formulation of behavioral objectives. Objectives are things that are always out of reach. They are goals towards which one works, targets we are urged to keep our eyes upon. Objectives are future-oriented, and when the future becomes increasingly important to us, we sacrifice the present in order to achieve it. In elementary schools both teachers and students are bedeviled by extrinsic rewards such as token economies. Children are rewarded for the achievement of objectives that themselves have little intrinsic appeal, and teachers may one day be paid in relation to their ability to produce certain measurable outcomes. When the future becomes all-important, it must be achieved at all costs. At the secondary level it leads to the pursuit of high scores on scholastic achievement tests and at the university level to the destruction of experiments and the stealing of books in pre-med programs. Not only must objectives be achieved, but one must also be sure that others do not achieve them. The present is sacrificed on the altar of tomorrow.

Third, scientific and technological approaches to schooling lead, as I have already said, to the attempt to "objectify" knowledge. Objectification almost always requires that at least two conditions be met. First, the qualities to which one attends must be empirically manifest, and second, they must be convertible to quantity. In this way both reliability and precision can be assured, hence conclusions about a state of affairs can be verified.

That these procedures themselves rest upon certain beliefs which cannot themselves be verified by procedures the beliefs espouse, does not seem to pose a problem for those who espouse them. But, in addition, these procedures, based as they are on a particular conception of truth, also bring with them some negative injunctions. For example, one must not emotionalize one's language when talking about children, educational practice, or educational goals. Intimation, metaphor, analogy, poetic insight have little place in such a view. For example, instead of talking about children, we are urged to talk about subjects. Instead of talking about teaching, we must talk about treatments. Instead of talking about aims and aspirations, we must talk about dependent variables, performance objectives, or competencies. And to increase "objectivity," instead of talking in the first person singular, the third person singular or first person plural is better form. Somehow, if "the author," or "we" conclude something, it is more objective than if "I" do.

This shift in language would not present much of a problem if it only represented a shift in language, but the problem exceeds the matter of language per se. It is a symptom of a larger difficulty encountered in trying to understand human beings. The problem is that in de-emotionalizing expression and proscribing suggestive language, the opportunity to understand empathically and to communicate the quality of human experience diminishes. As long as measurable forms of manifest behavior are our exclusive referent, the quality of experience will be neglected. Inference about experience has little place in radical behaviorism, but radical behaviorism, exemplified in the work of Thorndike, Watson, Hull, and Skinner has held a central place in American educational psychology. To know what people feel, to know what behavior *means*, we must go beyond behavior.[3]

Fourth, when one seeks laws governing the control of human behavior, it is not surprising that one would also seek the achievement of a common set of goals for that behavior. When one combines this with the need to operationalize such goals quantitatively, the use of standardized tests becomes understandable. The standardized test *is* standard; it is the same for all students. It not only standardizes the tasks students will confront, it standardizes the goals against which they shall be judged. These tests, de facto, become the goals. When this happens, uniformity becomes an aspiration; effectiveness means in practice that all students will achieve the same ends. Individualization, regardless of what it might mean, becomes defined in terms of providing for differences in rate; differentiation in pace rather than in goal, content, or mode of expression is the general meaning of individualization. Standardized achievement tests do not now provide the means for assessing the significant personalization of teaching and learning. In a technological orientation to educational practice, the cultivation of productive idiosyncrasy – one of the prime consequences of work in the arts – becomes a problem.

The major points that I have been trying to make thus far are two. First, the forms of evaluation that are now employed to assess the effectiveness of school programs have profound consequences upon the character of teaching, the content of curriculum, and the kinds of goals that schools seek to attain. Evaluation procedures, more than a reasoned philosophy of education, influence the educational priorities at work within the schools. Second, these evaluation procedures rest upon largely unexamined assumptions that are basically scientific in their epistemology, technological in their application, and have consequences that are often limited and at times inhospitable to the kinds of goals the arts can achieve.

Recognition of the assumptions, character, and consequences of conventional forms of educational evaluation is insufficient to bring about change in the ways in which we evaluate. Something more must be provided. That something more is an alternative or a complement to what now prevails, and it is the articulation and testing of this alternative that my present work aims at.

I have chosen to start with a set of premises about education that are quite different from those underlying the dominant conventional approaches to educational evaluation and to the study of educational practice. I do not believe that education as a process, or schooling as an institution designed to foster that process, or teaching as an activity that most directly mediates that process is likely to be controlled by a set of laws that can be transformed into a prescription or recipe for teaching. I do not believe we will ever have a "Betty Crocker" theory of education. Teaching is an activity that requires artistry, schooling itself is a cultural artifact, and education is a process whose features may differ from individual to individual, context to context. Therefore, what I believe we need to do with respect to educational evaluation is not to seek recipes to control and measure practice, but rather to enhance whatever artistry the teacher can achieve. Theory plays a role in the cultivation of artistry, but its role is not prescriptive, it is diagnostic. Good theory in education, as in art, helps us to see more; it helps us think about more of the qualities that constitute a set of phenomena. Theory does not replace intelligence and perception and action, it provides some of the windows through which intelligence can look out into the world. Thus one of the functions that theory might serve in educational evaluation is in the cultivation of *educational connoisseurship*.[4]

Educational connoisseurship, about which I will have more to say momentarily, is but half of a pair of concepts that I believe to be particularly promising for thinking about the conduct of educational evaluation. The other half of this pair is the concept of *educational criticism*. Each of these concepts, educational connoisseurship and educational criticism, have their roots in the arts – and for good reason. Because I believe teaching in classrooms is ideographic in character, that is, because I believe the features of classroom life are not likely to be explained or controlled by behavioral laws, I conceive the major contribution of evaluation to be a heightened awareness of the qualities of that life so that teachers and students can become more intelligent within it. Connoisseurship plays an important role towards this end by refining the levels of apprehension of the qualities that pervade classrooms. To be a connoisseur of wine, bicycles, or graphic arts is to be informed about their qualities; it means being able to discriminate the subtleties among types of wine, bicycles, and graphic arts by drawing upon a gustatory, visual, and kinesthetic memory against which the particulars of the present may be placed for purposes of comparison and contrast. Connoisseurs of anything – and one can have connoisseurship about anything – *appreciate* what they encounter in the proper meaning of that word. Appreciation does not necessarily mean liking something, although one might like what one experiences. Appreciation here means an awareness and an understanding of what one has experienced. Such an awareness provides the basis for judgment.

If connoisseurship is the art of appreciation, criticism is the art of disclosure. Criticism, as Dewey pointed out in *Art as Experience*, has at its end the reeducation of perception.[5] What the critic strives for is to articulate or render those ineffable qualities constituting art in a language that makes them vivid. But this gives rise to something of a paradox. How is it that what is ineffable can be articulated? How do words express what words can never express? The task of the critic is to adumbrate, suggest, imply, connote, render, rather than to attempt to translate.[6] In this task, metaphor and analogy, suggestion and implication are major tools. The language of criticism, indeed its success as criticism, is measured by the brightness of its illumination. The task of the critic is to help us to see.

It is thus seen from what I have said that connoisseurship provides criticism with its subject matter. Connoisseurship is private, but criticism is public. Connoisseurs simply need to appreciate what they encounter. Critics, however, must render these qualities vivid by the artful use of critical disclosure. Effective criticism requires the use of connoisseurship, but connoisseurship does not require the use of criticism.

What is also clear, when one thinks about it, is that education as a field of study does not have – as does literature, music, the visual arts, drama, and film – a branch called educational criticism. Yet educational practice and the outcomes of such practice are subject to critical techniques. We do not have, for example, journals of educational criticism or critical theory. We do not have programs in universities that prepare educational critics. We do not have a tradition of thought dealing with the formal, systematic, scholarly study and practice of educational criticism. My work at Stanford is aimed at precisely these goals. With a group of doctoral students I have, over the past two years, been attempting to flesh out the issues, the concepts, the criteria, the techniques, and the prototypes of educational connoisseurship and educational criticism. To do this we have been visiting schools around Stanford to study classrooms and to create criticism, and we have been creating educational criticism within Stanford University itself by critically describing the classrooms and courses offered within the School of Education. In addition, we have been making videotapes of classrooms and have been using these as a basis for our own education and the testing of our own criticism. Thus far two doctoral dissertations[7] have been completed in which educational criticism is the major conceptual tool. And two more doctoral students will receive their degrees in June of 1976 whose dissertations also employ educational criticism as a dominant mode of inquiry. In short, we have been working at the task of creating a new way of looking at the phenomena that constitute educational life within classrooms.

In pursuing these aims we have engaged in a kind of dialectic between the conceptualization of educational connoisseurship and educational criticism as theoretical categories and the actual writing of criticism and its attendant problems, such as what the role of the educational critic is when that person is in a classroom. This dialectic has informed both aspects of our work, the theoretical and the practical. Before I share with you an example of our work, let me say a few words about three major aspects of educational criticism.

What is it that one does when one writes educational criticism of a classroom, or a set of curriculum materials, or a school? There are three things that one does. One describes, one interprets, and one evaluates or appraises what one sees.

The descriptive aspect of educational criticism (and these three distinctions are not intended to suggest that they are independent or sequential) is an effort to characterize or render the pervasive and purely descriptive aspects of the phenomena one attends to. For example, critical description might tell the reader about the number or type of questions raised in a class, the amount of time spent in discussion, or the kind of image or impression the teacher or the room gives to visitors. Descriptive educational criticism is a type of portrayal of the qualities that one encounters without getting into – very deeply, at least – what they signify. Following Clifford Geertz, the descriptive aspect of criticism is fairly thin, although we recognize that all description has some degree of thickness to it. Let me give you an example of what is largely descriptive educational criticism written by one of my students.

Last Thursday morning I visited the auditorium of San Francisco's James Lick Junior High School. I had already stood in this room many times, for many years, in many schools. Recent visits remind me how my body has grown taller and heavier. The scuffed floorboards' squeaks feel less congenial. The looming balcony now appears less exotic. My eyes no longer trace geometric patterns in the familiar tan ceiling.

Although I lean on the rear wall, I feel close up to the stage. Between it and me wait twin sections of permanent wooden seats, each twelve across and maybe twenty-five rows deep. In front of the first row I watch the busy pit area, where several adults, some with flash cameras, mingle purposefully amid a baby grand piano, a drum set, several stools and benches, three conga drums, a folding table holding a tenor saxophone in its open case, and two microphone stands. Dark curtains close the raised stages.

About half the seats, those in the rear, are empty. The front half of the auditorium contains an exquisite kaleidoscope of several hundred junior high kids – standing, sitting, turning, squirming, tugging, slapping, squealing, calling, talking, clapping, laughing, waving. A few stare silent and motionless. Most smile. They make a multicultural mix, of obscure proportions. Here and there an adult, probably a teacher, joins the crowd or stands back to oversee.

Their combined voices swell ceaselessly, like the ocean's face, as though smiling in rhythm with the crowd's surging spirit. Occasionally a single voice calls or whistles to jar this bussing blanket's penetrating caress.

From behind the curtain, a grinning, slim, gray-haired man in a dark blue suit walks down to the audience, talks briefly with someone, picks up the tenor sax, and returns backstage. He leaves the curtains parted about a foot, revealing there people hurrying across the bright stage in last-minute urgency. Indistinct musical sounds from backstage join the audience's hum.

Small groups of kids from nearby schools file in quickly, filling all the remaining seats.

A man carrying a guitar peers out through the curtain, and then walks down to the pit, followed by the tenor sax man. They greet several adults already standing there in the right-hand corner.

A spotlight focuses several different size circles on the curtain. The lights onstage darken. The kids quiet, and their adults come to stand along the walls.

A serious-looking man of average build and thin, straight, gray hair, wearing dark slacks, a dark brown turtleneck shirt, and a beige sport-coat, strides directly to the microphone in the center of the pit. In the next ten minutes he and two other adults greet the audience and progressively, systematically introduce the morning's program and their guest, Mr. John Birks Gillespie. The last speaker – Mr. Smith, the school's music director – is the tenor sax player. His final words succumb to the kids' impatient applause.

Now, from the right corner, Dizzy Gillespie struts playfully across to the microphone – a middle-aged Tom Sawyer in a bulky, white, knit cap that hints broadly toward mischief. A brash musical rebel and innovator thirty-five years ago, now Dizzy is a jovial, stocky, Black man, with faint white hairs on his chin. Clutching his spangled trumpet against a black-and-white checked sport-coat which reveals his dazzling red shirt, he thanks Mr. Smith and greets his audience.

Hearing his first words, I expect to see Louis Armstrong's eyes and Bill Cosby's grin. Dizzy savors his voice; it flows gently – slow-paced and melodic. His audience sits rapt. Their posture shifts with his frequent vocal pitch and tempo modulations. I can barely recall the kids' homogenized chatter from a few minutes earlier.

For about ten minutes, he shares comfortable, chuckly stories about his trumpet and his own music education. Everyone seems to be listening, alert and smiling, and commenting with commotion, which Dizzy encourages.

Abruptly, he announces "What we're gonna do now is play for you," and with one foot he taps 1 . . . 2 . . . 1, 2, 3, 4. The drummer and two guitar players, who followed his entrance, now lean into a comfortable number which Dizzy leads in a moderate tempo. The piece seems unfamiliar to the kids, and they respond to the contrast between its tasty, pattering verse and the soaring chorus. All through the tune, the kids focus their attention on Dizzy, himself. Perhaps sensing this, he plays with their enthusiasm, making games for all to share. For example, turning to face the lead guitar player toward the end of the tune, he dances and sways while the guitar solos a chorus. Simultaneously, many kids are bouncing in their seats.

As the applause following this number dwindles, Dizzy cries out "Como estas usted?" and, responding to the kids' shouted replies, he announces that the next selection will be Latin. As though addressing a favorite toy, he sits behind the conga drums, develops a minute-long monologue about rhythm in jazz, and clowns with his face and voice while adjusting the microphone stand.

He describes a call-and-response routine for the song, demonstrates the kids' part (they fling their right fists while shouting "Oh!") and its cue (he sings a call), and drills them in the routine a few times. The kids conclude each practice with applause, laughter, and chatter, and they seem eager for more. Continuing, Dizzy announces that many people clap their hands on the wrong beats. They should clap on "two and four, as in 'oom-*cha*, oom-*cha*, oom-*cha*'." By now the kids are clapping solidly on the off-beats. Dizzy lets them take a few more measures and, with the other three musicians, begins the song.

He arches over the three congas with eyes closed, eyebrows raised, mouth slack open, and head pointing up to the right corner of the balcony. As though keeping six apples submerged in three pails of water, he moves his hands intently, rapidly, and gracefully. The kids find themselves creating part of the music they hear. Many clap, smile, talk, watch, and listen. Few are quiet. No one seems bored. Everyone seems involved.

Leaning toward the mike, Dizzy leads several repetitions of the kids' call-and-response routine. He returns briefly to the congas, before stepping up with his trumpet, which he plays, eyes closed, pointing the horn's bell to the same corner of the balcony. Returning to the mike, he chants a hushed "Swing low, sweet chariot, . . ." Opening his eyes and raising his hands, he replies " . . . coming for to carry me home." The kids join this response, and continue singing these familiar lyrics to their conclusion. Now standing upright, Dizzy sings a series of scat breaks – bursts of explosive syllables cogently declaring an impromptu rhythmic notion. Many kids answer each break by singing back its echo. Finally, he surprises us with an extended, complicated break. The kids respond with applause and laughter, and Dizzy ends the number here, laughing himself.[8]

The interpretive aspect of educational criticism represents an effort to understand the meaning and significance that various forms of action have for those in a social setting. For example, just what do the extrinsic rewards for reading mean to the third graders who keep charts of the number of books that they have read? What do the eager, outstretched, waving arms and hands signify to both teacher and students when students compete for the opportunity to provide the teacher with the right answer? What kinds of messages are being given to students by the allocation of time and its location in the school day to the various subject matters that constitute the curriculum? To answer these questions requires a journey into interpretation, an ability to participate empathically in the life of another, to appreciate the meanings of such cultural symbols as lists of books read, hand-waving, and time allocation. The interpretive aspect of educational criticism requires the judicious and informed use of a variety of social sciences and the practical wisdom born of experience in schools.

The third aspect of criticism is evaluative. It asks, "What is the *educational* import or value of what is going on?" To deal with the educational import of classroom life is, of course, to do more than to describe or to interpret it; it is to make some value judgments about it with respect to its educational significance. It is this aspect of educational criticism that most sharply differentiates the work of the educational critic from the work of an ethnographer, psychologist, or sociologist. Educational critics ultimately appraise what they encounter with a set of educational criteria; they judge the educational value of what they see. To make educational value judgments requires not only the ability to see educational subtleties occurring in the classroom and to be able to interpret their meaning or explain the functions they serve, it is also to have a background sufficiently rich in educational theory, educational philosophy, and educational history to be able to understand the values implied by the ongoing activities and the alternatives that might have otherwise been employed.

This latter aspect of the evaluative character of educational criticism – to be able to consider the alternatives that might have been employed – requires also a sense of the practical realities of classroom life. Each of us undoubtedly holds some pristine vision of educational virtue that we would like to see schools display, yet most of us realize that these images of educational virtue are seldom fully realized. Practical contingencies keep intruding. Lest we come down too hard on situations that do not live up to our highest hopes, it is important to recognize what is, and what is not possible in the course of daily educational life.

Thus the ultimate consequence of educational criticism is evaluative in the sense that something must be made of what has been described and interpreted. The task of the critic is not simply one of being a neutral observer (an impossible position in any case), nor is it one of disinterested interpretation. The critic uses what he or she sees and interprets in order to arrive at some conclusions about the character of educational practice and to its improvement.

Although I have said that educational connoisseurship can have as its subject matter anything that can be perceived or experienced, and by implication that educational criticism can describe what connoisseurship provides, it is time now to be more specific about what can be attended to in educational practice. What are the potential candidates for critical attention? Obviously the particular functions criticism is to serve and the particular audience to which it is directed will influence, if not determine, what is criticized and how it is shared. Yet, in general one can focus upon the qualities of the relationship that exists between teacher and student and the kinds of devices that the teacher employs to stimulate interest, to reward, to explain, and to manage. Teachers seldom have the opportunity to get informed feedback on their teaching. They read how they are doing in the reflections found in the eyes of children. Although this is a relevant source of information, it is neither an exhaustive nor an adequate one. Informed educational criticism may give teachers a view of their teaching that they simply would never otherwise possess.

The character of the discourse within the classroom is another candidate for critical attention. How do the children participate? What is the quality of what they and the teacher have to say? To what extent do they participate both psychologically and verbally in what transpires? Is their enthusiasm feigned or real? Is what they are learning worth their time and effort? And just what are they learning? Is it what is being taught, or are they learning other things that are conveyed by the manner of teaching and the organization and structure of the school day? What about the materials they use, the textbooks, the learning kits, the visuals with which they come in contact? What do these materials teach? How are they laid out? What does their format suggest? What messages are held between the lines of textbooks which for so many children occupy central roles in their school experience?

What about the relationships among the children themselves? Is it competitive or cooperative? Is the class a collection of individuals or a community? What is the pervasive quality of educational life that children in this particular classroom lead? How is time allocated within the school day? How are the various subjects taught? What values are conveyed by the ways in which time and space decisions have been made?

What is the quality of the work that children create? What is the character of their expression – verbal, written, visual, and musical? Over time, what kind of development is evident? In what ways is the development of intellectual curiosity and autonomy displayed? In what ways are they treated when they are expressed?

These questions represent some of the potential candidates for attention in the effort to create telling educational criticism. To be sure, these very questions reflect a conception of educational value. Only a fool would choose to attend to the trivial.

Finally, I wish to say a few words about the problems of validity, or, put another way, can educational criticism be trusted?

In determining the validity of educational criticism – that is, whether there is any justification for what the critic says is happening, what it means, and what its educational worth is – we discover three possible sources of disagreement between two or more critics. You will recall that I said that educational criticism has three aspects: descriptive, interpretive, and evaluative. Two critics, for example, might agree on what is occurring, agree on what it signifies, but disagree on what its educational value is. Or two critics might agree on what is occurring, disagree on what it signifies, but agree on its educational value. This occurs when two people like what they see, but for different reasons. Still another source of disagreement is when two critics see two different things, but agree upon their significance and agree upon their educational value. I am sure you can play out the rest of the hand, but the point is that the reasons why critics might agree or disagree in their critical disclosures are several. One cannot know them without analyzing the grounds or basis of what they have to say.

Although these conditions make the problems of validating educational criticism complex, there are still some useful criteria to apply. One of these criteria deals with determining the extent of structural corroboration within the criticism itself, and another deals with the criticism's referential adequacy.

Structural corroboration is a process that seeks to validate or support one's conclusions about a set of phenomena by demonstrating how a variety of facts or conditions within the phenomena support the conclusions drawn. It is a process of demonstrating that the story hangs together, that the pieces fit. One of the best examples of structural corroboration can be found in Agatha Christie's *Murder on the Orient Express*. What the detective did to solve the puzzling crime was gradually to piece the puzzle together so that the conclusion that all of the passengers on the train had a hand in the murder was cogent. The evidence was persuasive because each component corroborated the other. In the end a structure was created whose parts held together.

American jurisprudence is largely based upon a combination of structural corroboration and multiplicative corroboration. Structural corroboration is sought as two lawyers present the facts of the case to prove or disprove the innocence or guilt of their client, and multiplicative corroboration is practiced when twelve members of a jury concur or fail to concur that the evidence is sufficiently coherent and cohesive to remove any reasonable doubt.

But one of the liabilities of structural corroboration, as Geertz has pointed out, is that nothing can be so persuasive and coherent as a swindler's story. Something more must be added.

It is here that referential adequacy comes into play. Since criticism's aim is the reeducation of perception, good educational criticism, like good criticism of anything else, should help readers or listeners see more than they would without the benefit of the criticism. In this sense, the test of criticism is empirical, more empirical than numbers usually signify. The test of criticism is empirical in the sense that one asks of the criticism whether the referents it claims to describe, interpret, and evaluate can be found in the phenomena to which it attends. Is the teacher's enthusiasm really infectious? Do the children really support each other? Is the room really a celebration of the senses? The referential adequacy of educational criticism is determined by looking at the phenomena and finding what the critic has described. To the extent that criticism is effective, it should illuminate qualities of teaching and learning that would otherwise go unseen. By making these aspects of educational life visible, the teacher, supervisor, school administrator, or school board member is in a position to make judgments about them. Thus, educational criticism provides educational policy and the more narrowly defined aspects of educational decision making with a wider, more complex base of knowledge upon which to deliberate.

I would like to conclude by coming back full circle to the issues with which I began. Educational evaluation has had a particular tradition in this country. It is one that conceives of knowledge as scientific and believes that precision is a function of quantification. This tradition has made important contributions to the conduct of education, but as an exclusive mode of inquiry it possesses limits which in the long run exclude more from our understanding than they include. The time is ripe for broadening the base from which inquiry in education can go forward. It is time for a more catholic sense of possibility; we need, in my opinion, to widen our epistemology. In practice this means recognizing that the forms which humans create, the forms of art as well as the forms of science, afford unique opportunities for conceptualization and expression, and hence for communication. What we can know is shaped by the intellectual structures we are able to use. Many of those structures are framed in forms of knowledge that are nondiscursive. Since educational evaluation has, I assume, as its ultimate objective the improvement of the quality of educational life students lead, I see no reason why we should not exploit the various forms of understanding that different knowledge structures can provide. Educational connoisseurship and educational criticism represent two modes through which we come to understand and express what we come to know. But those modes themselves represent only a small portion of the possibilities in the conduct of educational evaluation. Some day we will make use not only of criticism in a poetic or artistically discursive mode, we will exploit the possibilities of film, video, photography, graphic displays, and the like. But that story will have to wait for another paper and another time. What we need today is a breakthrough in conception, a wedge in the door of possibility. Educational connoisseurship and educational criticism, it seems to me, offer some promising possibilities, not only for broadening the base of educational evaluation, but for those of us in the arts committed to the improvement of the process of education.

## Notes

1   Raymond Callahan, *Education and the Cult of Efficiency* (Chicago, IL: University of Chicago Press, 1962), *passim*.
2   George Hendrik von Wright, *Explanation and Understanding* (London: Routledge and Kegan Paul, 1971), p. 5.
3   Clifford Geertz, *The Interpretation of Culture* (New York: Basic Books, Inc., 1973).
4   Elliot W. Eisner, "The Perceptive Eye: Toward a Reformation of Educational Evaluation" (Invited address, Division B, Curriculum and Objectives, American Educational Research Association, Washington, DC, March, 1975).
5   John Dewey, *Art as Experience* (New York: Minton, Balch & Co., 1934).
6   Max Kozloff, *Renderings* (New York: Simon and Schuster, 1969).
7   Elizabeth Vallance, "Aesthetic Criticism and Curriculum Description" (PhD dissertation, Stanford University, 1974); Dwaine Greer, "The Criticism of Teaching" (PhD dissertation, Stanford University, 1973).
8   This descriptive educational criticism was written by one of my doctoral students, Robbie Schlosser. I am grateful for his permission to use his work in this article.

## CHAPTER 5

# ON THE USES OF EDUCATIONAL CONNOISSEURSHIP AND CRITICISM FOR EVALUATING CLASSROOM LIFE

*Teachers College Record*, 1977, 78(3): 345–358

That there is an intimate relationship between the assumptions and procedures employed to assess educational effectiveness and the kinds of programs schools offer is known to all familiar with the forces affecting schools.[1] It is my argument that the assumptions and procedures used in conventional forms of educational evaluation have, in the main, been parochial. They represent an extremely narrow conception of the way in which educational evaluation can be pursued. A wider, more generous conception of educational evaluation is badly needed. This paper defines the contours of such a conception.

Those familiar with the evolution of the evaluation field already know that it has been significantly influenced by the assumptions and procedures employed in doing educational research. And educational research in turn took as its model the natural sciences and had as its aspiration development of theory and methods that would make educational practice scientific. This aspiration is alive and well today. We still aspire to create a scientifically managed form of educational practice.

Yet, scientific procedures are not the only forms through which human understanding is secured and scientific methods are not the only ways through which human influence can be confidently created. What I shall do in this paper is to suggest perhaps not so much an alternative, as a needed supplement to the use of scientific procedures for describing, interpreting, and evaluating educational settings. I call this new, non-scientific approach to educational evaluation an approach that requires *educational connoisseurship and educational criticism*.[2,3] The remainder of what I have to say will be devoted to defining the meaning of these terms and to describing the way in which they can be used to evaluate educational settings.

## What is educational connoisseurship and criticism?

What I propose starts not with a scientific paradigm but with an artistic one. I start with the assumption that the improvement of education will result not so much from attempting to discover scientific methods that can be applied universally to classrooms throughout the land, or to individuals possessing particular personality characteristics, or to students coming from specific ethnic or class backgrounds, but rather by enabling teachers and others engaged in education to improve their ability to see and think about what they do. Educational practice as it occurs in schools is an inordinately complicated affair filled with contingencies that are extremely difficult to predict, let alone control. Connoisseurship in education, as in other areas, is that art of perception that makes the appreciation of such complexity possible. Connoisseurship is an appreciative art. Appreciation in this context means not necessarily a liking or preference for what one has encountered, but rather an awareness of its characteristics and qualities.

Take an example of connoisseurship in a realm simpler than education, that of wine. The wine connoisseur has through long and careful attention to wine developed a gustatory palate that enables him to discern its most subtle qualities. When he drinks wine it is done with an intention to discern, and with a set of techniques that he employs to examine the range of qualities within the wine upon which he will make his judgments. Body, color, nose, aftertaste, bite, flavor – these are some of the attributes to which the wine connoisseur attends. In addition, he brings to bear upon his present experience a gustatory memory of other wines tasted. These other wines, held in the memory, form the backdrop for his present experience with a particular vintage. It is his refined palate, his knowledge of what to look for, his backlog of previous experience with wines other than those he is presently drinking that differentiate his level of discernment from that of an ordinary drinker of wine. His conclusions about the quality of wines are judgments, not mere preferences. Judgments, unlike preferences which are incorrigible, can be grounded in reasons, reasons that refer back to the wines' qualities and to other wines of the same variety.

Connoisseurship in other fields shares principles similar to those of wine connoisseurship. Connoisseurship in cabinet-making, for example, requires a similar ability to place what one currently examines into a context of cabinets one has already seen. What is the quality of the varnish that has been used? How many coats have been applied? What about the construction? Have the joints been mitered, dovetailed, doweled, finger-lapped, or tenoned? Are the edges banded and so on. Knowing what to look for, being able to recognize skill, form, and imagination are some of the distinguishing traits of connoisseurship.

When it comes to the fine arts, even more is required for connoisseurship to be exercised. Works of art have a history, develop in a social context, and frequently possess a profundity in conception and execution that surpasses wine and cabinets. The poetry of e. e. cummings, the music of Stravinsky, the cinematography of Fellini and Bergman, the plays of Ibsen and Genet, the paintings of Rothko; connoisseurship with respect to these creations goes well beyond the use of awakened sensibility. Such works require an ability to recognize both how and why they depart from conventional modes in their respective art forms. To recognize such departures requires an understanding not only of the forms the various arts have taken in the past but also an understanding of the intentions and leading conceptions under-lying such works. The problems the artist formulates differ from period to period: the problems of Cezanne are not those of Duccio or Bellini or Motherwell. To appreciate the work of such men requires, therefore, not only attention to the work's formal qualities, but also an understanding of the ideas that gave rise to the work in the first place. This in turn requires some understanding of the socio-cultural context in which these artists worked, the sources from which they drew, and the influence their work had upon the work of others.

If connoisseurship is the art of appreciation, criticism is the art of disclosure. What the critic aims at is not only to discern the character and qualities constituting the object or event – this is a necessary but insufficient condition for criticism – the critic also aims at providing a rendering in linguistic terms of what it is that he or she has encountered so that others not possessing his level of connoisseurship can also enter into the work. Dewey put it nicely when he said, "The end of criticism is

the reeducation of the perception of the work of art."[4] Given this view of criticism –
a view I share – the function of criticism is educational. Its aim is to lift the veils that
keep the eyes from seeing by providing the bridge needed by others to experience
the qualities and relationships within some arena of activity. In this sense criticism
requires connoisseurship but connoisseurship does not require the skills of criticism. One can function as a connoisseur without uttering a word about what
has been experienced. Enjoyments can be private; one can relish or feel disdain in
solitude. Criticism, on the contrary, is a public art. The critic must talk or write
about what has been encountered; he must, in Kozloff's terms,[5] provide a rendering
of the qualities that constitute the work, its significance, and the quality of his
experience when he interacts with it.

Let's look at a piece of criticism by Max Kozloff as he describes his visit to an
exhibition of paintings by the contemporary British painter Francis Bacon:

> Wandering up and down the ramp of the Francis Bacon exhibition at the
> Guggenheim Museum on a sunny afternoon is a grisly experience. The joys of
> painting and the presence of a brilliant mind are not enough to dispel one's
> morbid embarrassment, as if one had been caught, and had caught oneself,
> smiling at a hanging.
>
> Earlier I was aware of his velvety, featherlike white strokes, which tickle the
> navy blue ground and form an urgent image all in their own time, only as an
> irritant. It is irritating, that is, to be cajoled, wheedled and finally seduced into
> an enjoyment of a painted scene whose nature connotes only horror or repul-
> sion. Such are his various tableaux of crucifixion and murder, although his
> merely voyeuristic glimpses of male orgies arouse guilt in this same way.[6]

Kozloff's language is notable on several grounds. First, the language itself,
independent of its relationship to Bacon's paintings, is sufficiently rich and vivid
almost to enable the reader to experience the quality of what Bacon's work must
be like even if one had never seen Bacon's paintings. Like a good storyteller,
Kozloff himself paints linguistically a visually vivid picture of what he has encountered. Second, Kozloff not only tells us about the quality of the paint, the feathery
character of the artist's brush strokes, the quality of the color that the paintings
possess, he also attends to his own experience – its quality, its mood, its voyeuris-
tic feelings, "as if one had been caught smiling at a hanging." Kozloff lets us in not
only on the qualities of the work, but on the qualities of his experience when he
interacts with it. Third, notice the kind of language that Kozloff uses to render the
work. It is a language filled with metaphor and with unlikely analogies – "smiling
at a hanging." This use of metaphorical language is at base poetic. Metaphor is the
recognition of underlying commonality in what is usually considered discrete and
independent. The sudden recognition of such commonalities through the use of
metaphor provides a bridge between the critic's language and the work and
provides the conditions through which insight is generated.

Both connoisseur and critics use, of course, an array of values that focus their
perception. One of the essential characteristics of human perception is that it is
selective. One cannot look at everything at once and although characteristics of the
perceptual field itself play a role in guiding perception, the leading ideas one holds
about the arts, wine, or cabinetmaking also perform a role in focusing attention.
These leading ideas and values about what counts grow from tradition and habit
as well as from implicit and explicit theories about the nature of artistic virtue. In
the fine arts such theories are explicitly created by aestheticians and implicitly by

the critics themselves. When Roger Fry lauds "significant form," he calls the critics' attention to the formal structure of the work; when Bernard Berenson applauds "tactile qualities," he reminds us that solidity and volume are crucial considerations in works of visual art; when Leo Tolstoy tells us that good art is sincere, clear, and that it establishes a communion among men's feelings he draws our attention to moral and ethical considerations that flow from our encounters with art.

The lesson to be learned here is that sheer description unguided by value considerations is rudderless. Seeking and selecting require guideposts. In the arts aesthetic theory provides them.

## What is the relationship of connoisseurship and criticism to the study of educational phenomena?

Thus far I have devoted my attention to the concepts of connoisseurship and criticism as applied to the arts. But what is the relationship of these concepts to education? How can practices useful in the arts be usefully employed in studying the conduct of classrooms? It is to these questions that we now turn our attention.

It is an old truism that scientific studies in education are as often defined by the form of research one has learned to use as by the substantive problems one believes to be significant. Becoming familiar with correlation procedures too often leads simply to questions about what one can correlate; the existence of statistically reliable achievement tests too often leads to a conception of achievement that is educationally eviscerated. Our tools, as useful as they might be initially, often become our masters. Indeed, what it means to do any type of research at all in education is defined, stamped, sealed, and approved by utilizing particular premises and procedures. A brief excursion into the pages of the *American Educational Research Journal (AERJ)* will provide living testimony to the range of such premises and procedures. For example, during the past three volume years the *AERJ* has published over 100 articles. Of these only three were nonstatistical in character.

Yet the range, richness, and complexity of educational phenomena occurring within classrooms are wider than what can be measured. Some phenomena can only be rendered. It is this richness and this complexity to which educational connoisseurship addresses itself.

Imagine a ninth grade class in algebra. The school, in an upper-middle-class suburb, is one of those single story, try-hard modern school buildings that looks like the district ran out of funds before it could be finished. The classroom is a boxlike environment, anonymous except for the sundry array of hand-carved initials that decorate the wooden desks that line it. Not even a nod is given to visual interest. The only visual art in it is a dog-eared poster of Smokey the Bear, reminding students to put out their campfires. The rest is blackboard, light green plaster walls, and small windows well above the level through which students can look out onto the world. Suddenly the buzzer pierces the atmosphere with a baritone voice that startles even the geraniums. To the students it is only a familiar reminder that class is ready to begin.

How do these tightly zipped, vivacious youths enter the room? What expressions do they wear on their faces? What do their posture, their pace, their eyes say about Algebra I to which they return each day at 10:05? How does the class begin? Is the procession of discourse one that stimulates, satisfies? Is it one of dutiful routine, one of feigned enthusiasm that so many students of the well-to-do do so well?

How does the teacher respond to students? What does the tone of his voice say to those who do not understand? Do you detect the tinge of impatience that humiliates?

How is the class paced? Does it have a sense of movement and closure? Is competitiveness engendered by the subtle but pointed reminders of extra credit, of the quiz the day after tomorrow, and of grades for college? What is the quality of the ideas and the analyses with which the students venture forth into the life of the mind? What is this teacher, in this setting, saying about algebra *and* about education to the students who meet him every day at 10:05?

These are some of the qualities, ideas, and practices to which an educational connoisseur might attend. But educational connoisseurship is not reserved for those outside of the teaching profession. Educational connoisseurship is to some degree practiced daily by educational practitioners. The teacher's ability, for example, to judge when children have had enough of art, math, reading, or "free time" is a judgment made not by applying a theory of motivation or attention, but by recognizing the wide range of qualities that the children themselves display to those who have learned to see. Walk down any school corridor and peek through a window; an educational connoisseur can quickly discern important things about life in that classroom. Of course judgments, especially those made through windows from hallways, can be faulty. Yet the point remains. If one knows how to see what one looks at, a great deal of information – what Stephen Pepper refers to as "danda" in contrast to "data"[7] – can be secured. The teacher who cannot distinguish between the noise of children working and just plain noise has not yet developed a basic level of educational connoisseurship.

Listen to the shop talk of teachers, the kind of discourse they carry on in the lounge; their shop talk reveals the application of their own levels of connoisseurship to the settings in which they work. If teachers and school administrators already possess educational connoisseurship, then why try to foster it? There are several reasons. In the first place connoisseurship, like any art, is capable of refinement. Teachers on their own – like all of us – develop whatever connoisseurship they can or need. What is obvious, by definition, we learn to recognize easily and early. What is subtle and complex we might never perceive. As Ryle[8] has pointed out, seeing is not simply an act, but an achievement. Seeing is a realization secured. Unfortunately, one of the consequences of familiarity is the development of obliviousness. We learn not to see, we turn off what we have become accustomed to. Thus, a teacher with years of experience in the classroom or a school administrator with a decade behind the desk might develop only enough educational connoisseurship to enable them to cope at minimal levels within the classroom and school in which they work. Being oblivious to a large portion of their environment they are in no position to bring about change, to rectify educational ills they cannot see, or to alter their own behavior. What is even worse, the conditions and qualities they do see they might believe to be natural rather than artifactual. We often come to believe, because of habit reinforced by convention, that the way things are is the way they *must* be. More refined levels of educational connoisseurship could militate against such seductive comforts.

In the second place connoisseurship when developed to a high degree provides a level of consciousness that makes intellectual clarity possible. Many teachers are confronted daily with prescriptions and demands from individuals outside the teaching profession – demands that are intended to improve the quality of education within the schools. Many of these the teachers feel in their gut to be misguided or wrong-headed; the demands somehow fly in the face of what they feel to be possible in a classroom or in the best interests of children. Two examples should suffice. The pressures toward accountability defined in terms of specific operational objectives and precise measurement of outcomes are pressures that many teachers dislike. Their distaste for these pressures is not due to professional laziness, recalcitrance, or stupidity, but is due to the uneasy feeling that as rational as a means–ends concept of accountability appears to be, it doesn't quite fit the educational facts with which they live and work. Many teachers, if you ask them, are unable to state why they feel uneasy. They have a difficult time articulating what the flaws are in the often glib prescriptions that issue from state capitols and from major universities. Yet the uneasiness is often – not always but often – justified. Some objectives one cannot articulate, some goals one does not achieve by the end of the academic year, some insights are not measurable, some ends are not known until after the fact, some models of educational practice violate some visions of the learner and the classroom. Many teachers have developed sufficient connoisseurship to feel that something is awry but have insufficient connoisseurship to provide a more adequate conceptualization of just what it is.

In the third place the development of higher levels of connoisseurship than we have in general at present might provide new subject matters not only for theoretical attention, but for conventional empirical research. Of what use is it to test a new method for the teaching of spelling to third graders if 15 percent of the children, because of where their desks are placed, cannot see the blackboard? Significant effects in schooling might be the result of factors that experimenters do not see and cannot, therefore, control. Jackson notes,[9] for example, that in elementary school classrooms when students come up to the teacher's desk for help, the teacher visually scans the classroom every forty seconds or so. He also notes that children seated on the periphery of the room tend to withdraw more – out the window as it were – than children seated up front or in the middle of the room. What do such behaviors mean for teaching and learning? What do they reveal about how children and teachers cope with the demands made upon them? These questions and others that could be raised grow out of the perceptive, critical observations that Jackson was able to make. These variables and others like them could provide new and productive leads for educational research. Such leads depend for their existence on the realizations that educational connoisseurship provides.

The end of criticism, unlike connoisseurship, is that of disclosure. Criticism applied to classroom phenomena is the art of saying just what it is that is going on in that setting. Take, for example, that mode of human performance called teaching. What is it that teachers do when they teach? How do they use themselves? How do they move? What level of tension, of affect, of spontaneity do they display? To what extent do they reveal themselves as persons to the students with whom they work? Are they approachable? In what ways? What kinds of values, ideas, and covert messages do they emphasize? How, given questions such as these, can the qualities to which such questions guide us be disclosed? How can they be disclosed in a way that does not rob them of their vitality as experienced? Here the educational critic has a task similar to his counterpart dealing with live theater. The critic's task in each case is to provide a vivid rendering so that others might learn to see what transpires in that beehive of activity called the classroom. What the educational critic employs is a form of linguistic artistry replete with metaphor, contrast, redundancy, and emphasis that captures some aspect of the quality and character of educational life.

In this task the educational critic does far more than describe behavior. A strictly behavioral description of what teachers do would not only avoid dealing with the intentions of the teacher, it would also describe in quantitative terms the number of behavioral moves made by the teacher. One such description goes like this:

> Launching is primarily the function of the teacher rather than the pupil. The teacher speaks 85.2 per cent of all structuring components; in contrast, the pupil speaks only 10.2 per cent. The range for the teacher is from a high of 96.8 per cent in Class 6 to a low of 73.5 per cent in Class 13, with a median of 86.2 per cent. The range for the pupil, on the other hand, is from 23.6 per cent in Class 13 to zero in Classes 9 and 10, with a median percentage of 11.8 per cent.
>
> Halting-excluding is strictly a function of the teacher; in no class does the pupil perform this function. When the teacher does halt or exclude a subgame, he usually does so in a multiple component move in which he also launches a new sub-game. More frequently, however, the teacher does not explicitly halt or exclude sub-games; rather, he signals the end of one sub-game by launching a new sub-game.
>
> Speakers perform the function of launching by using one of three methods: announcing, stating propositions or announcing and stating propositions. The most frequent method is announcing; that is, giving public notice about one or more dimensions of the game or sub-game. Speakers launch by announcing in 45.2 per cent of all structuring components, by announcing and stating propositions in 34.1 per cent and by stating propositions in only 16.1 per cent.

Such a description is, of course, useful for some purposes, but it is not likely to capture the meaning or character of the teaching that has occurred. Such a description of behavior is "thin" and can be contrasted to what Geertz[10] refers to as "thick" description. Thick description aims at describing the meaning or significance of behavior as it occurs in a cultural network saturated with meaning. For example, a behavioral description of an eyelid closing on the left eye at the rate of two closures per second could be described in just that way. But a thick description of such behaviors within the context of a cultural subsystem could be described as a wink. The meaning of a wink, especially if the person at the other end is someone of the opposite sex, is entirely different from a description of eyelid closures at the rate of two closures per second. To fail to recognize the difference in the critical description of behavior is the same as neglecting the iconography used in works of visual art. The splash in the ocean in Breughel's painting *The Fall of Icarus* can be critically described only if one knows the story of Icarus. Once aware of the story, the significance of the painting and the meaning of the splash become clear.

It is obvious that the creation of effective criticism requires the artful use of language. Good critics use language in a way that requires a certain poetic and fluid range of words and phrases. Since the artful use of language is so important in the creation of criticism, wouldn't it be reasonable to use professional writers or critics in fields other than education to create educational criticism? The answer to that question is no. While it must have a sense of linguistic fluency and imagination, good criticism requires more than simply using language artfully. In all fields, but especially in education, the need to understand the values and history beneath practices being employed is crucial. In educational settings the critic must be in a position not only to perceive the superficial and apparent but the subtle and covert. What is subtle and covert in classrooms is not by definition visible to an educationally naive eye. But even more, the educational critic needs to know what form of educational practice the particular practice he encounters represents so that the criteria he employs in describing that practice are appropriate to it. One does not give low marks to a cubist painting because of a paucity of color; one does not condemn Monteverdi because his music does not have the melodic line of the romantics. Each form of an art needs to be appraised by the style it represents and the criteria appropriate to it. A lecture is not intrinsically bad and a discussion intrinsically good, regardless of the number and types of interactions in a discussion. There are many types of educational excellence and an educational critic should be familiar with them.

In addition to these competencies of the creation of adequate educational criticism, the educational critic needs to be able to recognize what was neglected or rejected as well as what was accepted when a teacher uses a particular approach in a classroom. What values are being embraced? What values are being rejected when one decides to use particular educational procedures? Given the values that appear to animate classroom practices, how might they have been employed? In short, competent educational criticism requires far more than the writing skills possessed by a good novelist or journalist. It requires a broad grasp of educational theory and educational history and it would be a distinct advantage for critics to have had experience as classroom teachers.

It is instructive to note that the type of connoisseurship and particularly the type of criticism I am describing does not have a firm or well-developed tradition in schools of education. Such traditions do of course exist in highly sophisticated forms in literature, drama, the visual arts, poetry, and music. And cinematography, the art form of the twentieth century, is rapidly developing a tradition of criticism. The study of education in this country has evolved from different roots, those of the natural and social sciences. To do research in education has meant to do scientific work. To have evidence regarding educational practice has meant to have scientific evidence. Those whose interests and aptitudes for studying educational phenomena veered toward the humanistic or artistic modes of conception and expression have, unfortunately, too often been thought of as woolly headed, impressionistic romantics. Educational connoisseurship and criticism have not been encouraged. An ounce of data, it seems, has been worth a pound of insight.

## Can educational criticism be trusted?

One of the persistent concerns of those who do conventional forms of educational research and evaluation centers around the reliability of the instruments used. How can one be confident that the performance of individuals or groups being sampled is representative or consistent? How can one be sure that the judgments made by experts are reliable? The question of the dependability of criticism is, too, a concern of those doing criticism. How can we be sure that what educational critics say about educational phenomena is not a figment of their imagination? How can we know what confidence we can place in the critic's description, interpretation, and evaluation of classroom life?

The problem of determining the reliability of the critic's language is addressed by judging the referential adequacy of what he has to say. This is done by empirically testing his remarks against the phenomena he attempts to describe. Criticism has as its major aim the reeducation of perception. Therefore, the language used to describe educational phenomena, such as teaching, should disclose aspects of that performance that might otherwise not be seen. The critic's language is referentially adequate when its referents can be found in the work or event itself. If a group of readers cannot find these referents in what has transpired, it may be due to (1) poor critical talk, (2) critical talk that is inappropriate for the competencies of the audience listening to it or reading it, or (3) because the audience is so unprepared to perceive that a much more powerful educational program for that audience is needed. Poor critical language or inappropriate language for a given audience are problems from which any type of study can suffer. Conventional forms of educational research might also be so poorly articulated that they become incomprehensible. The technical level of the discourse of conventional research might, similarly, be inappropriately sophisticated or prosaic for a given audience. Insofar as the products of man are to have educational consequences, the fit between the audience and the message needs to be taken into account.

It is possible for critics to bring such bias to an encounter that they misread the situation. Their prior commitments function under exceptional circumstances as blinders rather than guides for seeing what is happening. But this liability, too, is not absent from conventional research. Theoretical convictions can lead one to gross misinterpretations of classroom life, and biases toward particular modes of statistical analyses or forms of testing can also create distortions in the state of affairs encountered. The tools we use are not simply neutral entities but have distinctive effects on the quality of our perceptions and upon our understanding.

When one deals with works of visual art and works of literature, there exists a certain stability in the material studied. But what do we do with things and events that change over time – classrooms, for instance? How can something as fluid as a classroom be critically described and how can such descriptions be tested for their referential adequacy? It should be noted that stage plays and orchestra performances, too, share some of the fluidity of the classroom or school, yet these art forms have a long critical history. What I believe must be done to fairly test the referential adequacy of critical discourse is two-fold. First, the classroom being studied needs to be visited with sufficient persistency to enable the critic to locate its pervasive qualities, those qualities through which aspects of its life can be characterized. Classrooms or schools are not so fugitive that their pervasive qualities change on a daily basis. What is enduring in a classroom is more likely to be educationally significant than what is evanescent. These enduring or pervasive qualities can become objects of critical attention. An educational connoisseur should be able to perceive what the critic has described when given the opportunity to do so.

Second, the availability of videotape recordings and cinematography now make it possible to capture and hold episodes of classroom life that can be critically described. Such videotaped episodes can then be compared with the criticism created and its referential adequacy determined. In addition, playback features of videotape make it possible to scrutinize expression, tempo, explanation, and movement in ways that live situations will not permit. Disputes about the adequacy of the criticism can be resolved, at least in principle, by reexamining particular segments of the tape. The technology now available lends itself exceedingly well to the work to be done.

One might well ask whether educational connoisseurship and criticism are likely to lead to useful generalizations about educational practice. Can the study of a handful of non-randomly selected classrooms yield conclusions that apply to classrooms other than the ones studied? The answer to these questions is complex. Insofar as the application of critical procedures discloses subtle but important phenomena that other classrooms and teachers share, then of course the gist of critical disclosure is applicable. But the only way to know that is to be able to learn from critical discourse what might be worth looking for in other educational situations. In other words, if it is true that the universal does indeed reside in the particulars which artistic activity constructs, the renderings of those constructions in critical language should open up aspects of classroom life that participate in such universals. To know that requires itself a sense of connoisseurship. Unlike the automatic application of a standard, what one learns from effective criticism is both a content within a particular classroom and a refined sensibility concerning classrooms that is useful for studying other educational situations.

There is another way in which effective connoisseurship and criticism might yield warranted generalizations and that is as cues useful for locating phenomena that might be subsequently pursued through conventional educational research. Creative scientific work in any field depends upon new realizations, new models, or new methods to guide inquiry. Insofar as effective criticism reveals aspects of educational phenomena that were previously unnoticed or underestimated, a fresh focus for conventional scientific study could be provided.

Thus far I have emphasized the similarities between criticism in the arts and criticism in education. But the fine arts are not identical with educational settings and determining the extent to which criticism in the arts can also be applied to education is something that needs to be determined. For example, art critics deal with completed works of art, not work in progress. The art critic looks at a completed painting, the music critic a finished symphony, and so forth. An educational critic has no such complete whole. Classroom activities flow into one another; seldom do classroom events form a completed whole. If this is true, what bearing does it have upon the doing of educational criticism?

Critics in the arts work within a long tradition;[11] they have at their disposal a tradition of critical writing, a language that is sharable, and a set of terms that have conventional meaning within the arts: impressionism, surrealism, constructivism, baroque, line, color, value, composition are conventional signs that those working in the arts understand. To what extent do we in education have similar terms and a comparable tradition? Is such a tradition possible and desirable in describing educational settings? Why hasn't one comparable to the arts been created? Are there differences between the criticism of the arts and of classrooms that make such a tradition unlikely?

In the world of the arts, critics have established themselves as inhabitants; art critics and art criticism are expected. Will teachers, school administrators, parents, educational theoreticians, and educational researchers accept educational criticism and educational critics? Will commitment to scientific objectivity lead to a rejection of criticism as a method of studying in education? Will teachers be able to use what critics provide? To what extent can educational criticism contribute to more effective teaching? What hampers critics from doing effective criticism when they have the opportunity to observe classrooms?

## Summary

What are the major points I have tried to make? First, I have pointed out that the methodology of educational evaluation has been dominated by scientific assumptions. These assumptions and the methods they yield, I have argued, do not exhaust the ways in which men come to know. Their exclusive use has led to a limited and parochial conception of how educational evaluation can proceed.

Second, I have described two concepts – educational connoisseurship and educational criticism – concepts embedded not in a scientific tradition, but an artistic one. I have argued that these concepts yield procedures that could provide a needed complement to the scientific approaches to evaluation used today.

Third, I have described the ways in which these concepts might be applied to describe, interpret, and evaluate educational settings, and I have identified some of the unanswered questions and potential problems that flow from their use.

But most importantly, I have tried to open up a new window through which educational practice might be studied and described. My hope is that the vision you secured through that window looks attractive and promising.

These are the things I have said. I would like to conclude by identifying some of the things I neglected saying. I have not talked about the possibility of creating courses in schools of education devoted to educational connoisseurship and criticism. I have not described the ways in which these concepts might be used to evaluate the products children create in schools. I have not discussed the training of educational connoisseurs and critics, nor have I mentioned the possibility of developing journals and books in education that present and analyze critical descriptions of educational settings. I have totally neglected talking about new forms through which the results of educational evaluations can be reported, forms that rely on film, videotape, taped interviews, logs, visual displays, and the like. I have not suggested the possibility that doctoral dissertations might someday not need to be bound in book form for library shelves, but shown on film with an accompanying perceptive narrative. I have not talked about what the promise of such dissertations might mean for that proportion of doctoral students who now feel compelled to be junior psychologists in order to do studies they do not believe in so that they can get their PhD's. I haven't talked about the potential long-term political consequences that might flow from opening up a new and legitimate approach to the study of education.

I have neglected talking about these things, and more. Yet all of them are possible. Whether they will be realized will depend upon the extent to which educational connoisseurship and criticism as concepts can capture the imagination of the field. It will also depend upon the usefulness of their application in practice. That application, it seems to me, is an appropriate agenda not only for those concerned with educational evaluation, but for anyone concerned with the design and improvement of educational programs.

## Acknowledgments

This paper has benefited from the perceptive criticism of more individuals than it would be possible for me to name. However, I want to express my special gratitude to my friends, Professors Alan Peshkin and Louis Rubin of the University of Illinois-Urbana, for particularly helpful suggestions.

## Notes

1 The material contained herein will appear in Elliot W. Eisner, *The Design and Evaluation of Educational Programs* (New York: Macmillan, 1979).
2 The term connoisseurship has some unfortunate connotations that I would like to dispel within the context of the work proposed. One such connotation is that of an effete, elite consumer or snob; something belonging to the upper classes. Connoisseurship, as I use the term, relates to any form of expertise in any area of human endeavor and is as germane to the problems involved in purse snatching as it is in the appreciation of fine needlepoint.

   Similarly, criticism gives some people the impression of a harping, hacking, negativistic attitude toward something. This is not the way in which the term is used here.

Criticism is conceived of as a generic process aimed at revealing the characteristics and qualities that constitute any human product. Its major aim is to enable individuals to recognize qualities and characteristics of a work or event that might have gone unnoticed and therefore unappreciated.

3 The concepts of educational connoisseurship and educational criticism have evolved from conceptual work extending over the past decade. Those interested in this work might refer to: Elliot W. Eisner, "Qualitative Intelligence and the Act of Teaching," *Elementary School Journal*, Vol. 73, No. 6 (March 1963); Elliot W. Eisner, "Instructional and Expressive Objectives: Their Formulation and Use in Curriculum," in W. James Popham, E. Eisner, H. Sullivan, and L. Tyler (eds), *Instructional Objectives*, American Educational Research Association Monograph No. 3 (Chicago, IL: McNally & Co., 1969); Elliot W. Eisner, "Emerging Models for Educational Evaluation," *School Review*, Vol. 80, No. 4 (August 1972); Elliot W. Eisner, *English Primary Schools: Some Observations and Assessments* (Washington, DC: National Association for the Education of Young Children, 1974); and Elliot W. Eisner, "The Future of the Secondary Schools: A Viewpoint," *Curriculum Theory Network*, Vol. 5, No. 3 (1975). These concepts are being operationalized by my students and me at Stanford University in the study of elementary and secondary school classrooms.

4 John Dewey, *Art as Experience* (New York: Milton Balch, 1934).

5 Max Kozloff, *Renderings* (New York: Simon and Schuster, 1969).

6 Ibid.

7 Stephen Pepper, *The Basis of Criticism in the Arts* (Cambridge, MA: Harvard University Press, 1945).

8 Gilbert Ryle, *The Concept of Mind* (New York: Barnes and Noble, 1949).

9 Phillip Jackson, *Life in Classrooms* (New York: Holt, Rinehart and Winston, 1968).

10 I first encountered the concepts of "thick" and "thin" description in listening to a paper by Clifford Geertz given at Stanford University in 1974.

11 The study of symbols as used in the arts is called iconography and is perhaps best exemplified in the work of Erwin Panofsky, *Meaning in the Visual Arts* (New York: Overlook Press, 1974).

# CHAPTER 6

# WHAT DO CHILDREN LEARN WHEN THEY PAINT?

*Art Education*, 1978, 21(3): 6–10

Although art educators have an abiding belief in the benefits art activity has for children, the grounds for holding this belief are often less than clear.[1] What is it that art activities provide to children? Why do children make visual images? What is it that nature provides and what is it that culture provides in the course of a child's development in art? But perhaps more specifically, what is it that children learn when they paint, draw, or make three-dimensional images? Questions such as these serve as the focus of this paper. In it I shall describe nine consequences or potential consequences for children who are given the opportunity to work with teachers of art. All of these consequences represent an attempt to answer the question: What do children learn when they paint? Before trying to answer this question, a word should be said about why the question itself is important.

Most art educators operate on the belief that drawing, painting, sculpting, and the like are good for children, but I believe few of us have formulated satisfying answers to the question of just why we consider it so good. Yet more and more people are asking for justifications for what we teach in the schools. Particularly as educational accountability becomes increasingly important to those who pay for the programs schools provide, the need to justify what is taught – but particularly in the arts – also becomes important. So from a pragmatic point of view knowing why children create and what they learn from working in art is important. But it is even more important for providing a kind of intellectual security for our work. We ought to be able to describe the value of what we do and place it within a framework for rationalizing the contributions of our work to the educational development of the students we teach. So let us start at the beginning. Let us ask what students learn when they paint, or sculpt, or draw. In short, what do children learn when they make visual images?

Perhaps the first thing that very young children learn is something that we often take for granted, namely they learn that they can, in fact, create images with material and that the activity of making such images can provide intrinsic forms of satisfaction. Knowledge that a person can alter the world through his or her own actions is not something that is incarcerated in the cortex prior to birth; such knowledge grows from experience. The making of a mark on paper or on wet sand or in moist clay is an alteration of the world, the forming of a new entity. When children are first given an opportunity to use materials, this is one of the first things they learn, namely that their actions can have consequences. Furthermore, the actions that brought about those consequences can themselves provide a source of satisfaction. The realization that actions can lead to consequences is what De Charms calls "personal causation."[2] Developing a sense of personal causation is not trivial; it represents a disposition towards the world, one that says that "I can make things occur, I am not simply at the mercy of the environment." The satisfaction that is received from action is what Charlotte Buhler refers to as "function pleasure." The rhythmic movement of the arm and wrist, the stimulation of watching lines appear where none existed before are themselves satisfying and self-justifying. They are intrinsic sources of satisfaction. The importance of intrinsic sources of satisfaction is often drowned in schools that beseige children with stars, grades, pats on the head, and other forms of extrinsic rewards used to motivate activity and to sustain "interest."[3] The token economy comes to replace activities that might have once been pursued for their own sake. Like sex, eating, and other basic functions, young children learn from making images that satisfactions inhere in the process of action and that they can be a source of personal causation, they can bring something into existence.

The second thing that young children learn is that the images they create can function as symbols. A symbol as distinct from a sign or signal is something that is intended to stand for something else. A sign, for example, might be the wetness on the pavement indicating that it had recently rained. A symbol, however, is a transformation of an idea into a public image that in some ways stands for it. Young children learn that the images that they are able to bring into existence can also stand for other things. First, images are made and then named, and later named and then made. In either case there is what Langer calls a "symbolic transformation"[4] occurring. The young child recognizes that visual concepts can be transformed into a public and stable form. To do this requires that two processes be employed. One, a child must form a visual concept of the object he or she perceives. Such concepts usually are the least conceptually ambiguous the child can form. Thus, the most telling view of a chair, a horse, or a person is imaginatively framed. Second, the child must invent a visual graphic image whose properties are in some way related to the visual concepts he wishes to symbolize. These public images are what Arnheim refers to as "representational concepts."[5] Thus we have a two-stage process occurring. First, the conceptualization of an image that articulates some object. Second, the invention of a graphic form whose elements in some way represent that image. This latter process is one of symbolization.

Now it is typically thought that the major function of symbols is to serve as a means of communication. While it is true that discursive language and pictographs do serve purposes of communication, Langer argues, and I think correctly, that symbol-making is first used *to form consciousness*, to articulate thought before it is used as a means of communication. She quotes Edward Sapir, one of the century's most able psycho/linguists as follows:

> The primary function of language is generally said to be communication.... The autistic speech of children seems to show that the purely communicative aspect of language has been exaggerated. It is best to admit that language is primarily a vocal actualization of the tendency to see reality symbolically, that it is precisely this quality which renders it a fit instrument for communication and that it is in the actual give and take of social intercourse that it has been complicated and refined into the form in which it is known today.[6]

What Sapir is saying here is that symbol-making, a process requiring abstraction and transformation of one thing into another, is a natural human capacity upon which thought and consciousness itself depend. To put the case this way implies that the roots of symbol formation are conceptual before they become public. To have ideas is, in a sense, to engage in a forming process in which conceptions are abstracted or created; that is, they are formed realizations. Given this view, the public manifestation of the image is a second order symbol, the first being the conceptualization itself.

Whether one embraces such a view or a less radical relative, the fact that children use the images they create as symbols for the world is clear. This activity is due to their need to construct a knowable world and later to convey what they know to others.

From the recognition that images can be made and that once made they can function as symbols, children learn something else as well. The third thing that they learn is that symbolic images can be used as vehicles for symbolic play. Children learn that the images and symbols they create can be used to transport them into a fantasy world, that they can create an imaginary world through the use of their own images and through them become a part of other situations in which they can play other roles.

For young children the taking of new roles through imagination is an important source of learning.[7] It allows them to practice in the context of play what they cannot actually do in "the real world." It affords them opportunities to empathetically participate in the life of another. Given that egocentricism is the psychological condition of the young child, the opportunity to learn to empathize, to feel like, as well as to feel for, others is an important ingredient in becoming a social being. The symbols that children create and manipulate afford them opportunities to learn such skills. Empathy requires the ability to imaginatively project; art is a means for cultivating such an ability.

The fourth thing that children learn from making images is that the process of image-making requires the making of judgments. The forming of images, particularly those that in some ways are intended to correspond to some aspect of the world, is a structure-seeking more than a rule-abiding activity. To create structures, the child must invent and judge. Unlike those activities of which spelling is a paradigm case, the young child, like the adult artist, must judge the adequacy and quality of his or her own work. Although he might have criteria for making such judgments, he has no standards, for none exist. A standard, as Dewey pointed out so vividly in *Art as Experience*, is an arbitrary, fixed convention.[8] In spelling, standards are clear: in the English language there are two ways to spell a word, correctly or incorrectly. In making symbolic images no such standards exist. The child must judge and in the process learn to exercise judgment in situations where standards are absent. This is no minor accomplishment, for it moves the locus of evaluation from the external to the internal. The child must learn to rely upon his or her own sensibilities and perceptions in order to determine the adequacy of the symbolic images he or she creates.

One of education's longstanding aims has been to enable children to think for themselves, to become intellectually independent, to develop autonomy of judgment so that they will not be manipulated by others. Yet, in how many fields are such opportunities afforded the young? And without opportunities what chance is there for potentialities to actualize and for learning to occur?

Much has been learned of late about the consequences of sensory deprivation on the perceptual development of animals. There are critical periods in the course of a kitten's development when the deprivation of certain stimuli, light, for example, creates an irreversible loss of capacity. Living organisms are born with a capacity to perform a variety of functions *provided* the stimulus conditions are available for the neurons related to those capabilities to be fired. Once the critical period is past without appropriate stimulation of specific capabilities, the likelihood of recovering those capabilities, even if the stimuli are present, is small or non-existent.

What are those capabilities that the young possess that are never actualized because the needed stimuli for their use are absent? Consider, for example, a process in the making of judgments called "flexible purposing." Children may initiate a project in art with one purpose and in the process shift purposes in order to exploit an unexpected opportunity; a new image presents itself, an array of colors looks particularly arresting, one color has run into another color to create a new shape. To exploit such opportunities purposes must be flexible and judgment must be exercised. In learning to paint, children learn to judge and learn to be flexibly purposive. Such opportunities for learning are virtually absent in the learning of arithmetic, spelling, and to a large degree in early reading.

A fifth thing that children learn when they create images is that images can be related to other images to form a whole. The task of relating one image to another is another thing that is often taken for granted. Yet the perception of subtle relationships within a complex visual configuration does not occur naturally. I will never forget my early days in a life drawing class when my teacher taught me that where a figure was placed on a sheet of paper was no minor consideration. I was so preoccupied with trying to create a persuasive rendering of the figure that I neglected considering the relationship of the figure to the ground. Young children also learn to "decentrate" their perception of the images they create, to use Piaget's phrase. They gradually learn to shift from local solutions to contextual solutions in the way they order relationships on a two-dimensional surface. The ability to decentrate perception, to consider relationships, not only isolated entities, is one of the conditions of maturity. Those who are immature focus on one item at a time. Long-term goals or second order effects are not considered. In spatial patterns, as in temporal ones, the child must learn to consider relationships as well. Having the opportunity to create visual images provides the occasion for such learning to take place, and the more sophisticated and complex the qualities in the picture, the more critical the teacher becomes in facilitating such learning. Thus, questions of balance, unity, color, and value become considerations through the guidance of the sensitive teacher of art. Human nature provides the potential, but culture contributes to its development.

Much of what goes on in schooling mitigates against such holistic and contextual thinking. Basal reading programs and programmed instruction often fractionate learning tasks so that the child seldom gets an opportunity to consider the relationships among parts, let alone have a hand in structuring such relationships himself. With increased tendencies to break up learning into discrete units reinforced by extrinsic rewards, meaning is secured from extrinsic rewards rather than from the construction of a whole whose relations themselves hold meaning for the child. When such instruction is salient in schools, art has a very special and particularly important role to play as a kind of educational antidote.

A sixth thing that children learn when they paint is that they can develop skills that make it possible for them to create illusion and to form images that are visually persuasive. Although the need to create symbolic images that articulate consciousness appears to be a natural aspect of the human condition, the skills with which those images are rendered are learned. Learning that skills can be used to transform ideas, images, and feelings into a public form is not trivial since consciousness is in part achieved through the public manifestation of what otherwise is evanescent and inchoate. The variety and sophistication of skills or techniques become vehicles for transforming those ideas, images, and feelings. It is by virtue of skills that the materials that the child uses become media for conceptualization and expression.

As children work with materials and have the benefit of intelligent and sensitive teaching in art, their power to conceptualize visual ideas and to use effective means for expressing them increases. Their range for expressive visual articulation increases. Their "vocabulary" of visual possibilities expands, and they become more confident because they become more competent in art.

The development of competence is one of the major sources of self-satisfaction for children. None of us likes to display our weaknesses, and none of us likes to remain at the same level of ability after substantial experience in the field of endeavor. The greatest spur to further work and to the setting of higher standards is the recognition that we have made progress. There is something that we can do now that we couldn't do before. Unfortunately many children do not recognize the genuine progress that they have made in art. Seldom do they have the opportunity to compare their current work with what they produced earlier, and while I do not want to imply that the quality of the product is the only relevant consideration, it is one important consideration. Much of what children have learned shows up in their work, and when it does it seems reasonable to let them in on it. But to do that would require a radical change in the way we evaluate and display children's work. Instead of mounting mini-Metropolitan exhibitions, we should show children's work over a time, we would take colored slides, or keep portfolios, we would talk to children about a body of their work, and when we displayed the work for parents or teachers we would provide educational interpretations of what the children were learning as evidenced in the work itself.[9]

Children learn to become competent when they paint. They learn skills that expand their power, and with that power they can say more both to themselves and to the world. The British philosopher R. G. Collingwood pointed out that expression is a process through which ideas are formed and clarified.[10] The writer in a sense does not know what he has to say until it is said. The process of forming ideas is also a process of clarifying one's thoughts. To what extent does the process of expressing feeling through the creation of visual images clarify the feelings that children have? To what extent do children learn from the images they make how they feel about aspects of the world or their own experience? Paintings, drawings, sculptures are, after all, public vehicles that provide feedback to the child. In a sense, paintings project back to the child the child's ideas. Yet there is, of course, an important interaction between the child's ideas and his skills. Ideas can be well in advance of the skills the child is able to use. When this occurs, frustration is likely. The child has something to express but does not have the means to express it in material form. Conversely, skills may be well developed, but the child (or adult artist) may have little or nothing to express. The point here is that there is an interaction between content and technique. The former without the latter leads nowhere, and the latter without the former is empty. Ideally the relationship is symbiotic.

A seventh thing that children learn from making images is that ideas and emotions that are not physically present can be symbolized by the images one can create. When children first engage in the making of images, the character of such images is wholly abstract. What they respond to is the joy of using their senses, the movement of the hands, wrists, and arms, and the emerging patterns that appear on paper. By the time children reach four years of age, the shift to symbolic forms of representation has occurred, and of course the symbols that are drawn are symbols of physical objects which although imbued with feeling, nevertheless are related to concrete forms; people, trees, houses, and the like. It is only later in the course of human development and learning that the child learns that images can be made that are non-representational and which can convey or stand for certain ideas or feelings that are literally non-empirical. The realization that ideas like "power" or "humor" or "crispness" can be represented in non-objective ways is a late development in children's art. Young children do not use abstract ideas as subject matter for their efforts. What they draw or paint is concrete, and by nine or ten they are interested in the persuasive rendering of concrete forms. Such rendering becomes for them an artistic virtue.

But as they get older, as they move into formal operations, they have the capacity to grasp the idea that ideas, even those that are temporal and abstract, can be transformed into a visual, non-objective analogue. The paradigm case of such art among mature artists is found in the work of Rothko, Kline, Pollack, and Barnett Newman and the like.

The achievement of such a realization is not, I think, common among children at either the elementary or secondary levels. Unfortunately the data that are available for elementary school children indicate that subject matter rather than style is the major focus to which children attend when looking at paintings.[11] Yet children and certainly adolescents can be helped to learn to see the strictly visual qualities of form and can come to realize the ways in which non-objective images can stand for qualities of experience that are not embodied in a concrete object.

One of the most sophisticated aspects of what children can learn when making visual images, is the fact that there are ideas, images, and feelings that can *only* be expressed through visual form. This is the eighth thing that children learn. What we have in this form of learning is the implicit, if not always explicit recognition of the epistemological contributions of art. The forms one uses to conceptualize and express are not neutral with respect to the content that one can know and understand. How one expresses what one knows, as well as the medium one chooses to use, influences profoundly the content of expression. Put more simply, eventually children and adolescents learn that the visual arts, or music, or poetry are not inferior substitutes for scientific and propositional knowledge. The expressive content of the visual arts cannot be duplicated in music; the expressive content of music cannot be duplicated in poetry; and poetry is no substitute for science. There is a significant relationship between the mode of conceptualization one employs, the forms of disclosure one chooses to use, and the character of understanding and experience one secures. It is one thing to conceptualize in an auditory mode, another in a visual mode, and still another in a discursive mode. Visual modes are more spatial than temporal, while auditory and discursive modes are temporal. The nature of these modes defines the parameters of conceptual possibility. For example, consider how easy it is to conceptualize and express suspense in music and how difficult it is in visual art. Suspense is a temporal phenomenon, visual art is not.[12]

The fact that the medium affects the message is an invitation to people to reflect upon the nature of non-discursive forms of understanding; indeed, experience in the arts provides the material needed for such reflection. One who has not experienced the unique contributions of the arts to human understanding is in no position to understand the variety of ways in which humans come to know. In this sense work in the arts provides a basis for philosophic inquiry into questions of what knowledge is, how it is secured, and how the utilities of its several species can be compared and contrasted. Such forms of learning are, of course, a far cry from the very young child's realization that he or she has the ability to bring images into existence, yet the whole range of what can be learned from making images should be explored and not only those germane to preschoolers.

Finally (for the purposes of this paper), the ninth thing that children learn when they paint is that the world itself can be regarded as a source of aesthetic experience and as a pool of expressive form.

This aspect of learning in art represents the development of a special relationship to the world, the cultivation of what might be called an aesthetic attitude. To create images that have expressive power and aesthetic quality one must forego exclusive attention to an object's literal meaning or to its instrumental use. One must attend to the form of the thing in order to perceive and explore the relationships among the qualities it presents. But perhaps even more, one must perceive the expressive character of the forms, not just their formal relationships, but what they convey in feeling. The ability to do this is to some degree natural. As Arnheim put it, "Expression is the primary content of vision."[13] Yet through acculturation the child's ability to perceive such qualities is diminished. As he gets older, discursive language takes over, and the instrumental use of forms supersedes their exploratory use.

Insofar as work in the visual arts fosters attention to qualities per se, it has the potential to develop what is absolutely critical for using the world as a source of aesthetic experience. That absolute necessity is the inclination and ability to relate to the world with an aesthetic attitude, a type of disinterested but not uninterested perception. Unless the individual can forsake the strictly literal or strictly utilitarian, the formal and expressive characteristics of objects, events, and situations remain unseen and inexperienced. What differentiates the aesthetically well developed individual from his or her opposite is that such an attitude has developed, first in relation to specific forms: ceramics, orchids, ten-speed bicycles, sculpture, and later as a generalized conceptual set toward a wide variety of forms. Eventually, the scope includes the world itself. Life becomes "an object" to be regarded with an aesthetic attitude. To say this is not to imply that individuals must constantly regard life as they would a Matisse. It is to say that the use of an aesthetic attitude toward a wide variety of forms in the world becomes an option that a person can employ when he or she so chooses.

Thus in one sense what children eventually learn when they paint is a way of looking at life – is a particular stance, a kind of perspective that frees them from the unrelenting demands of practicality. They learn how to savor the quality of experience that flows from the qualities they encounter. Such experience, in turn, become the sources for artistic expression. Work in the arts, in sum, provides children with the opportunity to develop the sensibilities that make aesthetic awareness of the world possible. And such awareness provides the content not only for aesthetic experience, but for art itself.

I would like to conclude by asking what all of this has to do with the relationship between what is natural and what is cultural in human development. Simply this. Some aspects of artistic thinking are inherent in the human condition, such as the need to confer form upon ideas and feelings in order to have them. The need to explore and be stimulated by images of our own making. The need to use our senses so that they actualize rather than atrophy. No culture has been found that does not use language or create images.

But what is not natural is the refinement of the images we make beyond the necessities of survival. What is not natural is the cultivation of the sensibilities beyond what is needed to get on in the world. What is not natural is the extension of the repertoire of skills that can be used to form conception and to articulate expression. For these forms of learning to occur, tuition is necessary. Teachers of art have a necessary role to play in bringing culture to nature. An unassisted course of maturation simply will not develop the potential that children possess. This assistance is what we call teaching, and to provide it I can think of no group of people more competent than those who are devoting their professional lives to its behalf. The people to whom I am referring are those we call teachers of art.

## Notes

1 This paper was originally prepared for presentation at the Canadian Society for Education Through Art, Calgary, Alberta, Canada, October 1977.

2 Richard de Charms, *Personal Causation: The International Affective Determinants of Behavior* (New York: Academic Press, 1968).

3 Mark Lepper and David Greene, "Turning Play into Work: Effects of Adult Surveillance and Extrinsic Rewards on Children's Intrinsic Motivation," *Journal of Personality and Sound Psychology*, 1975, Vol. 31, No. 3, 479–486.

4 Susanne Langer, "Intuition and Transformation in the Arts," *Problems of Art* (New York: Charles Scribner's Sons, 1957), pp. 90–107.

5 Rudolf Arnheim, "Growth," *Art and Visual Perception* (Berkeley, CA: University of California Press, 1954).

6 Susanne Langer, *Philosophy in a New Key* (New York: The New American Library, 1951), p. 99.

7 This is not to imply that children between two and five make a distinction between what is imaginative and what is "real." However, children beyond five generally do make such distinctions and will practice through play what they cannot do in actuality.

8 John Dewey, *Art as Experience* (New York: Minton, Balch & Co., 1934).

9 For an elaboration of this use of evaluation in art see Elliot W. Eisner, "Toward a More Adequate Conception of Evaluation in the Arts," *Art Education*, Vol. 27, No. 2 (February, 1974).

10 R. G. Collingwood, *Principles of Art* (London: Clarendon Press, 1938).

11 See Howard Gardner and Judith Gardner, "Developmental Trends in Sensitivity to Form and Subject Matter in Paintings," *Studies in Art Education*, 1973, Vol. 14, No. 2, pp. 52–56.

12 This observation was made by Rudolf Arnheim in a lecture at Stanford University's Art Education Lecture series in 1976.

13 Rudolf Arnheim, "Expression," *Art and Visual Perception* (Berkeley, CA: University of California Press, 1954).

# CHAPTER 7

# ON THE DIFFERENCES BETWEEN SCIENTIFIC AND ARTISTIC APPROACHES TO QUALITATIVE RESEARCH*

*Educational Researcher*, 1981, 10(4): 5–9

My intention in this paper is to identify 10 dimensions in which artistic and scientific approaches to qualitative research differ.

The term qualitative research does not have a long history in the field of education and in many ways it not only hides the important distinctions which need to be made, but it is, itself, misleading. The major distinction we seek is *not* between qualitative and nonqualitative forms of research since *all* empirical research must of necessity pay attention to qualities, but between what is studied in a scientific mode and what is studied artistically. There can be no empirical research, that form of research that addresses problems in a material universe, that does not aim to describe, interpret, predict, or control qualities. The major distinction to be made in the conduct of research is not located in the phenomenon of study but in the mode in which that study occurs. The difference that counts is between what is studied artistically and what is studied scientifically. These differences are the ones to which this paper is addressed.

At the outset it should be said that research flying under the flag of science is extremely wide. Indeed, it is so wide that some philosophers of science regard no form of research in the social sciences as scientific. For philosophers of science such as Nagel (1961) or Popper (1959), the so-called social sciences are not yet what they claim to be.

We need not, and I do not, embrace the strict conception of science that they advocate. I am willing to regard as scientific, inquiries ranging from the testing of formal mathematical models of learning through controlled laboratory experiments to the kind of studies done in the field of cultural anthropology by people like Redfield (1941). For the purposes of this paper, scientific research may be regarded as inquiries that use formal instruments as the primary basis for data collection, that transform the data collected into numerical indices of one kind or another, and that attempt to generalize in a formal way to some universe beyond itself. Although I recognize that there are forms of scientific research that differ from the characteristics I have just described, I believe that these characteristics are by far the most salient ones and hence should be regarded as modal characteristics.

As for the concept "artistic," it similarly has no single, simple definition. "Art" and "artistic" are terms that have been the subject of aesthetic debate and analysis for over 2,000 years. Plato, for example, viewed art as the creation of harmonious form whose mathematical relationships participated in the true, the good and the beautiful. Aristotle regarded art as the production of mimisis; Clive Bell as the presence in a work of significant form; Suzanne Langer as the creation of a nondiscursive symbol expressive of human feeling; John Dewey as coherent and emotionally moving experience (see Weitz, 1959). The point here is simply that neither the concept of science nor the concept of art are settled issues among those who have thought about them most deeply. I provide this caveat now because my remarks will of necessity be based on an arbitrary, but I hope not an unreasonable, conception of both art and science. To provide a philosophically adequate discussion of these concepts would exceed my competence and would, at the very least, require a manuscript of book length.

Following is a discussion of 10 dimensions in which scientific and artistic approaches to research differ.

(1) *The forms of representation employed.* One significant difference between research participating in a scientific mode and that participating in an artistic mode is the kind of form that each uses to represent what has been learned. Scientific work, of necessity, employs formal statements which express either empirically referenced quantitative relationships or communicate through discursive propositions. The language which is used is formal in the sense that it is literal. That is, the syntactical rules to which such statements abide allow little or no scope for the poetic or the metaphorical. This is not to say that the poetic and the metaphorical do not find their way into scientific research; they do in a multitude of covert ways. House (1979) provides some illuminating examples of how this occurs. It is to say that the meanings conveyed aspire to literal rather than figurative form. Perhaps a classic example of such work is to be found in Birdwhistle's (1970; see especially part IV, pp. 183–216) micro-analytic schemes for the recording and scoring of human gesture, posture and movement. His aim is to operationalize both the perception and recording of human behavior through codification. Once codified, the methods of data collection and analysis can be routinized and the results objectified.

Artistic forms of representation have no comparable codifications. They place a premium on the idiosyncratic use of form – visual and auditory form as well as discursive form – to convey in nonliteral as well as literal ways the meanings the investigator wishes to express. "One Flew Over the Cuckoo's Nest" is a brilliant example of how visual, musical, and verbal forms can be combined to convey significant insights into human and inhuman relationships. For the artistic, the literal is frequently pale and humdrum. What one seeks is not the creation of a code that abides to publicly codified rules, but the creation of an evocative form whose meaning is embodied in the shape of what is expressed.

(2) *The criteria for appraisal.* Scientific approaches to research ask whether or not the conclusions are supported by the evidence, and further, whether the methods that were used to collect the evidence did not bias the conclusions. In other words, scientific research is always concerned with questions of validity. For a research study to be judged valid, a variety of criteria need to be applied to it. These range from appraising the character of sampling procedures and the magnitude of instrument reliability to the less tangible areas of interpretation.

In artistic approaches to research, the cannons of test reliability and sampling do not apply. While one might question a writer's or film producer's reliability, there is no formalized set of procedures to measure writer reliability; one doesn't really want the mean view of four writer's observations about the mental hospital in Oregon which served as the subject-matter for Ken Kesey's play. One simply wants Ken Kesey's view. Its validity, if that is the appropriate term, is to be determined by our view of its credibility, and not by reducing his work to some average by using only that portion that it shares with the views of others. Validity in the arts is the product of the persuasiveness of a personal vision; its utility is determined by the extent to which it informs. There is no test of statistical significance, no measure of construct validity in artistically rendered research. What one seeks is illumination and penetration. The proof of the pudding is the way in which it shapes our conception of the world or some aspect of it.

(3) *Points of focus.* Scientific approaches to research tend to focus on the manifest behavior of the individual or group studied to a greater degree than artistic approaches. By this I mean that manifest behavior provides the primary data for research in the social sciences in which scientifically oriented research participates. What one attends to is what people do, how they behave, what they say. Such phenomena are open to experience, they are observable; their incidence can be counted, and once counted, they can be treated in a multitude of ways. Although one might make inferences from the behavior one observes and records, the farther the inference is from the behavior, the less trustworthy it is regarded to be. The distinction between "high inference" and "low inference" conclusions underscores this point.

Artistic approaches to research focus less on behavior than on the experience the individuals are having and the meaning their actions have for others. Just how does one focus on experience and meaning. How does one make sense of what is nonobservable? One way is to make inferences from observables to what is not observable. Manifest behavior is treated primarily as a cue, a springboard to get someplace else. The other way is to "indwell," to empathize; that is, to imaginatively participate in the experience of another. (For a vivid example of indwelling as a technique for describing the experience of others, see Barone, 1978.) The difference between the two is subtle but important. In the former, observables are used in a kind of statistical fashion; one intuitively (or statistically) estimates the probability that *this* behavior means one particular thing or another. There is no real need for empathy. The latter banks on the observer's ability to imaginatively project himself into the life of another in order to know what that person is experiencing. It is the content provided by this form of knowing that serves as a major source of understanding for artistic approaches to research. Thus, a major focus in artistic approaches to research is the meanings and experiences of the people who function in the cultural web one studies. As Geertz (1973) puts it with respect to his work, "Believing, with Max Weber, that man is an animal suspended in webs of significance he himself has spun, I take culture to be those webs, and the analysis of it to be therefore not an experimental science in search of law but an interpretive one in search of meaning" (p. 5).

(4) *The nature of generalization.* In the social sciences, the methodology required for generalizing from a set of specific findings to a universe is well defined. In this process the selection of a sample must be random and the parameters of the universe clearly articulated. Inferences from sample to population are acceptable only insofar as they meet these requirements. There is comparatively little interest in findings that deal only with the sample itself; social science research methods are after bigger fish. This orientation to generalization, one which is statistical in nature, is what Windelband has called nomethetic (see von Wright, 1971). Studies of single cases or the examination of the idiosyncratic are not considered good resources for generalizing. Indeed, in statistical studies "outlyers," individual scores that do not conform to the distribution of a sample or population, are often disregarded; they are considered part of the error variance. What one seeks are trends, robust central tendencies, or stable and statistically

significant differences in the variances between groups as a function of treatment. Research in the social sciences attempts to move from the particular to the general, and is interested in particulars only insofar as they represent the general. Random selection is the cornerstone of the process.

Artistic approaches to research have no comparable mechanism for generalization. But this should not be interpreted to mean that generalization is not possible. While it is sometimes said that ideographic research does not generalize, I think such a conclusion is incorrect. But if so, then how does one generalize from a nonrandomly selected single case? Generalization is possible because of the belief that the general resides in the particular and because what one learns from a particular one applies to other situations subsequently encountered (see Donmoyer, 1980). Consider literature as an example. Is it the case that Saul Bellow's novel *Mr. Sammler's Planet* is simply a story about Artur Sammler and no one else? Is Shakespeare's portrayal of Lady Macbeth simply about a particular Scottish noblewoman who lived in the later part of the eleventh century? Hardly. What these writers have done is to illustrate significant, common human attributes by the way they have written about particular individuals. Artistic approaches to research try to locate the general in the particular. They attempt to shed light on what is unique in time and space while at the same time conveying insights that exceed the limits of the situation in which they emerge. This is precisely what Aristotle meant when he said that "Poetry was truer than history."

Put into more contemporary psychological terms, the expectations we acquire from our examination of the particular become a part of our anticipatory schema; we shape our information pickup system by what we learn from individual cases (see Neisser, 1976). The artistically oriented researcher is interested in making the particular vivid so that its qualities can be experienced and because he believes that the particular has a contribution to make to the comprehension of what is general. The ability to generalize from particulars is one of the ways whereby humans cope with the world. I know of no one who forms the generalizations that guide his or her actions through a technically rigorous process of random selection.

(5) *The role of form.* In the sciences, the manner in which data are presented is interchangeable. For example, one can use numbers to display a pattern of scores which a population received or one can use a bar chart. The two methods are regarded as equivalent. Indeed, if one form designed to replicate the information provided in the other fails to do so, an error has occurred.

The matter of form in scientific work goes even farther. If the articles published in research journals are examined for style, it becomes quite apparent that the standardization of style is considered a virtue. One is supposed to identify the problem, review the literature, describe the instruments and population, report the treatment, present and discuss the results and, finally, project possible implications. If, in this format, any sense of the personality of the investigator shines through, it is to be neutralized. This is accomplished by requiring that writers use the third person singular or the first person plural instead of using the "I" form. The people studied are referred to as "subjects" or "Ss" and whatever uniqueness particular individuals might have are to be disregarded.

Not all research in the social sciences emphasizes so strict a formula as I have just described. Nevertheless, this is the dominant tradition in which social science research participates. The date an editor receives a manuscript is sometimes published with the manuscript, this being a clear indication of the effort editors of social science journals make to emulate their colleagues in the physical sciences where "who discovered what first" counts a great deal.

In artistic approaches to research, standardization of form is counterproductive. What artistic approaches seek is to exploit the power of form to inform. What those engaged in artistic work take as a given is the belief that form and content interact; some would say that form *is* content (Shahn, 1957). The opposite view is salient in scientifically oriented work. Standardization of form is sought so that it does not confound the content. Because of its rule-governed syntax, the same things can be said in several ways. Rules of equivalence are comparatively easy to apply. In artistic approaches the particular words chosen, the location of specific ideas within a report, the tone and tempo of the writing, the sense of voice which it possesses have no literal equivalent. The potential of form is not regarded as a liability but as an essential vehicle constituting a significant part of the content of the communication. In short, form is regarded as a part of the content of what is expressed and bears significantly on the kinds of meanings people are likely to secure from the work. Hence, being skilled at the making of artistically expressive forms – being able to write – is a critically important skill for those doing artistically oriented research in education.

(6) *Degree of license allowed.* Perhaps one of the most generally held beliefs about the differences between science and art is that the former deals with fact while the latter deals with fiction. The former is regarded as objective, the latter as subjective. Putting aside the point that scientific work is an artifact, that it is a human construction subject to all the human vicissitudes and foibles, there is a correct sense to the expectation that what is said in the name of science is to be more factual, less subject to imaginative fancy than, say, what is said by those who work within an artistic mode. We expect inventiveness and personal interpretation in the arts. We expect the artist to take liberties in order to drive home the point he or she wishes to make. These liberties – what we refer to as artistic license – are not intended to distract from artistic validity but to render more incisively and more persuasively what has been learned. Does such "bias" have a place in artistic approaches to research? Are the straight facts unencumbered by modulation more truthful? Is the longstanding expectation for pristine objectivity – even if such an aspiration were possible to achieve, which I think it is not – the most noble ideal for educational research?

One of the strengths that artistically oriented research possesses is that liberties in portrayal are wider than they are in scientifically oriented studies. Making things vivid through selective reporting and special emphasis occurs inevitably in any form of reporting, including scientific reporting. Artistically oriented research acknowledges what already exists and instead of presenting a facade of objectivity, exploits the potential of selectivity and emphasis to say what needs saying as the investigator sees it. Indeed, this orientation to writing has developed to such a degree of sophistication among the "new journalists" that a neologism has been created to designate the new genre: it is called *faction*, the marriage of fact and fiction. I regard this term as extremely illuminating. After all, what can be more biased than emotionally eviscerated fact describing conditions or situations that are emotionally significant to those in the situations being described. Distortion can result not only from what is put in, but also from what is left out.

(7) *Interest in prediction and control.* Scientifically oriented research aims at the production of ideas that will enable us to anticipate the future, if not to control it. The most rigorous form of scientific work, physics for example, makes both prediction and control possible and through them, the technological achievements that have captured the public's imagination. Some fields such as astronomy do not lead to control, but they do make accurate prediction possible. Most social science

fields neither control nor successfully predict, they explicate. Archeology and psychoanalysis are prime examples. As movement proceeds from the former to the latter, the affinity of scientifically oriented research to research that is artistically oriented grows stronger. Aside from the production of naturalistic-like generalizations (Stake, 1978), artistically oriented research does not aim to control or to produce formal predictive statements. It is after explication. It is closer in character to a hermeneutic activity than a technological one. What it yields at its best are ineffable forms of understanding which can only be conveyed through the figurative or nondiscursive character of the artistic image which such research yields (see Langer, 1957). The working assumption is that with such understanding, both cognitive differentiation and the ability of individuals to grasp and deal with situations like those portrayed in the research will be increased. It is not an algorithm that artistically oriented research seeks as much as a heuristic.

(8) *The sources of data.* In artistic approaches to research, the major instrument is the investigator himself. By this I mean that although the investigator might use some formal instruments to collect data, the major source of data emanates from how the investigator experiences what it is he or she attends to. There are several utilities of such an approach. In the first place, many things that might be significant might not find a place on a formal observation schedule. One might now know in advance what is significant. Second, the meaning of an incident within a social situation might only be revealed by putting it in its historical context. No instrument which I know of can do this. Third, the expressive character of action and speech – their muted messages – are often so subtle that only a perceptive eye and an informed mind are likely to recognize their significance. Balance, tradeoff, context, and other features of social life must be considered if the interpretation of socially shared meanings is to have validity. These are precisely what are so difficult to standardize on test instruments or interview and observation schedules. The ideal of the hermetically sealed test, which is administered according to a standardized procedure and whose ticks are optically recorded and computer-scored and then mailed with standardized interpretations to anxious students, is very far from the ideal in artistically oriented research.

Not only are standardized methods of data collection marginal rather than central, but the way in which what has been learned is shared with others is also nonstandardized. Reporting is guided by considerations of how the message is likely to be interpreted by those who receive it. In short, not only is there no standardized way of getting information, there is no standardized acontextual way of communicating what has been learned. What and how one says something depends on whom the message is for. Each report is, in this sense, a custom job.

(9) *The basis of knowing.* In artistic approaches to research, the role that emotion plays in knowing is central. Far from the ideal of emotional neutrality which is sought in much of social science research, the artistically oriented researcher recognizes that knowing is not simply a unidimensional phenomena, but takes a variety of forms. The research knows also that the forms one uses to represent what one knows affect what can be said. Thus, when the content to be conveyed requires that the reader vicariously participates in a social situation context, the writer or filmmaker attempts to create a form that makes such participation possible.

This orientation to knowledge embraces an epistemology that rejects the positivistic view which holds that only formal propositions can, in principal, provide knowledge (Ayer, n.d.). It rejects the view that affect and cognition are independent spheres of human experience. Instead, it gives to Rome what is Rome's; when you want to know how many students dropped out of a high school class you don't want a set of sonnets, you want a set of numbers. And it gives to others what they need to have in order to understand. Methodological pluralism rather than methodological monism is the ideal to which artistic approaches to research subscribe. To know a rose by its Latin name and yet to miss its fragrance is to miss much of the rose's meaning. Artistic approaches to research are very much interested in helping people experience the fragrance.

(10) *Ultimate aims.* This brings me to the last dimension I wish to discuss regarding the differences between scientific and artistic approaches to research: the question of differences in ultimate aim. Historically, one of the traditional aims of science is the discovery of truth. The Greeks had a word for it: episteme, the discovery of true and certain knowledge. Although many modern philosophers and historians of science such as Thomas Kuhn (1962) take a softer, more nominal view of science, not all philosophers of science do, and for a great many researchers in the social sciences, the correspondence theory of truth still holds sway. Propositions about reality are believed to be true to the extent to which those propositions correspond to the reality that they attempt to describe or explain. Given this view, science aims at making true statements about the world.

Artistic approaches to research are less concerned with the discovery of truth than with the creation of meaning. What art seeks is not the discovery of the laws of nature about which true statements or explanations can be given, but rather the creation of images that people will find meaningful and from which their fallible and tentative views of the world can be altered, rejected, or made more secure. Truth implies singularity and monopoly. Meaning implies relativism and diversity. Truth is more closely wedded to consistency and logic, meaning to diverse interpretation and coherence. Each approach to the study of educational situations has its own unique perspective to provide. Each sheds its own unique light on the situations that humans seek to understand. The field of education in particular needs to avoid methodological monism. Our problems need to be addressed in as many ways as will bear fruit. Interest in "qualitative research" is symptomatic of the uneasiness that many in the research community have felt with the methods of inquiry promulgated by conventional research tradition. I have suggested in this paper that looking to qualitative methods to reduce this uneasiness will prove inadequate. The issue is not qualitative as contrasted with nonqualitative or quantitative, but how one approaches the educational world. It is to the artistic to which we must turn, *not* as a rejection of the scientific, but because with both we can achieve binocular vision. Looking through one eye never did provide much depth of field.

## Note

* This is a modified version of a paper presented at the annual meeting of the American Educational Research Association, Boston, MA, April 1980.

## References

Ayer, A. *Language, Truth and Logic.* New York: Dover Publications, n.d.
Barone, T. *Inquiry into Classroom Experiences: A Qualitative, Holistic Approach.* Unpublished PhD dissertation, Stanford University, 1978.
Birdwhistell, R. L. *Kinesics and Context.* New York: Ballantine Books, 1970.
Donmoyer, R. *Alternative Conception of Generalization and Verification for Educational Research.* Unpublished PhD dissertation, Stanford University, 1980.
Geertz, C. *The Interpretation of Cultures.* New York: Basic Books, 1973.

House, E. "Coherence and Credibility: The Aesthetics of Education." *Educational Evaluation and Policy Analysis*, 1(5): 5–17; 1979.

Kuhn, T. S. *The Structure of Scientific Revolution*. Chicago, IL: The University of Chicago Press, 1962.

Langer, S. K. *Problems of Art*. New York: Scribners and Sons, 1957.

Nagel, E. *The Structure of Science: Problems in the Logic of Scientific Explanation*. New York: Harcourt, Brace and World, 1961.

Neisser, U. *Cognition and Reality*. San Francisco, CA: W. H. Freeman, 1976.

Popper, K. *The Logic of Scientific Discovery*. London: Hutchinson, 1959.

Redfield, R. *The Folk Culture of Yucatan*. Chicago, IL: The University of Chicago Press, 1941.

Shahn, B. *The Shape of Content*. Cambridge, MA: Harvard University Press, 1957.

Stake, R. "The Case Study Method in Social Inquiry." *Educational Researcher*, 7(7): 5–8; 1978.

von Wright, H. *Explanation and Understanding*. Ithaca, NY: Cornell University Press, 1971.

Weitz, M. *Problems in Aesthetics*. New York: Macmillan, 1959.

# CHAPTER 8

# THE ROLE OF THE ARTS IN COGNITION AND CURRICULUM

*Journal of Art & Design Education, 1986, 5(1 and 2): 57–67*

My thesis is straightforward but not widely accepted. It is that the arts are cognitive activities, guided by human intelligence, that make unique forms of meaning possible. I shall argue further that the meanings secured through the arts require what might best be described as forms of artistic literacy, without which artistic meaning is impeded and the ability to use more conventional forms of expression is hampered.

To talk about the cognitive character of the arts or about the kind of meaning that they convey is not particularly common. The models of mind that have typified US educational psychology (particularly that aspect of psychology concerned with learning and knowing) have made tidy separations between thinking and feeling, feeling and acting, and acting and thinking.[1] The view of thinking that has been most common is rooted in the Platonic belief that mind and body are distinct, and, of the two, body is base while mind is lofty.[2] Feeling is located in *soma*, idea in *psyche*. The literature distinguishes between cognition and affect, and we tend to regard as cognitive those activities of mind that mediate ideas through words and numbers. We consider words more abstract than images, icons less flexible than propositions. We regard words as high in that hierarchy of cognitive achievement we use to describe cognitive growth. Jean Piaget, for example, regarded formal operations, those mental operations that deal with logical relationships, as the apotheosis of cognitive achievement.[3] For some cognitive psychologists, thinking is a kind of inner speech that allows one to reason.[4] Since reason is a condition of rationality and since reasoning is believed to require the logical treatment of words, operations of the mind that do not employ logic are placed on the margins of rationality.

In this view the arts, if not considered irrational, are thought of as *a-rational*. As for meaning, it is most commonly regarded as an attribute of propositions, the property of assertions for which scientific warrant can be secured. The arts are considered emotive forms that might provide satisfaction – but not understanding.

The consequences of this view of mind have, in my opinion, been disastrous for education. First, this view has created a dubious status hierarchy among subjects taught in schools. Mathematics is the queen of the hill; other subjects, especially those in which students 'work with their hands', are assigned lower intellectual status. Simply recall the standard whipping boy of school activities, basket weaving. Basket weaving epitomises low status and mindlessness. Let me state quickly that I reject mindless forms of basket weaving in school. But let me add just as quickly that I also reject mindless forms of algebra and that I find nothing inherently more intellectually complex in algebra than in basket weaving; it depends upon the nature of the algebra and the nature of the baskets we choose to weave.

Besides making some subjects the targets of verbal abuse, the status hierarchy among subjects that emanates from such an indefensible conception of mind has practical day-to-day consequences in schools. Consider how time is allocated in school programmes. Time is surely one of the most precious of school resources. As researchers of time on task have told us,[5] the relationship between the amount of time allocated and learning is a significant one. Partly because of our view of intellect, however, some subjects – the fine arts, for example – receive very little attention in school programmes. On the average, elementary school teachers devote about 4 per cent of school time each week to instruction in the fine arts.[6] And this time is not prime time, such as the so-called cognitive subjects command. For the fine arts, Friday afternoons are very popular.

Space does not permit a lengthy recital of sins that have been committed by schools in the name of cognitive development. Yet it is important to remember that the conception of giftedness used in many states excludes ability in the fine arts, that tax dollars support programmes whose criteria discriminate against students whose gifts are in the fine arts, and that colleges and universities do not consider high school grades in the fine arts when making admissions decisions.[7] We legitimate such practices by distinguishing between intelligence and talent, assigning the former to verbal and mathematical forms of reasoning and the latter to performance in activities we deem more concrete: playing a musical instrument, dancing, painting.

I could elaborate at length on each of these points. But I mention them simply to highlight the model of mind that has been so widely accepted and to provide a context for my remarks concerning the role of the arts in cognition and curriculum.

If you were to consult the *Dictionary of Psychology* regarding the meaning of cognition, you would find that cognition is 'the process through which the organism becomes aware of the environment'.[8] Thus cognition is a process that makes awareness possible. It is, in this sense, a matter of becoming conscious, of noticing, of recognising, of perceiving. It is a matter of distinguishing one thing from another: a figure from its ground, the various subtleties and nuances that, when perceived, become part of one's consciousness.

In this process, the functions of the senses are crucial. They bring to awareness the qualitative world we inhabit. To become aware of the world, two conditions must be satisfied. First, the qualities must be available for experiencing by a sentient human being. Second, the individual must be able to 'read' their presence. When both of these conditions are met, the human being is capable of forming concepts of the world. These concepts take shape in the information that the senses have provided.

The process of forming concepts is one of construing *general* features from qualitative particulars. The perception of the qualitative world is always fragmented: we never see a particular immediately, in an instant. Time is always involved.[9] General configurations are formed – that is, built up from parts to wholes. Through time they yield structured patterns that constitute a set. The patterns formed in this way are concepts. They are root forms of experience that we are able to recall and to manipulate imaginatively.

The importance of the senses in concept formation is that: (i) no concepts can be formed without sensory information;[10] (ii) the degree to which the particular senses are differentiated has a large effect on the kind and subtlety of the concepts that are formed; and (iii) without concepts formed as images (whether these images are visual, auditory, or in some other sensory form), image surrogates – words, for example – are meaningless.[11]

It is easy to see how such concrete concepts as dog or chair, red or blue, depend upon sensory information. But what about such abstract concepts as justice, category, nation, infinity? I would argue that these words are nothing more than meaningless noises or marks on paper unless their referents can be imagined. Unless we have a conception of justice, the word is empty. Unless we can imagine infinity, the term is nothing more than a few decibels of sound moving through space. I do not mean to imply that we conjure up an image every time we hear a word. Our automatic response mechanisms make this unnecessary. But when I say, 'The man was a feckless mountebank', the statement will have meaning only if you have referents for 'feckless' and 'mountebank'. If you do not, then you turn to a friend or a dictionary for other words whose images allow you to create an analogy. It is through such analogies or through illustrative examples that so-called abstract concepts take on meaning. Concepts, in this view, are not linguistic at base; instead, they are sensory. The forms concepts take are as diverse as our sensory capacities and the abilities we have developed to use them.

The process of concept formation is of particular importance in the development of scientific theory. In the social sciences, for example, theoreticians form concepts by construing social situations in ways that others have not noticed. Terms such as class, social structure, adaptation, role, status, and reinforcement are meaningful because they bracket aspects of the social world for us to experience.[12] They call to our attention qualities of the world that otherwise would have gone unseen. But the reality is in the flesh and blood of experience, not simply in the words. Put another way, there is an icon – a stylised image of reality – underlying any term that is meaningful. The makers of such icons are people we regard as perceptive or insightful. Indeed, the Latin root of 'intuition' is *intueri*, meaning to look upon, to see. In the beginning there was the image, not the word.

One important characteristic of concepts is that they can be not only recalled but imaginatively manipulated. We can combine qualities we have encountered to form entities that never were but that might become: hence unicorns, helixes, ideals of perfection towards which we strive, and new tunes to whistle. We can construct models of the world from which we can derive verbal or numerical propositions or from which we can create visual or auditory images. The point is that, while the sensory system provides us with information about the world in sensory form, our imaginative capacities – when coupled with an inclination towards play – allow us to examine and explore the possibilities of this information.[13] Although our imaginative lives might be played out in solitary fantasy or daydreaming, imagination often provides the springboard for expression. How is experience expressed? What vehicles are used? What skills are employed? And what do the arts have to do with it? It is to that side of the cognitive coin that I now turn.

Thus far I have emphasised the cognitive function of the sensory systems, and I have pointed out that concepts formed from sensory information can be recalled and manipulated through imagination. But thus far, this manipulation of concepts has been private, something occurring within the personal experience of individuals. The other side of the coin deals with the problem of externalisation. In some way an individual must acquire and employ a form that can represent to self and to others what has been conceptualised. This task requires what I call a *form of representation*.[14] The problem of representing conceptions is a problem of finding or inventing equivalents for those conceptions. In this task, the form or forms to be employed must themselves appeal to one or more of the senses. A visual concept, for example, might be externalised in a form that is visual, or the form might instead be auditory, verbal, or both. Thus, for example, we could represent an imaginary stream of rolling and flowing blue amoebic shapes either visually or through sound. The stream might be described through words, or it might be represented through movement – perhaps dance. Regardless of the form we select, it must be one that the sensory systems can pick up. Put another way, the form must be empirical.

The kind of information that we are able to convey about what we have conceptualised is both constrained and made possible by the forms of representation that we have access to and are able to use. Some of the things an individual knows are better represented by some forms than others. What one can convey about a river that slowly wends its way to the sea will be significantly influenced by the form of representation one chooses to use. The same holds true for portrayals of classrooms, teaching, love affairs, and memorable cities one has visited.

Consider suspense. Almost all of us are able to invent a way of conveying suspense through music. From old cowboy movies and mystery dramas on radio and television, we already have a repertoire of models to draw upon. But think about how suspense would be represented through painting or sculpture. Here the problem becomes much more difficult. Why? Because suspense is a temporal experience, and painting and sculpture are largely spatial. It is more difficult to use the latter to represent the former than to use music, which itself is temporal.

Some forms of representation can illuminate some aspects of the world that others cannot. What a person can learn about the world through visual form is not likely to be provided through auditory form. What an individual knows takes shape in the empirical world only through a vehicle or vehicles that make knowing public. The vehicles we use for this purpose are the forms of representation.

Although I have described the externalisation of concepts as one-directional – that is, as moving from inside out – the process is actually reciprocal. For example, what a person knows how to do affects what he or she conceptualises. If you walk around the world with black and white film in your camera, you look for contrasts of light and dark, for texture, for patterns of shadow against buildings and walls. As Ernst Gombrich put it, 'Artists don't paint what they can see, they see what they can paint.' The ability to use a form of representation skilfully guides our perception. The process flows, as it were, from representation to conception as well as from conception to representation.

Dialectical relationships between conception and representation occur in other ways as well. For example, the externalisation of a conception through a form of representation allows the editing process to occur. By stabilising what is evanescent, the conception can be modified, abbreviated, sharpened, revised, or discarded altogether. Further, in the process of representation new concepts are formed. Indeed, the act of discovery through expression is so important that R. G. Collingwood describes its presence as the difference between art and craft.[15] The craftsman knows how to do a job well, but produces nothing essentially new. The artist not only has the skills of the craftsman but discovers new possibilities as work progresses. The *work* of art is to make expressive form become a source of surprise, a discovery, a form that embodies a conception not held at the outset.

The selection of a form of representation does not adequately resolve the question of how that form, once selected, becomes 'equivalent' to the conception. I suggest that we secure equivalence by treating forms of representation in one of three ways. The first of these modes of treatment is *mimetic*, the second is *expressive*, and the third is *conventional*.

Mimetic modes of treatment are efforts to imitate the surface features of perceived or conceptualised forms, within the constraints of some material. Early examples of mimesis are the running animals found on the walls of the Lascaux Caves. According to Gombrich, the history of art is replete with efforts to create illusions that imitate the visual features of the environment as it was or as it was imagined.[16] But mimesis as a way of treating a form of representation is not limited to what is visual. Mimesis occurs in auditory forms of representation, such as music and voice, and in movement through dance. Mimesis is possible in any of the forms used to provide information that the senses can pick up.

As I have already said, the creation of an equivalent for a conception is always both constrained and made possible by the medium a person employs. Different media appeal to different sensory systems. Thus, when a person transforms visual conceptions into sound or movement, he or she must find what Rudolf Arnheim calls the 'structural equivalent' of the conception within the medium he or she elects to use.[17] Such transformation requires the invention of analogies.

In language, analogic functions are performed by metaphor. When we move from the auditory to the visual, however, we must create a structural equivalent between the auditory and the visual. For example, the sounds 'ooo loo loo' and 'eee pee pee' are represented best by two very different kinds of graphic lines – one waving, the other pointed or jagged. Humans have the capacity to perceive and grasp these structural equivalences even when they take shape in different forms of representation – one visual, the other auditory. Thus mimesis, the business of imitating the surface features of a conceptualisation within the limits of some medium, is one way to secure equivalence between a conception and its forms of representation.

The second way to do this is by treating the forms expressively. By expressively, I mean that what is conveyed is what the object, event, or conception expresses – not what it looks like. Thus 'sorrow' can be represented mimetically, but it can also be represented expressively. In the arts, this expressive mode of treatment is of particular interest: the tense nervousness of Velasquez's *Pope Innocent X*, the celebration of colour in a Sam Francis, the asceticism of a late Barnett Newman, the ethereal quality of Helen Frankenthaler's work, the symbolic undertones of an Edward Hopper, the crisp architecture of Bach's fugues, the romantic expansiveness of Beethoven's *Seventh Symphony*, the lighthearted whimsy of the poetry of e. e. cummings. What these artists have created are expressive images. In general, mimesis is a minor element in their works, used only to complement the dominant intent. Pablo Picasso succinctly stated the importance of the expressive mode of treatment in art when he said, 'A painter takes the sun and makes it into a yellow spot, an artist takes a yellow spot and makes it into the sun.'

By contrast, the conventional model of treatment uses an arbitrary sign, on whose meaning society has agreed, to convey that meaning. Thus words and numbers are meaningful, not because they look like their referents but because we have agreed that they shall stand for them. The use of convention is, of course, not limited to words and numbers. Swastikas, crosses, six-pointed stars, the iconography of cultures past and present are all examples of visual conventions. Conventions in music take such forms as anthems, wedding marches, and graduation processionals.

In much of art the three modes of treatment are combined. Erwin Panofsky made his major contribution to the history of art – to the study of iconography – by describing these relationships.[18] The works of Jasper Johns, Marc Chagall,

Joseph Cornell, Jack Levine, Robert Rauschenberg, and Andy Warhol demonstrate the ingenious ways in which visual artists have exploited all three modes of treatment in their effect to convey meaning.

I hope that I have made my point clear: any form of representation one chooses to use – visual, auditory, or discursive – must also be treated in some way. Some forms tend to call forth one particular mode of treatment. The treatment of mathematics, for example, is essentially conventional, even though we may recognise its aesthetic qualities. The visual arts, by contrast, tend to emphasise the mimetic and the expressive. Language tends to be treated conventionally and expressively (save for occasional instances of onomatopoeia, which are obviously mimetic). The forms we choose provide potential options. The options we choose give us opportunities to convey what we know and what we are likely to experience.

Just as any form of representation we elect to use must be treated in a particular way, the elements within that form must also be related to each other. This relationship constitutes a syntax, an arrangement of parts used to construct a whole. Some forms of representation, such as mathematics and propositional discourse, are governed rather rigorously by publicly codified rules, through which the operations applied to such forms are to be performed. To be able to add, one must be able to apply correctly a set of prescribed operations to a set of numerical elements. To be able to punctuate, one must follow certain publicly articulated rules so that the marks placed within a sentence or paragraph are correct. Similarly, in spelling, rules govern the arrangements of elements (letters) that constitute words. There are only two ways to spell most words in English: correctly or incorrectly. Forms of representation that are treated through convention tend to emphasise the rule-governed end of the syntactical continuum. When forms are treated in this way, the scoring of performance can be handled by machines, because the need for judgement is small.

Forms of representation that are treated expressively have no comparable rules. There are, of course, rules of a sort to guide one in making a painting of a particular style or designing a building of a particular architectural period. But the quality of performance in such forms is not determined by measuring the extent to which the rules were followed (as is done for spelling and arithmetic). Instead, quality is judged by other criteria – in some cases, criteria that do not even exist prior to the creation of the work. Syntactical forms that are open rather than closed, that allow for the idiosyncratic creation of relationships without being regarded as incorrect, are figurative in character. Thus it is possible to array forms of representation not only with respect to their modes of treatment but in relation to the ends of the syntactical continuum towards which they lean. In general, the arts lean towards the figurative. That is why, given the same task, 30 students in music, poetry, or visual art will create 30 different solutions, all of which can be 'right', while 30 students in arithmetic will – if the teacher has taught effectively – come up with identical solutions. That is also why the arts are regarded as subjective: one cannot apply a conventionally defined set of rules to determine whether the meanings that are conveyed are accurate. Idiosyncratic arrangements are encouraged when figurative syntaxes are employed.

The importance of this distinction between rule-governed and figurative syntactical emphases becomes apparent when we consider the kinds of cognitive processes that each type of syntax elicits. Learning of rules fosters acquiescence: one learns to *obey* a rule or to *follow* it. Figurative syntaxes, by contrast, encourage invention, personal choice, exploratory activity, and judgement. The use of forms whose syntax is figurative is an uncertain enterprise, since there are no formally codified rules to guide judgements. The student, like the artist, is thrown on his or her own resources. How does one know when the painting is finished, the poem completed, the story ended? There is no predefined standard by which to check a solution. There is no correct answer given in the back of the book, no procedure for determining proof. The necessary cognitive operations are what were known, in earlier psychological jargon, as 'higher mental processes'. At the least, tasks that emphasise the figurative give people opportunities to form new structures, to make speculative decisions, and to act upon them. Such tasks also enable people to learn to judge – not by applying clear-cut standards, but by appealing to a form of rationality that focuses on the rightness of a form to a function.

It would be well at this point to recall the theme of this article, the role of the arts in cognition and curriculum. I began by describing a commonly held view: cognition requires that ideas be linguistically mediated, whereas the arts are expressive and affective activities depending more upon talent than intelligence or cognition. I next analysed the role of the senses in concept formation, arguing that all concepts are basically sensory in character and that concept formation requires the ability to perceive qualitative nuances in the qualitative world and to abstract their structural features for purposes of recall or imaginative manipulation. From there I moved to a discussion of the task of representation. An individual who wishes to externalise a concept must find some way of constructing an equivalent for it in the empirical world. To do this, people invent new forms of representation or borrow from those already available in the culture. Because these forms can be treated in different ways and because they appeal to different sensory systems, the kind of meanings each yields is unique. What we can convey in one form of representation has no literal equivalent in another. I have labelled the modes of treating these forms as mimetic, expressive, and conventional. Because the elements within forms of representation can be ordered according to different rules, I have identified a syntactical continuum, highly rule-governed at one end and figurative at the other. The rule-governed end of the continuum prescribes the rules of operations that must, by convention, be followed in ordering those elements. The figurative end allows maximum degrees of latitude for idiosyncratic arrangement. The former is more of a code; the latter, more of a metaphor.

But what is the significance of such analysis for education? What bearing does it have on what we do in school? What might it mean for what we teach? There are four implications, I believe, for the conduct of education and for educational theory.

First, the view that I have advanced makes it impossible to regard as cognitive any mental activity that is not itself rooted in sensory forms of life. This expands our conceptions of intelligence and literacy. Any conception of intelligence that omits the ordering of qualities through direct experience is neglecting a central feature of intellectual functioning. But no intelligence test that is published today includes such tasks. The models of mind that underlie current tests assign only marginal intellectual status to what is an intellectual activity. One no more plays the violin with one's fingers than one counts with one's toes. In each case, mind must operate, and the kind and number of opportunities a person is given to learn will significantly affect the degree to which his or her ability develops. The concepts of talent and lack of talent have been used too long to cover up weak or non-existent programmes in the arts. To be sure, individual aptitudes in the arts vary, but such differences also exist in other content areas. So-called lack of talent is too often nothing more than an excuse for absent opportunity. It also serves as a self-fulfilling prophecy.

Second, the view that I have advanced recognises that the realm of meaning has many mansions. Science, for example, despite its enormous usefulness, can never have a monopoly on meaning because the form of representation it employs is only one among the several that are available. It is not possible to represent or to know everything in one form. The way Willy Loman conveys his inability to cope with a sinking career can only be represented through the expressive treatment of form that Arthur Miller employed in *Death of a Salesman*. The quality of space in the paintings of Georgio De Chirico or Hans Hoffman depends on the artists' arrangements of visual images; it cannot be rendered through number. When Dylan Thomas wrote, 'Do not go gentle into that good night, /old age should burn and rage at close of day;/rage, rage against the dying of the light',[19] he conveyed a message about being in the anteroom of death that cannot be translated fully, even in propositional prose.

What this means for education is that – insofar as we in schools, colleges, and universities are interested in providing the conditions that enable students to secure deep and diverse forms of meaning in their lives – we cannot in good conscience omit the fine arts. Insofar as we seek to develop the skills for securing such meanings, we must develop multiple forms of literacy. Such meanings do not accrue to the unprepared mind. The task of the schools is to provide the conditions that foster the development of such literacy. At present, for the vast majority of students, the schools fail in this task.

Third, educational equity is one consequence for students of the change in education policy that my arguments suggest. As I have already pointed out, the benefits derived from excellence in differing forms of representation are not equal. Students who perform at outstanding levels in the fine arts do not have these grades taken into account when they apply for admission to colleges and universities. The beneficiaries of the funds allocated to education for the gifted often do not include students whose gifts are in the fine arts.[20] The amount of school time devoted to cultivating abilities in the arts is extremely limited; hence, students with abilities and interests in the arts are denied the opportunities that students in science, mathematics, or English receive.

Such policies and practices amount to a form of educational inequity. This inequity would cease if the arguments I have presented were used as grounds for decisions about the allocation of school time, about the criteria used to identify gifted students, and about the aptitudes suitable for college and university study. It is an anomaly of the first order that a university should confer credit in the fine arts for courses taken on its own campus and deny credit to students who have taken such courses in high schools. At present, that is the way it is.

Finally, the view I have presented implies that the cultivation of literacy in, for example, visual and auditory forms of representation can significantly improve a student's ability to use propositional forms of representation. The ability to create or understand sociology, psychology, or economics depends on the ability to perceive qualitative nuances in the social world, the ability to conceptualise patterns from which to share what has been experienced, and the ability to write about them in a form that is compelling. Without such perceptivity, the content of writing will be shallow. Without the ability to manipulate conceptions of the world imaginatively, the work is likely to be uninspired. Without an ear for the melody, cadence, and tempo of language, the tale is likely to be unconvincing. Education in the arts cultivates sensitive perception, develops insight, fosters imagination, and places a premium on well-crafted form.

These skills and dispositions are of central importance in both writing and reading. Without them, children are unlikely to write – not because they cannot spell but because they have nothing to say. The writer starts with vision and ends with words. The reader begins with these words but ends with vision. The reader uses the writer's words in order to see.

The interaction of the senses enriches meaning. The arts are not mere diversions from the important business of education; they are essential resources.

## Acknowledgement

This paper has been reproduced, with the kind permission of the author, from his collection of essays entitled *The Art of Educational Evaluation* (London and Philadelphia, PA: Falmer Press, 1985), chapter 13.

## Notes

1  These distinctions are reified most clearly in the customary separation between the cognitive and the affective domains, which are typically discussed as if they were independent entities or processes.
2  See especially *The Republic* (trans. F. M. Cornford) (New York: Oxford University Press, 1951).
3  B. Inhelder and J. Piaget, *The Growth of Cognitive Thinking from Childhood to Adolescence* (trans. A. Parsons and S. Milgram) (New York: Basic Books, 1958).
4  See, for example, A. Schaff, *Language and Cognition* (New York: McGraw-Hill, 1973).
5  B. Rosenshein, 'Classroom Instruction', in N. L. Gage (ed.) *Psychology of Teaching*, 75th Yearbook of the National Society for the Study of Education, Part 1 (Chicago, IL: University of Chicago Press, 1976), pp. 335–371.
6  If an elementary teacher provides one hour of instruction in art and one hour of instruction in music each week, the percentage of instructional time devoted to both is about 7%. Many teachers provide less time than this.
7  The University of California System, like many other state universities, provides no credit for grades received in the fine arts when computing grade-point averages for students seeking admission.
8  *The Dictionary of Psychology* (Cambridge: Riverside Press, 1934).
9  The acquisition of visual information over time is a function of micromovements of the eye and brain called saccades.
10  Insofar as something is conceivable, it must, by definition, be a part of human experience. Experience without sensory content is an impossibility.
11  This view argues that the reception and organisation of sensory material require the use of intelligence. Intelligence is not something that one applies after experiencing the empirical world. Rather, it is a central factor in the process of experience.
12  See M. Weitz, 'The Role of Theory in Aesthetics', *Journal of Aesthetics and Art Criticism* (September 1956), 27–35.
13  In a sense, play is the ability to suspend rules in order to explore new arrangements. See B. Sutton-Smith (ed.) *Play and Learning* (New York: Halsted Press, 1979).
14  This concept is elaborated in greater detail in my 1982 book, *Cognition and Curriculum. A Basis for Deciding What to Teach* (New York: Longman Inc).
15  R. G. Collingwood, *Principles of Art* (New York: Oxford University Press, 1958).
16  E. H. Gombrich, 'Visual Discovery Through Art', in J. Hogg (ed.) *Psychology and the Visual Arts* (Middlesex: England Penguin Books, 1969).
17  R. Arnheim, *Art and Visual Perception* (Berkeley, CA: University of California Press, 1954).

18  E. Panofsky, *Meaning in the Visual Arts: Papers in and on Art History* (Garden City, NY: Doubleday, 1955).

19  D. Thomas, 'Do Not Go Gentle into That Good Night', *The Collected Poems of Dylan Thomas* (New York: New Directions, 1953), p. 128.

20  Until a couple of years ago the Mentally Gifted Minor Program (MGM) in California – now Gifted and Talented Education (GTE) – did not include students who were gifted in the fine arts.

## CHAPTER 9

# CAN EDUCATIONAL RESEARCH INFORM EDUCATIONAL PRACTICE?*

*Phi Delta Kappan*, 1984, 65(7): 447–452

That enterprise known as educational research is predicated on the supposition that research is vital to the improvement of educational practice. As a former vice president of one of the divisions of the American Educational Research Association (AERA), I suppose I should endorse that supposition. As a member of the faculty of a school of education committed to the belief that educational research informs educational practice, I might be expected to embrace that belief as a matter of institutional loyalty. Yet I have worked in the field of education for 26 years, 23 of them in universities – Ohio State for 1 year, the University of Chicago for 5 years, and Stanford for 17 years – and, despite efforts to socialize me to the prevailing norms, I still have questions about the relationship of research to practice. I would be less than honest to accept as a matter of faith a belief about which I have serious doubts. Hence I write this article not to proclaim that educational research informs educational practice, but to ask whether it *can* inform educational practice.

By *educational research* I mean correlational and experimental studies of the type typically published in the *American Educational Research Journal*. And by *educational practice* I mean the things that teachers and administrators do when they formulate educational aims, plan curricula, manage a class or a school, teach a lesson, motivate a group of students or staff, and attempt to discern what progress they have made.

I raise this question of the relationship of research to practice in good will. I have no intention of harping on the gap between what we know and what we do, on the reluctance of teachers to use the information that researchers provide, or on the fact that educational research is only 80 years old and that the breakthrough on teaching and learning is right around the corner. My aim is to seriously inquire about the relationship of what we do as educational researchers and what practitioners do in schools. Since I assume that the conduct of educational research is intended to do more than to advance the careers of educational researchers, asking about the relationship of research to practice is not altogether irrelevant.

Let me confess that I have long been intrigued about the relationship of theory to practice in education, but was motivated to write about this topic because of my experience as a faculty member at three research-oriented universities. This experience made it increasingly clear to me that research findings, and even the theories from which they are derived, seldom – indeed, hardly ever – enter into the deliberations of faculties, regardless of the area of education about which these faculties deliberate. Of course, this experience might be unique to my tenure at Ohio State, Chicago, and Stanford. Other institutions might be different.

At the institutions where I have worked, questions having to do with curriculum planning, the evaluation of teaching, or the identification of institutional strengths and weaknesses are hardly ever answered in light of educational research. Thus those who are best informed about educational research seldom use the fruits of their labors either to make practical decisions or to shape institutional policy within the institutions where they work. If educational researchers do not use research findings to guide their own professional decisions, why should we expect those less well informed to use research findings to guide theirs? This anomaly and others like it moved me to raise the question that is the title of this article: Can educational research inform educational practice?

Some readers may justifiably wonder if I could really know whether or not my colleagues use educational research in their own activities as teachers or as planners of curricula. Even if the fruits of educational research do not emerge in faculty deliberations, perhaps they are used by individual faculty members as they plan and teach their courses.

To get answers to these questions, I asked one of my research assistants to interview faculty members in the School of Education at Stanford. The interviewees were guaranteed anonymity, and I do not know who provided which response. What I do know is that, although my colleagues in the School of Education say that they "use" research in their planning and teaching, they find it extremely difficult to give any examples of how they use it. The typical response is that research findings function in the background, as a sort of frame of reference.

I suspect that my colleagues are correct, but I wonder what they mean by educational research. Altogether, I find their remarks – as reported verbatim by my research assistant – vague and unconvincing. I would hate to have to make a case for the utility of educational research in educational practice to a school board or a congressional committee if it had to be based on statements of the kind that they provided. In addition, I collected from each faculty member who responded to my request a copy of the reading lists and introductory course materials for the course or courses that the faculty member offered in the autumn of 1982. I examined these materials to determine whether they contained any features that might have been influenced by educational research. Did these materials contain educational objectives, for example? Alas, only the materials from one professor contained anything resembling educational objectives. Perhaps this omission is a function of the other faculty members' having read the research on behavioral objectives, but I doubt it. I use this example simply to provide what I regard as further evidence that, although we prescribe to teachers and school administrators one thing, we do another thing for ourselves.

In commenting about the behavior of my colleagues, I in no way mean to depreciate them. My behavior is no different from theirs. Furthermore, I do not believe that our behavior is exceptional. On the contrary, I believe it to be typical of research-oriented professors of education.

Thirty elementary and secondary school administrators were also interviewed by my research assistant. Perhaps they use educational research in ways of which I was unaware. Perhaps they use what university professors of education appear to neglect. The story for teachers and school administrators is largely the same as it is for professors. Not one of the 30 people interviewed provided any examples of how they actually used research to make a decision or to shape a practice – although several assured my research assistant that research is useful. Some simply said that research has little to do with their work.

Readers might not be surprised by these findings. After all, research in education does not provide the kind of prescriptions that are employed, say, in medical practice as a result of research in medicine. The use of research in education is more heuristic; it provides a framework that we can use to make decisions, not a set of rules to be followed slavishly. Hence, to expect even my research-wise colleagues to use research in a prescriptive way is to expect too much. Had I expected less – or something other than a prescriptive use of research – I would not have been as disappointed.

This is a plausible view. It is one that I have advanced myself in a number of papers and books.[1] But in some ways this view is a bit too comforting. There are two problems with it that I wish to identify.

The first problem has to do with what it means to use research as a framework for making practical decisions. Does this mean knowing how to think about a problem, or does it mean having a research-supported theory to guide decision making? Does it mean that we have examined a body of research studies, extracted generalizations, determined that the theory is supported by the evidence, and then used the theory as a tool for shaping decisions? If this is what "using research to inform practice" means, then I think that it seldom occurs. Practitioners seldom read the research literature. Even when they do, this literature contains little that is not so qualified or so compromised by competing findings, rival hypotheses, or faulty design that the framework could scarcely be said to be supported in some reasonable way by research.

Or does "using research to inform practice" mean simply that practitioners have read the distillations found in reviews of research, in order to garner conclusions that they can then act upon? Can it be legitimately claimed that a teacher or a school administrator who seeks to increase students' time on task is using research to justify this decision? I suppose one might claim that popularized research conclusions that are employed by practitioners are a use of research. Yet, in popularization the findings are not only popularized, they are vulgarized as well. By *vulgarization* I mean that the qualifications that researchers specify in stating their conclusions are often absent in the versions used by practitioners. The specific limits within which these conclusions hold are seldom enumerated or described. What one then has is a vague apparition of the work that was done in the first place. Indeed, the conclusions of the practitioner are likely to look nothing like the conclusions of the researcher. Is this what we mean by using research to inform educational practice? Although such use of research might *influence* practice, whether it *informs* practice is quite another matter.

A second problem with the less strict (but more comforting) view of the uses of research in education is that, in principle, such uses should improve practice. Those practitioners who rely on decision-making frameworks that are supported by solid research findings should be better at their jobs. But here too the available evidence is altogether unconvincing. Those who are informed about educational research – i.e., professors of education who do research – are, in my view, in no way better at teaching or course planning than liberal arts professors who have never seen the inside of the *American Educational Research Journal* or the *Review of Educational Research*.

What shall we make of this? I recognize that teaching is complex and course planning difficult and that strong effects on tasks so demanding are not likely. But does educational research have *any* noticeable effects? I must confess that I believe the variance in teaching abilities to be as wide in schools of education as it is in history departments – and the mean no higher.

Despite these observations, it still does not seem intuitively correct to say that educational research does not inform educational practice. What researcher among us wants to entertain the idea, let alone conclude, that the research in education that we do or have done has no impact on the education of the young? Such thoughts are disquieting. Perhaps we can take some consolation in the idea that *some* educational practices have changed as a result of educational research – programs using operant conditioning to shape the behavior of autistic children, programs in the teaching of reading using, for example, the DISTAR materials. Surely there are dozens of others. Yet even these programs need to be intelligently interpreted and employed. Teachers have no algorithm to which to appeal. These programs are not easily generalized in prescriptive ways to large populations of students in a variety of schools and school districts. In addition, their benefits are far from clear.

But what about the impact of research on our image of the child, our conception of thinking, and our view of perception? Our images of the child, thinking, and perception are certainly different today from those held at the turn of the century. Research must surely have had something to do with shaping those images, and surely new images of the learner and of learning affect practice.

As plausible as these observations seem, we should not become too comfortable. In the first place, many – perhaps most – changes in practice emanating from new views of the learner *preceded* rather than followed the findings of educational research. We built architecturally open schools *before*, not after, we studied their effects. We unscrewed desks from the classroom floor *before*, not after, we researched the effects of small-group instruction. We embraced a problem-centered curriculum *before*, not after, we investigated the effects of problem-centered tasks on cognitive development. In short, I believe our propensity to change practice is a function of the attractiveness of a set of ideas, rather than of the rigor of a body of data-based conclusions.

Beliefs about how children should be taught, views of what knowledge is of most worth, positions on the use of rewards in schooling need not emanate from those in the research community, nor must they be based on empirical evidence to be found attractive. Much of what we do in the schools is influenced in some way by such beliefs, models, images, metaphors. But when it is, can we legitimately claim that it is educational research that is informing educational practice? Rhetoric might be informing practice – but research? I wonder. Thus you can see that when I think of educational practice – not only in the public schools but in my own School of Education – and of educational research, I find it difficult to articulate the way in which the latter informs the former.

Despite what some may think, I am not a nay-sayer for educational research. My motive is not to argue that research can have no place in educational practice. I have not chosen this theme to hound those who have committed their professional lives to the conduct of research in education.

I write with different motives. I am professionally committed to the improvement of education, and I would like educational research to be useful to those engaged in educational practice. If research is to inform both educational practice in the schools as well as our own teaching, I believe that researchers will need to do something quite different from what we have been doing over the past 80 years. I am not sanguine about forthcoming breakthroughs from cognitive science; I have enough gray hairs to have a sense of déjà vu when I hear such forecasts. I am not optimistic about the putative benefits of tightly controlled experiments; classrooms are complex places, and well-controlled experiments have little ecological validity.

I am not optimistic about achieving effects so robust as to vitiate interactions within classrooms.[2] Children have an enormous capacity to learn how to cope with treatments that they wish to manage for their own purposes.

Where does this leave us with regard to the place and function of research in education? Can we develop an approach to research that will be more useful for improving educational practice than what we have at present? What would such an approach look like? I believe that educational research ought to take its lead from the practices that pervade school programs. That is, those engaged in educational research should have an intimate acquaintance with life in classrooms. I say this because the tack that has been taken in educational research by educational researchers has, in the main, distanced itself from practice. We have imported concepts and theories from fields other than education and mapped them onto classroom phenomena. Thus, what has been learned from rat maze learning, the use of memory drums, and operant conditioning we have applied to teachers and students to explain how the former might go about shaping the behavior of the latter; teachers were to be guided in their work by what experimental psychologists have learned about the ways in which pigeons learned to play Ping Pong and rats learned to run mazes.

If one invokes the Sapir-Whorf hypothesis concerning the impact of language on perception, it seems reasonable to expect that educational researchers employing theories that were suitable for rats and pigeons – or for prisons and asylums, small communities and monasteries, the armed services and factories – are able to see those things that schools and classrooms have in common with pigeons, rats, prisons, asylums, small communities, monasteries, the armed services, and factories. To be sure, some relationships exist – even, I suspect, between pigeons and adolescents. Yet classrooms and schools are also distinctive places that use distinctive processes.

To see what is common to such settings and practices and other institutions is not necessarily to see what is unique or special about schools. To miss what is special about schools and classrooms is to diminish the probability that what will be learned will be useful to those who work in such settings. Like language, theory is both an asset and a liability. It is an asset because it provides guidelines for perception: it points us in directions that enable us to see. But it is also a liability because, while it provides the windows through which we obtain focus, it creates walls that hamper our perception of those qualities and processes that are not addressed by the concepts we have chosen to use. Our theoretical frameworks function as templates for perception – every template conceals some parts of the landscape just as it brings other parts to our attention.

To develop more relevant windows is, of course, a very difficult task. It is the task of theory construction. Theory construction, I am arguing, is more likely to be fruitful for educational practice when educational researchers become well acquainted with the life of schooling. Contact with such phenomena is more likely to yield useful concepts from which educational investigators can proceed than by extrapolating from frameworks that were designed for situations having other than educational missions.

Consider research on teaching. Most such research regards excellent teaching as a generic set of skills. The aims of most researchers are to identify the moves that effective teachers make in their classrooms, to understand the nature of their verbal behavior, and, through such analyses, to identify the factors that make for effectiveness. Often, the model of excellence is the recitation – one teacher talking, explaining something, or lecturing to students.[3] The dependent variables are frequently achievement in the three R's and satisfaction with school – typically elementary schools, where most studies of teaching occur.[4]

Is it really the case that excellent teaching of mathematics to 7 year olds requires the same sorts of pedagogical skills as excellent teaching of history to 17 year olds? Are kindergarten teachers excellent on the same criteria as teachers of algebra or English? What might we learn about the extent to which teaching skills are domain-specific, if we were to study excellent teachers within different disciplines and at different grade levels? What might we learn about the components of excellent teaching, if we were to carefully study artistic teachers in action? And to complicate matters further, what do different educational orientations held by teachers of different subject matters mean for what we regard as important to appraise in the study of teaching? There are a dozen ways to read a novel, eight major orientations to social studies education, over half a dozen rationales and teaching practices within art education. What might we learn by studying teachers in each of these ways, not to speak of the special conditions that different levels of schooling require?

Yet, in research on teaching, we tend to ignore the unique requirements that particular subject matters exact, the ages and developmental levels of the children being taught, and the aims to which a teacher is committed. Instead, we define our dependent variables – often using scores on standardized, norm-referenced tests of basic skills – and then try to find relationships between generic teaching skills and these outcomes. Thus we arrive at the astounding conclusion that the more time a student is engaged in studying a subject, the more likely he or she is to achieve high test scores in that subject.

What I am suggesting is that we have distanced ourselves from the phenomena that should be central to our studies, that we employ models that have been designed to deal with other than educational phenomena, and that we reduce what is a rich source of data into a pale reflection of the reality we seek to study. We do this by proscribing language that has the capacity to do justice to life as it is lived in classrooms and to teaching as it is practiced by excellent teachers.[5] For example, how can a typescript of classroom discourse that is dissected into units in order to locate patterns of speech provide robust generalizations that inform educational practitioners? Such material is radically eviscerated of most of the content of classroom life. Language exists in context; it is accompanied by gesture, expression, tempo, cadence, melody, silence, emphasis, and energy. A tape-recorded version of such activity already distorts by omission the reality it seeks to describe; it contains no visual content. When that tape is reduced even further by having it put into typescript, melody, cadence, tempo, emphasis, and energy are further obliterated. Then one more reduction into small speech units administers the coup de grâce.

Why do we use such procedures? Our absence from classrooms and our inveterate reliance on such methods as I have described are, I believe, a legacy of our own uneasiness with our status as social scientists. A great many in the educational research community wish to be known not as educators who research educational practice, but as psychologists, sociologists, or political scientists who happen to work in schools of education. As they see it, the better their work is, the more indistinguishable it will be from the work of their colleagues in the parent disciplines. Indeed, many educational researchers claim that education is not and can never be a discipline; it is an applied field – and what is applied is psychology, sociology, and so on.

If we continue the way we have been going the past 80 years, education will remain an applied field with, I fear, as much impact on educational practice in

2020 as it had on educational practice in 1980. I believe that this model and the assumptions on which it rests are inadequate. They are inadequate for dealing with the problems of practice, and they are inadequate for building a secure intellectual place for education as a field of study. As long as schools of education are nothing more than geographical conveniences for those whose work is indistinguishable from the work of specialists in the social sciences, schools of education will never have a secure place within the university. If the best work in education is indistinguishable from the work that is done in the social sciences, the best place to train educational researchers is not in schools of education but in the social science disciplines. If the social sciences define the criteria for excellence in educational research, the promotion and tenure of untenured professors of education who look like educationists is going to be very difficult indeed.[6]

To collect some information on this matter, I wrote to the deans of six research-oriented schools of education: those at the University of California–Los Angeles, Harvard University, Stanford University, the University of Chicago, the University of Illinois, and Teachers College, Columbia University. I asked the deans of these schools how many individuals were appointed as full-time members of the faculty during the Seventies, in what fields these individuals held doctorates, and of this group how many were promoted to tenure and in what fields those who attained tenure secured their doctorates. I indicated to the deans that the information that I received would be pooled and presented anonymously, as part of my vice-presidential address to the AERA. Only one institution responded – UCLA. When I mentioned to William Cooley, then president of the AERA, that I was not able to collect the data that I wanted, he sagely replied, "I think you have."

What I believe we need if educational research is truly to inform educational practice is the construction of our own unique conceptual apparatus and research methods. The best way I know of for doing this is to become familiar with the richness and uniqueness of educational life. If we are sufficiently imaginative, out of such familiarity can come ideas, concepts, and theories of educational practice. Out of these theories can come methods of inquiry that do not try to achieve levels of precision better suited to fields other than our own.

Consider, for example, our proclivity to avoid confounding in the experiments we conduct in the schools. What we do is to abbreviate experimental treatment time in order to maximize control and thus to increase our ability to interpret. Superficially, this does not seem to be an unreasonable goal. Yet its consequences are often unfortunate. Consider the length of treatment in educational experiments. I reviewed all of the 15 experimental studies published during 1981 in the *American Educational Research Journal*. Of the 10 studies out of the 15 that reported experimental treatment time per student, the median treatment time was 1 hour and 12 minutes. Seventy-two minutes to make a difference. We conduct educational commando raids to get the data and to get out. Yet 72 minutes is almost a 60 percent increase over the average amount of treatment time per student that educational researchers reported in 1978. The studies published that year in the *American Educational Research Journal* reported an average experimental treatment time of 45 minutes. How can we hope to achieve *educationally* significant results when the models of inquiry we employ virtually preclude achieving them?

As you can see, I am skeptical about the current impact of educational research on educational practice, and I am not sanguine about its future impact, if we continue to do what we have been doing in the past. If educational research is to inform educational practice, researchers will have to go back to the schools for a fresh look at what is going on there. We will have to develop a language that is relevant to educational practice, one that does justice to teaching and learning in educational settings, and we will need to develop methods of inquiry that do not squeeze the educational life out of what we study in such settings.

The achievement of these aims – and they are enormously difficult ones – will do much to contribute a sense of intellectual integrity to the field of education. It will do much to create the kind of knowledge that practitioners will find useful. But even with the development of the field's own language and with its own array of appropriate research methods, educational research will, in my view, always – in principle – fall short of what practitioners need. Let me explain why.

As it is now conceptualized, educational research is a species of scientific inquiry, and scientific inquiry couches its conclusions and its theories in a language of propositions. Science makes assertions, it provides explanations, and it specifies the means or criteria by which propositions about the world can be refuted or verified. Because in science it is propositions that must carry forward meanings about empirical matters and because propositions can never (in principle) exhaust the meanings of the qualities for which they stand, propositions are de facto reductions of the realities we hope to know.[7]

Because the realities of the classroom and of social life in general are, at base, an array of qualities for which meanings are construed, they will always present more to the perceptive teacher than propositional language can ever capture. The particularity of a set of conditions, the uniqueness of an individual child, the emotional tone of something said in love or in anger, the sense of engagement when a class is attentive will always elude the language of propositions. Yet it is precisely these qualities that the teacher must address in his or her own work. The language of propositions is a gross indicator of such qualities: it cannot capture nuance – and in teaching as in human relationships nuance is everything. It is nuance that converts repetition to repetitiousness, assertiveness to boorishness, diffidence to shyness, inquisitiveness to prying, dignity to aloofness. Theory in science cannot, I suggest, even in principle, replicate the qualities of life as it is lived. And yet it is these qualities upon which subtle pedagogical decisions must be made. The teacher who cannot see such qualities in his or her classroom cannot know what needs to be known to function effectively. Theory and generalizations from educational research can provide a guide – but never a substitute – for the teacher's ability to read the meanings that are found in the qualities of classroom life.[8]

Propositions and theory fall short for another reason as well. The rationality of action and the logic of exposition may very well appeal to different psychological bases. Exposition is sequential; action requires the perception of configurations in space. The simultaneity found in the patterns of context is lost in the sequence of propositions. Grasping these patterns of context and modifying one's decisions almost cybernetically, as patterns change, might depend on a kind of intelligence and a form of knowing that differ in kind from the kind of intelligence and form of knowing carried by words. To be sure, the two modes of grasping the world must overlap, but the extent of the overlap, particularly in situations that one cannot completely control, may be smaller than we imagine.

If this view makes sense to you, what might it suggest for our work as researchers in education? To me it suggests that, while we can increase the relevance of educational research to educational practice by becoming intimate with practice and by developing theories that are unique to what we see, such theories, because they are propositional, will always fall short of the mark in guiding practitioners who must deal not only with the qualitative, but with the qualitative *as a particular*.

To increase the capacity of educational research to capture the qualitative, a language capable of conveying qualities must be permitted to develop. Such a language needs permission because such a language is often regarded as impressionistic and nonscientific – and therefore unworthy of our respect or admiration. Such a language *is* both impressionistic and nonscientific, but it is nonetheless worthy of our respect and admiration when its instrumental utility is high. The language of criticism is such a language.

By a *language of criticism*, I mean a language rooted in the humanities. This is a language that does not shrink from metaphor, that does not make mute the voice of the writer, that recognizes that form is an inescapable part of meaning. By a *language of criticism*, I mean a language perceptive to what is subtle, yet significant, in classrooms and schools – a language that uses the artistic, when it must, to render the subtleties of classrooms vivid to the less discerning. When well crafted, such a language provides insight and the kind of guidance that the emotionally drained language of propositions cannot provide. A language of criticism will not provide prescriptions, but it can illuminate precisely those aspects of classroom life that propositional discourse cannot locate. It enables the teacher to see and therefore to have a basis on which his or her intelligence can operate.

In the past decade we have already moved forward to a wider view of research methodology in education. Anthropological inquiry is perhaps the most prominent step that has thus far been taken in that direction. But anthropological inquiry is still a species of social science; it is a useful but still too timid step. A full complement to the social sciences will be found when humanistic sources are drawn upon for describing, interpreting, and appraising educational life. It is the humanities to which we must turn to make the particulars of the life of schooling vivid.

I sincerely hope that readers will not regard this article as pessimistic. Education is an optimistic enterprise, and I write with a sense of optimism. What is pessimistic is a failure or unwillingness to recognize our condition – to look at our professional world through glasses that allow us to see only what we wish. *That* would be pessimistic. The identification of our problems is the important first step toward their resolution. My aim here is to suggest what some of the other steps might be.

I wish to emphasize that in identifying the need to create a critical language for describing educational practice, I do so not as a replacement for the equally important need for an *educationally relevant* scientific language. We need not one but two eyes through which to see and understand what concerns us. Both achievements, if they are to be realized, are iconoclastic in character. For the kind of educational science we need, we will have to design our own ship and sail it into the waters we seek to map. For the language of criticism we need, the philosophical and political space must be provided for new forms of disclosure to be developed. Educational research will come of age when we muster the courage to move ahead in both domains so that we can, without qualification, doubt, or hesitation, say with confidence that educational research truly does inform educational practice.

## Acknowledgment

I wish to acknowledge the assistance I received from David Flinders, who conducted the interviews with the Stanford faculty members and with the teachers and school administrators.

# Notes

* This article is a modified version of his vice-presidential address to the American Educational Research Association, Division B, delivered in Montreal in 1983. He wishes to thank Lee J. Cronbach, Arthur Applebee, and Myron Atkin for their critiques of this article in draft form.
1 See, for example, Elliot W. Eisner, *The Educational Imagination: On the Design and Evaluation of School Programs* (New York: Macmillan, 1979); and idem., "The Art and Craft of Teaching," *Educational Leadership* (January 1983), pp. 4–13.
2 Lee J. Cronbach, "Beyond the Two Disciplines of Scientific Psychology," *American Psychologist* (February 1975), pp. 116–127.
3 See, for example, Nathaniel Gage, *The Scientific Basis of the Art of Teaching* (New York: Teachers College Press, 1978).
4 For an extremely lucid and intelligent review of research on teaching, see Karen Kepler Zumwalt, "Research on Teaching: Policy Implications for Teacher Education," *Policy Making in Education: 81st Year-book of the National Society for the Study of Education* (Chicago, IL: University of Chicago Press, 1982), pp. 215–248.
5 It is not insignificant that, in reporting results of educational research, writers are encouraged to write in the third person, singular or plural, rather than in the first person and that students and teachers are regarded as "subjects," rather than as students or teachers.
6 For a lucid analysis of the state of graduate education in the US, see Harry Judge, *American Graduate Schools of Education: A View from Abroad*, a report to the Ford Foundation (1982).
7 For a discussion of these and related matters, see Elliot W. Eisner, *Cognition and Curriculum: A Basis for Deciding What to Teach* (New York: Longman, 1982).
8 Elliot W. Eisner, "Toward an Artistic Approach to Supervision," *1983 Yearbook of the Association for Supervision and Curriculum Development*; and idem, "On the Use of Educational Connoisseurship and Educational Criticism for Evaluating Classroom Life," *Teachers College Record* (February 1977), pp. 345–358.

# CHAPTER 10

# AESTHETIC MODES OF KNOWING

84th Yearbook of the National Society for the Study of Education, *Learning and Teaching the Ways of Knowing*, Chicago, IL: University of Chicago Press, 1985, pp. 23–36

So gorgeous was the spectacle on the May morning of 1910 when nine kings rode in the funeral of Edward VII of England that the crowd, waiting in hushed and blackclad awe, could not keep back gasps of admiration. In scarlet and blue and green and purple, three by three the sovereigns rode through the palace gates, with plumed helmets, gold braid, crimson sashes, jeweled orders flashing in the sun. After them came five heirs apparent, forty more imperial or royal highnesses, seven queens – four dowager and three regnant – and a scattering of special ambassadors from uncrowned countries. Together they represented seventy nations in the greatest assemblage of royalty and rank ever gathered in one place and, of its kind, the last. The muffled tongue of Big Ben tolled nine by the clock as the cortege left the palace, but on history's clock it was sunset, and the sun of the old world was setting in a dying blaze of splendor never to be seen again.

(Barbara Tuchman, *The Guns of August*, p. 1)

An examination of the relationship between the form and content of the opening paragraph in Barbara Tuchman's *The Guns of August* will help us understand what the phrase "aesthetic modes of knowing" alludes to. Before examining this relationship I wish to mention now a theme that I will return to later. The phrase, "aesthetic modes of knowing," presents something of a contradiction in our culture. We do not typically associate the aesthetic with knowing. The arts, with which the aesthetic is most closely associated, is a matter of the heart. Science is thought to provide the most direct route to knowledge. Hence, "aesthetic modes of knowing" is a phrase that contradicts the conception of knowledge that is most widely accepted. I hope to show in this chapter that the widely accepted view is too narrow and that the roads to knowing are many. Let us return to Tuchman.

"So gorgeous was the spectacle on the May morning of 1910 when nine kings rode in the funeral of Edward VII of England that the crowd, waiting in hushed and black-clad awe, could not keep back gasps of admiration." What does Tuchman do in this, the opening line of her book? In the initial phrase, "So gorgeous was the spectacle on the May morning," Tuchman creates a rhythm, which is then punctuated by a staccato-like "when nine kings rode in the funeral of Edward VII." She then follows with contrasts between "gasps" and the soft sound of "hush." And then again, with the phrase "in scarlet *and* blue *and* green *and* purple, three by three the sovereigns rode through the palace gates," Tuchman creates a syncopation that recapitulates the sound of hoofs pounding the pavement as the horses pass by. Again, "with plumed helmets, gold braid, crimson sashes and jeweled orders flashing in the sun" – another series of short bursts filled with images as well as sound. And later in the paragraph, the "muffled tongue of Big Ben tolled nine by the clock." Here, the paired contradictions of "hushed gasps" and "muffled tones" appeal to our sense of metaphor. And for a finale Tuchman writes, "but on history's clock it was sunset, and the sun of the Old World was setting in a dying blaze of splendor never to be seen again." Like the coda of a classical symphony, Tuchman brings the paragraph to a slow declining close.

What occurs in the paragraph occurs throughout the book, and what occurs throughout the book is what makes literature literary. It is in the use of form, especially in the cadence and tempo of language, that patterns are established among the "parts" of the sentence and between the sentence and the paragraph that create their counterpart in the reader's experience. "After them came five heirs apparent, forty more imperial or royal highnesses, seven queens – four dowager and three regnant – and a scattering of special ambassadors from uncrowned countries." Like a partridge in a pear tree, the cadence of the sentence captivates and carries the reader off on a ride.

What also occurs in the paragraph is the generation in the reader's mind's eye of an array of visual images. The writing is vivid and it is vivid because it is designed to elicit images of scarlet and blue and purple and of the plumed helmets and the gold braid. The writing evokes the scene Tuchman wishes the reader to see. We are able to participate vicariously in events that occurred when we were not yet born.

Consider again her use of language: "the muffled tones of Big Ben" and "black-clad awe." The language is shaped to help us see and feel the day and hence to know it as participants. Its form and content transport us to another time, another place. The literary in literature resides in the aesthetic capacities of language to influence our experience.

The reader should not assume that the aesthetic treatment of form for purposes of vicarious participation in events not directly available is limited to literature. Poetry, dance, the visual arts, and drama all employ form for such purposes. The drama within drama is created through the tensions that writers, actors, stage designers, lighting experts, and directors produce. What happens on the stage is the result of a collective effort. What occurs in literary works and in the visual arts is usually the product of individuals. Whether collective or individual, the common function of the aesthetic is to modulate form so that it can, in turn, modulate our experience. The moving patterns of sound created by composers, in turn, create their counterparts in the competent listener. The physically static forms produced by visual artists create in the competent viewer a quality of life analogous to those in the forms beheld. In sum, the form of the work informs us. Our internal life is shaped by the forms we are able to experience.

The phrase "we are able to experience" is a critical one. If the forms that constitute the arts or the sciences spoke for themselves we would need no programs in the schools to help students to learn how "to read" them. What we are able to see or hear is a product of our cultivated abilities. The rewards and insights provided by aesthetically shaped forms are available only to those who can perceive them. Not only is competence a necessary condition for experiencing the form in works we have access to, but the particular quality of life generated by the forms encountered will, to some degree, differ from individual to individual. All experience is the product of both the features of the world and the biography of the individual. Our experience is influenced by our past as it interacts with our present.[1] Thus, not only must a certain kind of competence be acquired in order to perceive the qualities of form in the objects available to us, but the nature of our experience with these forms is influenced not only by the form itself but by our past.

I have thus far directed my remarks to the aesthetic functions of form as a source of experience and understanding in the fine arts and in literature. But I do not wish to suggest that the aesthetic is restricted to the fine arts and literature. All scientific inquiry culminates in the creation of form: taxonomies, theories, frameworks, conceptual systems. The scientist, like the artist, must transform the content of his or her imagination into some public, stable form, something that can be shared with others. The shape of this form – its coherence – is a critical feature concerning its acceptability. The adequacy of theory is not simply determined by experimental results. Experimental results can often be explained by competing theories. The attractiveness of a theory is a central factor in our judgment of it.

Viewed this way, both artist and scientist create forms through which the world is viewed. Both artist and scientist make qualitative judgments about the fit, the coherence, the economy, "the rightness" of the forms they create. Readers of these forms make similar judgments. It was his recognition of the universal character of form-making in every sphere of human life that prompted Sir Herbert Read to say that the aim of education was the creation of artists. What he meant was that all students should be enabled to produce good forms. He writes:

> Having established the relevance of aesthetics to the processes of perception and imagination, I shall then pass on to the less disputed ground of expression. Education is the fostering of growth, but apart from physical maturation, growth is only made apparent in expression – audible or visible signs and symbols. Education may therefore be defined as the cultivation of modes of expression – it is teaching children and adults how to make sounds, images, movements, tools and utensils. A man who can make such things well is a well educated man. If he can make good sounds, he is a good speaker, a good musician, a good poet; if he can make good images, he is a good painter or sculptor; if good movements, a good dancer or laborer; if good tools or utensils, a good craftsman. All faculties, of thought, logic, memory, sensibility and intellect, are involved in such processes, and no aspect of education is excluded in such processes. And they are all processes which involve art, for art is nothing but the good making of sounds, images, etc. The aim of education is therefore the creation of artists – of people efficient in the various modes of expression.[2]

There is another sense in which form and the aesthetic experience it engenders can be considered. I have used the term "form" thus far to refer to the products made by both artists and scientists. Both, I have argued, create forms, and these forms have aesthetic features that appeal. But the term form can be conceived of not only as a noun, but as a verb. Following Read, we form groups, we form sentences, we form structures. "Form," in this sense, refers to something we do. Indeed, in Norway visual arts education is called "Forming." To form is to engage in an activity occurring over time, guided by attention to changing qualities whose end is to produce a structure, either temporal or spatial, that gives rise to feeling. To be able to produce such forms the qualities that constitute them must be appraised by their contribution to the life of feeling. The maker, in this case, must know what he has before him in order to make decisions that will yield the hoped for results. A satisfying end is achieved only if appropriate choices are made in process. To make such choices one must be aware of the qualities of form as well as the content as one proceeds. One must know the qualities of life that the qualitative components engender and how they will function within the whole when it is completed.

In this view the aesthetic is both a subject matter and a criterion for appraising the processes used to create works of science as well as art. The aesthetic is not simply the possession of completed works. The sense of rightness or fit that a scientist or artist experiences in the course of his or her work is crucial to the quality of the final work. But not only does the aesthetic function in this way. The ability to experience the aesthetic features of the process has been regarded as a prime motive for work. Alfred North Whitehead once commented, "Most people believe that scientists inquire in order to know. Just the opposite is the case. Scientists know in order to inquire." Scientists, Whitehead believed, are drawn to their work not by epistemological motives but by aesthetic ones. The joy of inquiry is the driving motive for their work. Scientists, like artists, formulate new and puzzling questions in order to enjoy the experience of creating answers to them.

The distinctions I have made concerning form and the aesthetic as a mode of knowing can be summed up thus far as follows. First, all things made, whether in art, science, or in practical life, possess form. When well made these forms have aesthetic properties. These aesthetic properties have the capacity to generate particular qualities of life in the competent percipient. In literature and in many of the arts such forms are used to reveal or represent aspects of the world that cannot be experienced directly. Second, form is not only an attribute or condition of things made; it is a process through which things are made. Knowing how forms will function within the finished final product is a necessary condition for creating products that themselves possess aesthetic qualities. Such knowing requires an active and intelligent maker. Third, the deeper motives for productive activity in both the arts and the sciences often emanate from the quality of life the process of creation makes possible. These satisfactions are related to the kinds of stimulation secured in the play process and from the aesthetic satisfactions derived from judgments made about emerging forms.

My comments thus far have been intended to free the aesthetic from the province of the arts alone and to recognize its presence in all human formative activity. All subjects have aesthetically significant features, from the process of making to the form the product finally takes. I have also argued that what we find satisfying in both art and science is a function of the coherence the things we make possess. The creation of coherence is a central aim in both art and science. The aesthetic as a mode of knowing therefore can be regarded in two senses. First, it is through aesthetic experience that we can participate vicariously in situations beyond our practical possibilities. The aesthetic in knowing, in this sense, performs a referential function; it points to some aspect of the world and helps us experience it.

Second, knowledge *of*, rather than knowledge *through*, the aesthetic is knowledge of the aesthetic qualities of form per se. We become increasingly able to know those qualities we call aesthetic by our developed ability to experience the subtleties of form. We come to know aspects of music and literature and science by being increasingly able to experience their nuances. The music of Mendelssohn and the paintings of Pollack contain certain unique features; they possess an "aesthetic." To know these features is to know aspects of the world. To achieve such knowledge the percipient must be aesthetically literate. He or she must be able to read their subtle and often complex aesthetic features. Knowledge within the aesthetic mode is therefore knowledge of two kinds. First, it is knowledge of the world toward which the aesthetic qualities of form point: we understand the emotional meaning of jealousy through the form that Shakespeare conferred upon

*Othello*. Second, it is knowledge of the aesthetic in its own right, for no other purpose than to have or undergo experience. Such motives are often the driving force in the creation of both science and art.

One might well ask why the aesthetic should play such an important role in the arts and sciences. What is it that confers such a significant function upon what is often regarded as an ornamental and unnecessary aspect of life? One reason is related to man's biological nature. I speak here of the deep-seated need for stimulation. Humans have a low toleration for homeostasis. We seek to use our capacities, to activate our sensory systems, to vary our experience. When our life is without stimulation, as it is in sensory deprivation experiments, we hallucinate. When we are sated with one type of experience, we seek other kinds. Rather than being a stimulus-reducing organism, the human is stimulus-seeking. The aesthetic is one important source of stimulation. Secured within the process of coping with the problematic, its satisfactions arise as the problematic is explored and eventually resolved. The making of a form from the simplest sandcastle to the most advanced architectural achievement is a process in which aesthetic satisfactions are pervasive. Our need for variety and for stimulation is met, in part, through the aesthetics of human action.

The aesthetic is not only motivated by our need for stimulation; it is also motivated by our own need to give order to our world. To form is to confer order. To confer aesthetic order upon our world is to make that world hang together, to fit, to feel right, to put things in balance, to create harmony. Such harmonies are sought in all aspects of life. In science it is extraordinarily vivid: theory is the result of our desire to create a world we can understand. The scientist conceptualizes a theoretical structure, defines its parts, and arranges them in a configuration that appeals to our sensibilities so that the theoretical form helps us make sense of our world.

The need for coherence in things made is not, of course, limited to science or art; it manifests itself in all walks of life from the setting of a table to our social interactions.[3] The exquisite creation of either is a very high aesthetic achievement.

The aesthetic, then, is motivated by our need to lead a stimulating life. Related to the need to explore and play, the aesthetic is part and parcel of what these processes are intended to yield, not only practical outcomes related to premeditated goals, but the delights of exploration. The aesthetic is also inherent in our need to make sense of experience. This sense-making is located in the choices we make in our effort to create order. Both scientists and artists, to take paradigm cases, are makers of order – the former through the relationships created within theoretical material and the other through the ordering of the qualitative. Our sense of rightness, like our sense of justice, is rooted in that ineffable experience to which the word "aesthetic" is assigned.

I said at the outset that I would return later to a theme I introduced at that time. That theme was the contradiction in our culture between the terms aesthetic and knowing. The polarities we encounter between these terms hark back to Plato's conception of the hierarchies of knowledge. Plato believed that episteme – true and certain knowledge – could not be secured if one depended upon the information the senses provided.[4] The reasons, he thought, were clear enough. Sensory information is dependent upon the stuff of which our universe is made, namely, material things. Since material things are in a state of constant decay, any knowledge derived from them must, of necessity, be short-term at best and misleading at worst. Second, sensory information is not trustworthy. To illustrate how the senses mislead consider how a perfectly straight rod placed in a glass of water appears to be bent. Knowledge derived from what the senses provide, as such a case reveals, is misleading. The rod is straight, not bent, even though it *appears* bent. To secure knowledge that is dependable, Plato believed, one must move away from the empirical world that our senses come to know and move into the world of abstraction. The most secure and dependable form of knowledge is achieved not through empirical investigation or sensory information, but through the exercise of our rationality. Through our rational powers we can conceive of a perfect circle even though we will never see one in the world in which we live. Dependable knowledge is more likely as we move from the concrete to the abstract. The more we advance toward the abstract the more we achieve episteme.

Plato's views have had a profound effect not only upon our conception of knowledge, but upon our conception of intelligence. To be intelligent means in our culture – especially the culture of schooling – to be able to manipulate abstract ideas. One of the most vivid examples of this is to be found in the status of mathematics as a school subject. Mathematical ability is commonly regarded as a prime manifestation of intelligence. Ability in mathematics is considered prima facie evidence of one's suitability for the rigors of university work. Mathematics, the queen of the sciences, is the apotheosis of human intelligence.

Subjects that depend upon empirical information such as the natural and social sciences are a step lower in the intellectual hierarchy. Again, the reason is clear. Truth in mathematics does not require empirical evidence but rather rational comprehension. Claims to truth in the sciences look toward a decaying empirical world for evidence of validity.

When it comes to the arts and to things made, the level of intelligence employed is even lower in rank. And should emotion or feeling enter the picture, the likelihood of achieving dependable knowledge is smaller still. For Plato the life of feeling was, like the passions, an impediment to knowledge.[5] What one wanted was pure mind, unencumbered by emotion or by the misleading qualities of the empirical world.

This view of knowledge and intelligence did not terminate with Plato's passing. Our current view of knowledge is based largely upon it. Consider, for example, the distinction we often make between intelligence and talent: talent is displayed primarily in things related to the body, the arts and sports, for example. Intelligence is used to describe those who are good at abstraction. The highly intelligent enroll in college preparatory courses – the more abstract the better. Those who are talented are good at making and doing things. We are less apt to view these doings and makings as examples of intelligence at work.[6] Consider further the typical distinctions between the cognitive, the affective, and the psychomotor. We create tidy psychological domains, keep our categories clean, and assign the aesthetic to affect: its presence in human experience, we tacitly hold, is not a function of thinking.

Consider still further what our tests assess in the way of achievement. The *Scholastic Aptitude Test*, for example, focuses upon two areas of human performance, verbal and mathematical. Both of these areas are regarded as abstract rather than concrete in character. We assess a student's aptitude for the heady work of college by defining aptitude in terms of verbal and mathematical skills. To be sure, verbal and mathematical skills are relevant for college; my point is not that they are irrelevant. It is that these abilities are considered the primary surrogates of human intelligence and symbolize an entire constellation of assumptions about the mind, knowledge, and human ability. These assumptions are so pervasive in western culture and so dominant in our own professional culture that few of us have the psychological distance to regard them for what they are, human constructions, something made and, therefore, something that could be otherwise.

Given these assumptions, the aesthetic becomes a casualty in American education. It is embedded in a historical context that has underestimated the role it plays in man's effort to know. The aesthetic aspects of human experience are considered luxuries. And luxuries, as we all know, can be rather easily foregone in hard times.

The aesthetic is also diminished by our belief that we *search for* knowledge. Knowledge is considered by most in our culture as something that one discovers, not something that one makes.[7] Knowledge is out there waiting to be found, and the most useful tool for finding it is science. If there were greater appreciation for the extent to which knowledge is constructed – something made – there might be a greater likelihood that its aesthetic dimensions would be appreciated. To make knowledge is to cast the scientist in the role of an artist or a craftsperson, someone who shapes materials and ideas. The making of something is a techne, and for good techne one must be artistically engaged, and if artistically engaged, then aesthetic considerations and criteria must operate to some extent.

What does the argument I have provided imply for education? One implication pertains to the way in which we think about what we teach. The curriculum of the school performs a variety of important functions. One such function is to convey to students what we regard as important for them to learn. These values are expressed in what we choose to assess in school, in the amount of time we devote to various subjects, and in the location of the time that is assigned to what we teach. Our educational priorities are not expressed by our testimonials or our publicly prepared curriculum syllabi, but in our actions. By our works we are known.

If we believe that the aesthetic values of a subject are important for students to appreciate and experience, then we must, it seems to me, try to figure out how these values can be purposely introduced to them. We often recognize, in our conversations at least, that mathematics has an aesthetic dimension. What does this mean for designing curriculum and teaching? Are students aware of the aesthetic aspects of mathematics, and if not, what can we do about it?

Mathematics is, in some ways, far removed from what we usually regard as a subject having aesthetic dimensions, but clearly literature is not. Yet, how do we help students experience the aesthetic aspects of language? What kind of work would they be asked to do if we gave the aesthetic aspects of writing and reading a significant priority in the teaching of English? What kind of sensibilities would we cultivate – indeed must we cultivate – if writing and reading are to be more than simple encoding and decoding? One cannot write well if one has a tin ear. It is necessary to hear the melodies of language (as Barbara Tuchman obviously does) in order to use language in graceful and informative ways. While few students will become as skilled as Tuchman, all students can learn how to attend to the cadences of language. How do we help them do this?

Do students recognize the aesthetic features of inquiry in science and in the social studies, or do they separate the aesthetic from what they study in general and assign it to the realm of the arts alone? What would we need to teach in each of the fields students study to help them understand the role that the aesthetic plays in a particular field? How might we design tasks within a field of study so that inquiry in that field provided aesthetic satisfaction? Such questions point in a direction quite opposite to the direction in which curricula and teaching have been moving over the past ten years. Pedagogical practices in American schools have become increasingly fragmented. Because of pressures upon teachers to become "accountable," there has been a widespread tendency to break curricula into small units of instruction.[8] The result of this fragmentation is to make it increasingly difficult for students to see how each piece is a part of a larger whole. When the content taught for each small fragment is tested, the test is a signal to the student that he or she can forget what has been "learned" after the test has been taken. By using such teaching and testing procedures it is believed the teacher will secure an objective record of what a student knows and the student will have unambiguous feedback of how well he or she is doing. The educational liability of such teaching and learning procedures is that they emphasize short-term memory; it is difficult to remember small bits and pieces of information when there is no larger conception or armature upon which they can be placed. Indeed, this orientation to teaching and testing is formidable; it may make it difficult for students to achieve meaningful learning.

Another factor that undermines the aesthetic is that the rewards that are emphasized in class are rewards emanating from test performance. What far too many teachers and students care about almost solely is how well they do on tests.[9] Again, the focus is on the short-term and the instrumental. Yet the enduring outcomes of education are to be found in consummatory satisfactions – the joy of the ride, not simply arriving at the destination. If the major satisfactions in schools are high test scores, the value of what is learned tends to decline precipitously after the tests are taken. The only confident way to have a bull market in schooling is to turn students on to the satisfactions of inquiry in the fields into which they are initiated.

There is another implication of signal importance that pertains to the formation of curriculum and teaching in our schools. The implication I described earlier regarding the place of the aesthetic in the school curriculum is related to what we convey to students about what we value for them. The absence of a subject or its de facto neglect in the curriculum teaches students implicitly that we do not value that subject.

There is, finally, one more implication regarding the absence of a subject. This implication has to do with the fact that the curriculum is a mind-altering device. When we define the content and tasks that constitute the curriculum, we also define the kind of mental skills we choose to cultivate. The absence of attention to the aesthetic in the school curriculum is an absence of opportunities to cultivate the sensibilities. It is an absence of the refinement of our consciousness, for it is through our sensibilities that our consciousness is secured. If our educational program put a premium on the aesthetic as well as on the instrumental features of what is taught, students would have an opportunity to develop mental skills that for most students now lie fallow. Attention to the aesthetic aspects of the subjects taught would remind students that the ideas within subject areas, disciplines, and fields of study are human constructions, shaped by craft, employing technique, and mediated through some material. Works of science are, in this sense, also works of art.

Such an orientation to knowledge would reduce the tendency for students to regard the textbook as sacred and knowledge as fixed – not a bad outcome for a nation that prides itself on being a democracy. The more students conceive of their roles as scholars and critics, as makers and appraisers of things made, the less tendency they will have to regard the world as beyond their power to alter.

But for me the most important contributions of the aesthetic to education pertain to what I have called its referential and its consummatory functions. The referential function is performed as students acquire the ability to read the forms that aesthetic qualities convey: we can learn from aesthetically rendered lives what words, paradoxically, can never say. As Langer puts it:

> The arts, like language, abstract from experience certain aspects for our contemplation. But such abstractions are not concepts that have names. Discursive speech can fix definable concepts better and more exactly. Artistic expression abstracts aspects of the life of feeling which have no names, which have to be presented to sense and intuition rather than to a word-bound, note-taking consciousness.[10]

The consummatory function of the aesthetic provides delights in the inquiry itself. The durable outcomes of schooling are not to be found in short-term, instrumental tasks. Such outcomes must penetrate more deeply. When school programs neglect attention to the aesthetics of shaping form, they neglect the very satisfactions that reside at the core of education. If students are not moved by what they study, why would they want to pursue such studies on their own? But one has a hard time keeping them away from things that do provide them with deep satisfactions. Can we aspire for less in education?

The aesthetic in education has two major contributions to make, neither of which is yet a purposeful part of our educational agenda. First, it tells us about the world in ways specific to its nature. Second, it provides the experiential rewards of taking the journey itself. These potential contributions must surely be important to those who wish, as we do, to improve the quality of schooling for the young.

## Acknowledgment

I wish to acknowledge with gratitude the very useful critique of this chapter by my student, Lynda Stone.

## Notes

1  The concept that most succinctly captures this notion is John Dewey's term "interaction." See his *Experience and Education* (New York: Macmillan, 1938).
2  Herbert Read, *Education through Art* (New York: Pantheon Books, 1956), p. 10.
3  John Dewey, *Art as Experience* (New York: Minton, Balch & Co., 1934), especially chapter 1.
4  Plato, *The Republic*, translated into English by B. Jowett (New York: Modern Library, 1941).
5  Ibid., Book Six.
6  It is telling, I believe, that the best overall prediction of intelligence test scores is the vocabulary section of group intelligence tests. The ability to know and use words is, in our culture, a mark of intelligence. This view is now being challenged by several psychologists. See, for example, Howard Gardner, *Frames of Mind* (New York: Basic Books, 1983).
7  Even some constructionist views of knowledge employ terms, in the books in which they appear, suggesting that knowledge is discovered. See, for example, Barney G. Glaser and Anselm Strauss, *The Discovery of Grounded Theory* (Chicago, IL: Aldine Publishing Co., 1967) and Karl Popper, *The Logic of Scientific Discovery* (New York: Harper and Row, 1968).
8  Recent studies of classroom practices in secondary schools have revealed this tendency. See John I. Goodlad, *A Place Called School* (New York: McGraw-Hill, 1984).
9  Current studies of secondary schools undertaken at Stanford University suggest this quite clearly.
10  Suzanne Langer, *Problems of Art* (New York: Charles Scribners Sons, 1957), pp. 94–95.

# CHAPTER 11

# THE CELEBRATION OF THINKING

*Educational Horizons*, 1987, 66(1): 1–4

## Schools without celebration

Celebration has a spirit that is rare in discussions of American schooling. Celebration connotes joy, ceremony, something special in experience. Celebrations are events we look forward to and prize. The celebration of thinking suggests an honoring of, and a joy in, a process we all consider central to education. Yet those of us who work in education today are admonished to get serious, to tighten up, to excise the so-called soft side of school programs. One way to do this is to specify a common curriculum. Another is to prescribe to teachers the steps that should be taken to teach the students in our classrooms. The former solution neglects student idiosyncracy and aptitude differences by assuming that in curricular matters one size fits all. Both Alan Bloom,[1] in *The Closing of the American Mind*, and E. D. Hirsch,[2] in *Cultural Literacy: What Every American Needs to Know*, come close to such solutions, the former in the name of intellect, the latter in the name of culture.

The specification of teaching method appeals to our sense of techne,[3] a technology of practice that is deduced from research that aims to assure, if not guarantee, results. The most common pedagogical procedure for such a technology is the breaking up of content into small units, prescribing a uniform sequence among those units, and using an objective, multiple-choice test to measure learning. Both approaches to school improvement have little place in their lexicons for celebration. Both, if they celebrate anything, celebrate standardized content, standardized method, and standardized objectives measured by standardized tests.

The idea that education is best served by standardizing method, content, goals, and evaluation procedures leads to another consequence. It tends to convert education into a race. Those who achieve goals most quickly win. This attitude is expressed in the proliferation of preschools, the academic formalization of kindergarten, the creation of "better baby" institutes, and the all-too-common syndrome David Elkind[4] refers to as the hurried child (see his book *The Hurried Child*, 1981). At more advanced levels, this attitude is represented in the growth of Stanley Kaplan schools and the special high school courses on the SATs. Yet speed in accomplishing tasks is not particularly compatible with the concept of celebration. Events that we celebrate are events that we like to prolong. Efficiency and speed in completing a task are characteristics of tasks that are distasteful. We like to clean our kitchen or the toilet bowl efficiently, but who likes to eat a great meal efficiently? What we enjoy we wish to savor.[5]

My argument here is not to slow up teaching and learning for its own sake but rather to recognize that speed is no necessary virtue. Getting through the curriculum in the shortest possible time is a virtue primarily when the program is noxious.

Thinking, which we celebrate here today, should be prized not only because it leads to attractive destinations but also because the journey itself is satisfying.

## Language and knowledge

It is the nature of thinking and the forms through which it occurs that I wish to focus upon. In American schools, like their counterparts in Europe, thinking is often conceptualized as a process that is both abstract and linguistic in nature. Thinking, like knowledge itself, is argued by some to depend upon language. To truly have knowledge, one must be able to make a claim about the world that is capable of being verified. The truth or falsity of a belief can be determined only if the belief can be stated in words; and not just any words, but propositions. Without propositions there is no claim. Without a claim there is no test; without a test, there is no verification. Without verification there is no knowledge. (For elaboration of this point, see Denis Phillips's[6] "After the Wake: Postpositivistic Educational Thought," *Educational Researcher*, May 1983.)

The argument goes further. To state propositions, one must be able to think in a propositional form. Indeed, some claim that language itself makes thinking possible. Consider the following statement by Adam Schaff,[7] a prominent student of language:

> When we adopt the monistic standpoint, we reject the claim that language and thinking can exist separately and independently of one an other. Of course, we are talking about specifically *human* thinking, in other words about *conceptual* thinking. Thus we assert that in the process of cognition and communication, thinking and using a language are inseparable elements of one and the same whole.

What such a view has meant for school is that language has been assigned a place of privilege in our educational priorities, in our time allocations, and in our concept of intelligence itself. I need not remind you that the best predictor of IQ is the vocabulary subtest on the IQ test. The SATs have two sections, verbal and mathematical. So do the GREs. Human intellectual ability, the ability to think, is made almost isomorphic with the ability to use language or number.

My aim is to challenge that view. I wish to portray a conception of mind, of thinking, of intelligence that is not restricted to language. Any view of intellect that is limited in scope will penalize those students whose aptitudes reside outside of its boundaries. If schools are aimed at the cultivation of intellect, those students whose aptitudes lie in forms of thinking excluded from the accepted conception of intellect will themselves be excluded from a place of our educational sun. So, too, will others whose aptitudes are in the use of language for language itself, I will argue, depends upon forms of thinking and intelligence that relate to the qualitative aspects of our experience.

## A biological basis for thinking and learning

I start with the claim that humans do not enter the world with minds but with brains. The task of education, acculturation, and socialization is to convert brains into minds. Brains are born and minds are made, and one of the privileges of the teaching profession is to have an important part to play in the shaping of minds.

The major means through which this fête is accomplished is through the programs we offer in schools – the curriculum – and the quality of the process through which it is mediated – teaching.

When we define school curricula, our definition reflects views of mind that we believe are important. Our culture regards language skills as important and defines intelligence as being able to handle abstract, language-based tasks. I wish to develop another view of thinking and intelligence and, hence, another basis for deciding about the content and goals of our school programs.

Traditionally we have separated mind from body. The separation is Platonic. For Plato[8] mind was lofty and body was base. Working with one's head was different and more noble than working with one's hands. Today we have manual trade schools for those who are good with their hands, but the really bright take physics. The separation, this unfortunate dichotomy, is philosophically naive, psychologically ill-conceived, and educationally mischievous. There is no competent work of the hand that does not depend on the competent use of mind. The mind and senses are one, not two.

Consider the world in which we live. It is first and foremost a qualitative world: that is, a world consisting of qualities we are able to experience; color, texture, smell, sounds are qualities that permeate our world. Becoming conscious of that world or some aspect of it depends upon a skilled and intact sensory system. I emphasize *skilled*. We often do not think of the senses as being skilled; they are just there. But if you think about it, the qualities of the world are not simply given to human experience; they must be won. Experience is not simply an act or event; it is an achievement. We learn to see and hear. We *learn* to read the subtle qualitative cues that constitute the environment. We learn to distinguish and differentiate between the small furry creatures we call kittens, squirrels, and puppies. Eventually, if we care enough, we are able to see qualities in Irish setters, golf clubs, fine wines, antique cabinets, Japanese pots, and the complex nuances of American football that others miss. If we care enough and work hard enough we *achieve* experience. We become connoisseurs of some aspect of the world.

It is through cultivated or refined sensibilities that the nuances and pleasures of a Beethoven quartet are experienced; the differences between a smile and a smirk are noticed; the achievements of a fine craftsman are appreciated. It is through a cultivated and refined sensibility that patterns in nature and culture are distinguished. It is from these patterns that the works of science and art are built.

## Remembering and imagining

The development of the sensibilities not only provides us with access to the qualities of the world. It is through the content of such experience that we are able to perform two very important cognitive operations: we are able to remember and we are able to imagine.

Recall, or remembering, is the ability to reconstruct in our mind's eye images encountered earlier. The sensibilities, a part of our *minding*, provides recall with its content. What we have noticed we are more likely to be able to recall. What we have not experienced we cannot under normal circumstances remember. The ability to remember, therefore, is significantly influenced by the qualities of the world we are able to experience in the first place. The differentiation of the sensibilities is a key process in providing the mind with a content.

The ability to remember is clearly a critical aspect of our cognitive capabilities, but to remember without the ability to imagine would leave us with a static culture. The engine of social and cultural progress is our ability to conceive of things that never were, but which might become. The central term in the word imagination is *image*. To imagine is to create new images, images that function in the development of a new science, the creation of a new symphony, and the invention of a new bridge. It is a process critical for the creation of poetry and for innovation in our practical lives. But imagination, like recall, works with qualities we have experienced. What was not first in the hand cannot be later in the head. Try to imagine something you have never experienced. You will find that while you are able to imagine new forms of animals, autos, devices for seating, and the like, the components of these entities are qualities you once encountered. Our imaginative life is built out of experience.

One would think, given the importance of imagination, that it would be regarded as one of the basics of education. It is not on anyone's list of basics, at least not in any national report on the state of our schools. We are far more concerned with the correct replication of what already exists that with cultivating the powers of innovation or the celebration of thinking. Perhaps a little parity among these educational goals would be appropriate.

Everything that I have said thus far about the sensibilities and about recall and imagination pertain to events that occur inside our heads. Recall and imagination are qualities of human experience that are internal and private. I can enjoy my own fantasies and you can enjoy yours, but you cannot access mine, nor I yours. If things were left that way, culture would be static; even worse, it would eventually cease to exist, because culture depends on communication. Communication requires the externalization of what is internal, a shift through which what is private is made public.

## Using forms of representation

This process of making the private public is a process we take too much for granted. It is an extraordinary achievement, one that is still evolving and, although language is our prime vehicle, we have over time found it necessary to create other means through which what we have thought, felt, and imagined could be given a public face. In my book *Cognition and Curriculum* (1982), I have called these means "forms of representation." Becoming acculturated means acquiring the multiple forms of literacy that enable one to encode or decode such forms of representation.

Forms of representation are visual, auditory, tactile, gustatory, and even olfactory. They manifest themselves in pictures, speech, the movements of dance and gesture, in words and in number. Each of these social devices carries meanings that represent qualities we have experienced directly or through recall or imagination. Hence, experience that is visual may be uniquely represented by forms of representation that exploit the visual; if we want to know what someone looks like, a picture is better than a paragraph. If we want to know about a sequence of events over time, a story is usually better than a picture. If we want to convey the vital and dynamic experience of our emotional life, dance and music are probably better than a string of numbers. Our curricula could be designed to help children acquire the multiple forms of literacy.

The use of any form of representation has at least four important educational functions. First, it is important to recognize that there is nothing so slippery as a thought. Working with a form of representation provides the opportunity to stabilize what is ephemeral and fleeting. Second, it gives students an opportunity to hold onto their thinking. Thoughts written on a paper, portrayed on a canvas, arrayed in a notation, or reproduced on a recorded tape can be edited, and the process of editing allows one to refine one's thinking, to make it clearer and more powerful and, not least, to appreciate the happy achievements created.

The editing process, whether in writing, painting, or making music, is not much emphasized in our schools. Students typically write not to communicate what they care about but to answer questions, posed by the teacher, that the teacher already has answers to.

The third function of using a form of representation to externalize the internal is to make communication possible. For our thoughts to be known, they must be given public status: they must, somehow, be made public. Imagine how impoverished our musical life would be if Mozart at age 13 decided not to notate his magnificent music, or if Cezanne simply enjoyed the views of Mount St. Victoire rather than painting them, or if Isaac Newton decided not to tell. The history of art and western science would have been ineluctibly altered.

The fourth function of using a form of representation is to provide opportunities for discovery. The creation of anything is more like a dialogue than a monologue. The act of making something is not only an occasion for expressing or representing what you already know, imagine, or feel; it is also a means through which the forms of things unknown can be uncovered. The creative act is an act of exploration and discovery.

Thinking should be celebrated by giving students opportunities to try to represent what they think they know. And because what they know cannot always be projected in a single form of representation – say, the logical use of language – they should have a variety of options available and the skills with which to use them.

## Forms of representation have a syntax

There is one other feature about forms of representation that is relevant to our discussion concerning the celebration of thinking. All forms of representation have a syntactical structure. The term syntax comes from the Latin *syntaxis*, which means to arrange. For example, forms of representation used in painting or drawing require the student to arrange the qualities within the work so that they cohere. The same is true of musical composition or choreography. What the individual seeks is a coherent, satisfying form. Other forms of representation such as the use of word and number must also be arranged. However, mathematics and much of language, particularly in the early grades, is more rule abiding than structure seeking. (For a discussion of this distinction see G. L. Rico's *Writing the Natural Way*.)[9] That is, there are strict conventions that work within these forms must meet. To use the English language correctly requires that one obey the rules for language use. To spell correctly requires that one put letters in the proper order. To calculate correctly requires that operations be performed according to rule.

However, the problem in our schools is that activities whose syntactical structure is rule-abiding dominate the curriculum to the virtual exclusion of figural or structure-seeking activities. As we all know, students never learn one thing at a time. While they are learning to write and to compute they are also learning to be good rule followers. They are also learning that for most tasks, and especially the most important ones, the correct answer is known. The teacher knows it or, if not, it can be found in the back of the book.

I believe we should be concerned about a curriculum that places such a heavy emphasis on such limited forms of learning and thinking. When these forms of learning dominate a curriculum, they also cultivate a disposition and that disposition is one that does not match the kinds of problems with which most people must deal in life outside of school. Life's problems are seldom solved by following rules or applying algorithms. They almost always have more than one solution, and they typically require judgment and trade-off. They are problems that more often demand a satisfying sense of closure than a single correct answer. The paucity of such problems in our programs creates a disjuncture between what we emphasize in the short-term and what we seek as the long-term goals of schooling. Ironically, one area of thinking that has the most to offer is often the most neglected in our schools. I speak of the arts. The arts are models of work that do emphasize the creation of coherent structure, that do encourage multiple solutions to problems, that do prize innovation, that do rely upon the use of judgment, and that do depend upon the use of sensibility. In short, the arts, a realm of thinking typically neglected in our school programs, constitute our potentially most important means of celebrating thinking.

Now I am painfully aware that the current education climate for the ideas I have expressed are not as hospitable as they might be. As I indicated when I began, we do not typically pay much attention to celebrating thinking, or curiosity, or imagination, or creativity in our schools. In addition, we have a strong tendency to want to monitor the quality of schooling by implementing a common program and applying common standards to determine who comes in first. The results, like the results at the Belmont race track and the Kentucky Derby, are published in the newspapers.

## Developing multiple forms of literacy in our schools

Consider the matter of content and the ways in which students display what they have learned. The content that we care about, let's say, is helping students understand the life and times of the slaves just prior to and during the Civil War. This material, as you know, is common fair for fifth-graders in many elementary schools in our country. What students learn about slavery will be shaped by the kind of messages they are given. In turn, these messages are shaped by the forms of representation that we choose to use. If the students read an artistically crafted historical text, not only will they be given access to facts, but the language itself, its style and form, will enable them to learn something about how the slaves felt and what those who kept slaves felt about their own lives. Through narrative and prose that exploits the capacity of language to generate images and to foster feeling, an effective picture of the period can be rendered and secured. Of course, to secure this picture students must know how to read. They must know how to read not only clipped, factual accounts but also literary accounts. They must be sensitive to the melody, cadence, and metaphor of language if the text contains them.

But even when students possess such high levels of reading comprehension, literary text cannot tell all. The music of the period, the hymns, the chants, the rhythms of Africa can also help students gain access to the period. And so can Matthew Brady's photos and Lincoln's Emancipation Proclamation and Gettysburg Address. So, too, can the mythology of the slaves and their homespun stories. Further, it would be useful for students to create their own plays about the period and to act them out. It might be useful for them to perform the dances and to eat what the slaves of the period ate.

A model of curriculum that exploits various forms of representation and that utilizes all of the senses helps students learn what a period in history feels like. Reality, whatever it is, is made up of qualities: sights, smells, images, tales, and moods. First-hand experience is simply a way of getting in touch with reality. In our schools we often rely upon conceptually dense and emotionally eviscerated abstractions to represent what in actuality is a rich source of experience. To compound things further, we require students to tell us what they have learned by trying to fit it into one of four alternatives to a multiple-choice question.

The use of multiple forms of representation in the construction of curriculum is not limited to social studies; good math teachers use them in the teaching of math. Graphics, charts, histograms, and number diagrams are ways of helping students access mathematical ideas through forms that many find easier to grasp. The fact that charts, diagrams, schematics, and spreadsheets are very useful ways to display information has been quickly understood by IBM, Apple, and Toshiba. They waste no time pointing out to prospective customers how much more readable and saleable their products will be if they use graphics. In this respect, they are far ahead of educators.

The hegemony of language on our curriculum, and a narrow version at that, limits what students can come to know and restricts thinking processes to those mediated mainly by language. What language can carry is not all that we can know. Ultimately, what we know is rooted in qualities encountered or images recalled and imagined.

The celebration of thinking should be returned to our classrooms. It should be given a seat of honor in its own right, for its own rewards. The forms in which thinking occurs should not be subjected to the status differences and inequities of our society. Is a first-rate piece of science really better or more important than a first-rate symphony? Is knowledge of geometry more important than understanding and appreciating poetry? I am not urging a displacement of science for art or math for poetry. I am not arguing for the creation of a new privileged class, but rather for a decent conception of what our students are entitled to. Without opportunities to acquire multiple forms of literacy, children will be handicapped in their ability to participate in the legacies of their culture. Our children deserve more than that.

## Notes

1   Alan Bloom, *The Closing of the American Mind*, New York: Simon and Schuster, 1987.
2   E. D. Hirsch, *Cultural Literacy: What Every American Needs to Know*, Boston, MA: Houghton, Mifflin, 1987.
3   Technological approaches to teaching and school improvement is represented by much of the research on effective teaching and on effective schools. In both cases factors are identified that purportedly constitute effectiveness in these areas and teachers and policy-makers are encouraged to replicate those factors in their own teaching. The operating assumption is that the factors that make for educational effectiveness are common across situations, replicable, and relatively context independent. In addition, little or no attention is paid to matters of interaction or curvilinearity.
4   See David Elkind, *The Hurried Child: Growing Up Too Fast Too Soon*, Reading, MA: Addison-Wesley Publishing Co., 1981.
5   Unless students receive satisfaction from their work, the likelihood of pursuing such work outside of the classroom is low. The only robust outcomes of schooling are those internalized by students and pursued because of the satisfaction they provide.
6   Denis Phillips, "After the Wake: Postpositivistic Educational Thought," *Educational Researcher*, May, Vol. 12, No. 5, 1983, pp. 4–12.
7   Adam Schaff, *Language and Cognition*, in Robert S. Cohen (ed.), Linguistics: From Herder to the Theory of the "Linguistic Field", New York: McGraw-Hill, 1973, p. 118.
8   See, for example, Plato's *Republic*, especially Book Seven, Cleveland, OH: Fine Editions Press, 1946.
9   The distinction between structure-seeking and rule-abiding is found in Gabrielle Lusser Rico, *Writing the Natural Way*, Los Angeles, CA: J. P. Tarcher, Inc., 1983.

## Bibliography

Arthur Applebee, *Writing on the Secondary School: English and the Content Areas*, Research Report No. 21, Urbana, IL: National Council of Teachers of English, 1981.
Elliot W. Eisner, *Cognition and Curriculum: A Basis for Deciding What to Teach*, New York: Longmans, Inc., 1982.
Elliot W. Eisner, *What High Schools Are Like: An Inside View*, Stanford, CA: School of Education, Stanford University, 1986.
Howard Gardner, *Frames of Mind*, New York: Basic Books, Inc., 1983.
Suzanne Langer, *Philosophy in a New Key*, Cambridge, MA: Harvard University Press, 1942.

## CHAPTER 12

# THE PRIMACY OF EXPERIENCE AND THE POLITICS OF METHOD*

*Educational Researcher*, 1988, 17(5): 15–20

Knowledge is rooted in experience and requires a form for its representation. Since all forms of representation constrain what can be represented, they can only partially represent what we know. Forms of representation not only constrain representation, they limit what we seek. As a result, socialization in method is a process that shapes what we can know and influences what we value. At base it is a political undertaking. This article addresses the politics of method and its effects on the character of educational research.

## Experience as achievement

To what extent do the research methods we use shape what we can learn about educational practice? To what degree do the forms we employ to describe what we have learned constrain what we are able to say? To what extent do our conceptions of art and science, knowledge and belief, truth and falsity influence how we go about our work? These questions adumbrate the major themes addressed in this article. How these questions are answered have profound implications for the future of educational research. Consider what we mean by experience.

One of our most widely accepted beliefs is that experience is an automatic condition of living. We plan programs in schools and talk about the experiences our students will have. We take our children to the country or to the zoo to enrich their experiences during their childhood. We see someone making the same mistakes over and over again and comment to ourselves that the person doesn't seem to learn from experience. Like breathing, we regard experience as a condition that is ineluctably associated with being alive. To live is to experience.

It is true, of course, that living creatures, humans perhaps more than most, experience the world in which they live. But experience is more than a simple given of life. It is not only an event; it is also an achievement. The qualities of the world are there for those who have the skills to take them. It is one of our culture's most significant tasks, one for which our schools have a special responsibility, to provide the tools and to develop the skills through which the child can create his or her own experience.

The main agency for human experience is the senses, those biologically given information pickup systems through which we make contact with the world. If not congenitally impaired, the young infant has the capacity to experience the qualitative world into which it is born. For some functions such as sucking, the response to the mother's breast is instinctive. But the skills that are needed to negotiate the world must be learned. These skills develop slowly and become increasingly refined throughout the course of living. The young infant learns to see, and the process of learning to see, to hear, to taste, and to smell, continue throughout the life cycle. Perceptual differentiation and sensory memory provide the major vehicles through which qualities are identified and contrasts and comparisons are made possible.

The kind of experience we have depends on a host of factors, but two that are central are the qualities themselves and the conceptual structures we bring to them. For example, redness, sweetness, and even kindness are words whose semantic content is located in experience we call qualitative. If our senses were impaired, whether through injury, genetic defect, or miseducation, our ability to experience the qualities of the world would suffer. Qualities we cannot experience, we cannot know.

But if our experience were simply a function of what the world presented to us, the simple presence of an event or object would guarantee its occurrence. It clearly does not. The conceptual tools we have acquired are critical for "reading" the qualitative world around us. These tools consist of language, intention, and schema. Language functions not only as a means for conveying our ideas to others, but also as an agency that shapes what we see.[1] Our way of dividing the world and classifying its components is significantly influenced by the linguistic system that we have learned to use. Theories, for example, in psychology and education, just as in physics and chemistry, provide their own portraits. The terms they employ slice the pie in different ways and harbor their own assumptions. When the term *stimulus* entered the lexicon of psychological discourse, we began to think about humans as responding to what the stimuli evoked. Our major aim was to discover the connections between stimulus and response. Mind did not mediate. It was not, except in physiological terms, a part of the picture. When consciousness re-emerged in the language of psychology, when information processing became a salient paradigm, when the mind was likened to a computer, a sponge, an iceberg, and a growing organism, our thinking about thinking altered and our way of seeing the world changed. What we experienced was shaped by the theoretical language through which we became professionally socialized. To this day, theories of nature and of culture provide powerful agents for guiding our perception. These theories are, in the sciences, propositional languages about how the world is and what is worth attending to.

Even as powerful as language is, it is by no means the only, nor necessarily the most powerful, vehicle affecting our experience. The images, around us, the forms we see in our art and the vernacular forms of our culture – our manners, architecture, dress, rituals, and ceremonies – provide potent prototypes through which we classify, compare, and appraise the qualities of the world we encounter. It is through the images of Monet that we can see what light can do to a summer field, how it can radiate an array of haystacks, and how it can convert the facade of a Gothic church into a prism. It is through the apparitions of an Edvard Munch that we can experience the psychological torment of the death bed and the anguish of the mental hospital. It is through the icons of the silver screen that we acquire models of physical beauty, moral courage, and sexual attractiveness. Images are there to be taken and those crafted by artists are among the most powerful that we are offered.

What the artist and the creative scientist have in common is that both are makers of form (Read, 1944), one qualitative, the other theoretical, who offer us images of the world. When the images are well crafted they provide compelling schemata that capture both our attention and our allegiance.

The forms we call art and science, rite and ritual, not only provide schemata through which we experience the world, they also are the forms through which we represent it. We have a strong tendency, I think, to regard these forms as if they had a life independent of their makers. We tend, perhaps especially in dealing with language, to reify concepts and to think about propositions as containing within them meanings of their own. Forms of representation, and science is such a form, re-present what a scientist has imagined. The meaning of language, when it is propositional in character, is substantially referential. Empirical claims and empirical theories refer to the world, and their truth ultimately is tested in the experience their claims and explanations make possible. Each form of representation has its own boundaries, its own constraints, and its own possibilities. Representation is an auxiliary process. It helps us convey, it helps us see, and it helps us formulate what we have imagined by providing a means through which what we have imagined can be made acute. The act of representation also provides the occasion for discovery, as both Collingwood (1938) and Croce (1909) have argued. Ultimately, however, representation must give way to the primacy of experience. In the end, it is the qualities we experience that provide the content through which meaning is secured. Meaning is not located in either propositional language or forms of art independent of a competent and creative reader who is able to secure from them a particular quality of life.

## The hegemony of propositions

In our schools and in our research communities in education, the language of science and propositional forms of discourse have been dominant. Knowledge is defined within these forms and the variety and quantity of our research journals, our books, and our conferences provide ample testimony to the seriousness with which we regard the written and spoken word.

There are very good reasons for the hegemony of propositional discourse in educational theory and research. Propositional language is the vehicle, par excellence, for precise communication. When terms are made conventional and the rules of syntax codified, the possibility of sharing meanings is increased. Mathematics is the ultimate expression of precision in such matters. Furthermore, the language of propositions is typically a class language. That is, it focuses upon categories of events and objects and thus generalizes more than particularizes. Since what we typically seek is a knowledge of classes, forms of representation that focus upon the particular or that are idiosyncratic to the user diminish both utility and comprehension. Those who use language in unique ways are hard to understand. Finally, knowledge, we are told, consists of making warranted assertions. To provide warrant, assertions must be as unambiguous as possible and the ability to specify the referents to support the claim must be demonstrated. We worry about claims that cannot be tested, and we believe that unless assertions are made in propositional terms, we have no good way to test their truth.[2]

I am sure that this ground is quite familiar to you. It is a view that has been dominant in American educational research since its inception in the field of education. We seem to believe that what we cannot say, we cannot know. Some go even further to claim that thinking itself depends upon the ability to put our thoughts into words, a kind of subvocal speech. Indeed, if we examine the tests we employ to assess thinking, particularly intelligence and academic aptitude, language competency is always a dominant form of the performance. Those whose language skills are low are regarded as not being intelligent enough to be admitted to our most prestigious institutions of higher education.

## The plurality of meaning

Despite these views and policies, language in the propositional sense does not exhaust either the limits of thought, the limits of knowledge, or the limits of intelligence (Gardner, 1985). It is only one of several ways through which what is not linguistic can be represented. As Michael Polanyi (1958) has pointed out, and Susanne Langer (1967, 1972) before him, and Ernst Cassirer (1957) before her, we know more than we can tell. Knowledge need not – and I would say should not – be restricted to what one can claim.

The corollary of such an assertion is that how we try to understand our schools, how we seek to learn how our classrooms work, and how our teachers teach should not be limited to the schemata, theories, or methods that a propositional conception of knowledge requires. If the schema shapes experience, should we not become versatile in the schemata we can use?

Understanding the way in which forms of representation represent is critical for assessing their epistemological utility. One major distinction between the meanings conveyed by art and those conveyed by science has been provided by that great German student of symbolic form, Ernst Cassirer. In his *An Essay on Man* (1945), Cassirer discusses the complementary contributions of art and science to our comprehension of the world:

> The two views of truth are in contrast with one another, but not in conflict or contradiction. Since art and science move in entirely different planes they cannot contradict or thwart one another. The conceptual interpretation of science does not preclude the intuitive interpretation of art. Each has its own perspective and, so to speak, its own angle of refraction. The psychology of sense perception has taught us that without the use of both eyes, without a binocular vision, there would be no awareness of the third dimension of space. The depth of human experience in the same sense depends on the fact that we are able to vary our modes of seeing, that we can alternate our views of reality. *Rerum videre formas* is no less important and indispensable a task than *rerum cognoscere causas*. In ordinary experience we connect phenomena according to the category of causality or finality. According as we are interested in the theoretical reasons for the practical effects of things, we think of them as causes or means. Thus, we habitually lose sight of their immediate appearance until we can no longer see them face to face. Art, on the other hand, teaches us to visualize, not merely to conceptualize or utilize, things. Art gives a richer more vivid and colorful image of reality, and a more profound insight into its formal structure. It is characteristic of the nature of man that he is not limited to one specific and single approach to reality but can choose his point of view and so pass from one aspect of things to another.
>
> (1945, p. 170)

The important lesson that Cassirer teaches is that language in its customary sense can divert our attention from the qualities of direct experience to their causes. It can easily be used to substitute concept for percept, the name of the thing for the thing itself. The point that Cassirer makes has also been made by the American philosopher John Dewey, who, in *Art as Experience* (1934), his final major philosophic work, distinguishes between seeing and recognizing. Seeing requires sustained attention to the qualities of an object or situation; it is exploratory in character. Recognition is the act of assigning a label to an object.

Once assigned and classification has occurred, exploration ceases. When in our teaching, our curriculum, and our research methods we emphasize the prompt classification and labeling of objects and events, we restrict our consciousness and reduce the likelihood that the qualities of which those objects and events consist will be experienced. Thus, our awareness is always limited by the tools we use. When those tools do not invite further sensory exploration, our consciousness is diminished.

The heavy emphasis on language skills in the early stages of schooling in America might have much to do with the limited vision and dulled sensibility that seems so pervasive in our culture. That language in its customary sense is less than optimal for conveying to others what we wish them to grasp is evident in the forms we have invented to overcome the limits of language. For example, we use diagrams to explain relationships within electronics, we invent models to describe the structure of nature, we create maps to determine our position on our planet, we produce scattergrams to discover the character of statistical distributions, we design graphs to portray trends in our data, pictographs to identify needed conveniences, holograms to see objects in the round, photographs to capture images we cherish, and painting and sculpture to tell others how we feel about them. As Cassirer said: "*Rerum videre formas* is no less important and indispensable a task than *rerum cognoscere causas.*" Knowledge of forms is as important and indispensable as knowledge of causes.

## Art as image of feeling

Forms of representation that are treated in an artistic mode convey not only knowledge of appearance, but also knowledge of feeling (Langer, 1942). Art can be said to be that activity concerned with the creation of images of feeling. The situations, people, and objects we encounter are never without affect. Classrooms, schools, teaching episodes, students struggling to learn and others resisting learning are emotionally charged slices of life. Human beings are, after all, sentient beings whose lives are pervaded by complex and subtle forms of affect. To try to comprehend the ways in which people function and the meanings the events in their lives have for them and to neglect either seeing or portraying those events and meanings is to distort and limit what can be known about them. The artistic treatment of forms of representation has the capacity to arouse such feelings. Such forms provide the conditions through which empathy can emerge, and generate the *nachleben* that gives us vicarious access to the lives of others. A language that does not permit us to see or to say what such matters mean to us is a language so limited in scope that it cannot, in principle, yield the kind of understanding needed to deal adequately with educational matters. If science states meaning, as John Dewey once said, the arts express them (1934). The artistic treatment of form provides what Langer calls a non-discursive form of knowledge. It is knowledge of the forms of feeling, secured by virtue of the way the artist has employed a technique to treat a medium so that it will have an effect upon those competent to read its message. The need for such messages, I am arguing, is as important in the conduct of educational research as in those forms that have for so long dominated our conception of how we are to go about our work.

Consider the following two descriptions of classroom practice. The first discusses the results of an empirical, quantitative study of teacher clarity, achievement, and student satisfaction. The latter is a qualitative description of an award winning art program in a small rural high school.

This research, conducted within the context of a college peer-teaching laboratory situation, found a number of highly significant and positive relationships between clarity measures taken of teachers and the outcome measures of student achievement and student satisfaction. These relations were relatively consistent across both a triangulation of measurement sources (observers, students, and teachers) and three different measurement levels of the clarity construct (low-, intermediate-, and high-inference). Further, as Doyle (1977) suspected, the use of students' perceptions of teacher clarity as a mediating process variable helped to illuminate the nature of relations between the clarity of teachers and the two examined outcome variables of student satisfaction and achievement.

The limitations of this descriptive study should be mentioned. As noted, observed teaching episodes were brief, and they were observed within reflective teaching situations. The use of this peer-teaching vehicle to examine didactic teaching possesses numerous advantages, the most obvious for research being the ability to affect a high level of control of a number of potentially confounding variables (e.g., diverse lessons, types of instruction, learners, etc.). However, the laboratory-like structure of reflective teaching prompts legitimate concerns about the external validity of research findings. The extent to which the findings reported here can be found in more natural classroom settings awaits future investigation. Also unresolved are questions pertaining to the value of using lower inference behaviors to train teachers to be clearer.

(Hines et al., 1985, pp. 87–99)

Now to the art program.

Just what does motivate these teenagers? It is an important question because its answer can provide a clue to the *educational* meaning and significance of the Swain County Arts Program's outcomes – the character of its impact on the lives of these students. Having spent only four days in the school, I will avoid pronouncements, and instead share my reasons for some strong suspicions. They are based on observations of student comportment, on the informal comments, on mass "whole-class" discussions over which I presided, and on interviews with individual students...

One discerns a personal pride emanating from their accomplishments. There are several facets to this pride, including a degree of vanity from the attention their talents attract. Occasionally a sense of self-importance could be detected among some of Forrister's senior students, an awareness of a kind of privileged status usually associated with talented athletes, or found among high school thespians backstage before the senior play. This status, as far as I could tell, was certainly not flaunted – and part of it might be explained by the fact that so many of Forrister's senior students were already part of (in Philip Cusick's term) the school's "power clique." But this status was also derived from the recognition of and admiration for their many awards and honors which the students (they readily admit this) welcome. That thrill of victory is heady stuff. The scent, from a drop or two, can apparently provide the momentum for many a painstaking and time-consuming project. This attention and excitement may be particularly impressive to the large percentage of Forrister's students who are (according to Ms. Lance) in other subjects less than academically able. Can we image the impact registered on the psyche of an eleventh grader who after years of frustration, boredom, and perhaps even derision in math and English classes, is suddenly flown to New York to receive a national award for his drawings?

(Barone, 1983, pp. 11–13)

Each of the foregoing narratives have different stories to tell and are useful for different purposes. But no one narrative alone can tell the story of the other. The identification of variables, the measurement of relationships between them, the abstracted and detached sense of language in the first description with its impersonal voice and distance between the language as written and the reality it represents were done for a purpose. That purpose is to objectify through depersonalization. It is one version. But one version of the world is one version still. As Nelson Goodman has said in *Ways of World-Making* (1978), "There may be one world, but there are many versions of it." And, as he says elsewhere, there are as many versions as there are languages to describe them. The research language that has dominated educational inquiry has been one that has attempted to bifurcate the knower and the known. We use a language that implies that it is possible for the organism to grasp the environment as it *really* is. Consider how we discuss our research efforts. We talk about our *findings*, implying somehow that we discover the world rather than construe it. We say in our discussion, "it turns out . . . ," implying that how things are is nothing for which we have any responsibility. We write and talk in a voice void of any hint that there is a personal self behind the words we utter: "the author," "the subject," "the researcher," or, miraculously, we somehow multiply our individuality and write about what "we" found. All of these linguistic conventions are, paradoxically, rhetorical devices designed to persuade the reader that we, as individuals, have no signature to assign to our work. As we say in the vernacular, "We want to tell it like it is." The motive for such locutions, ultimately, is found in our search for objectivity, that God's eye view of the world that sees comprehensively and without the encumbrances of feelings, motives, interests, or a personal biography. We distance ourselves from the phenomena we wish to understand so that we can see them from the knee of God – or at least somewhere close by.

The result is the creation of a language of research that only researchers can understand and that, even for them, is difficult to use to reconstruct images of classroom life having a semantic content. When such an orientation to research and knowledge becomes salient in our forms of professional socialization, the methods that accompany them become political in character. Legitimacy is conferred upon those who belong to the same church.

The politics of method breeds a sense of community among those who adhere to its principles. For those who do not, it can breed a sense of alienation. Describing the feeling of alienation, of being torn between the canons of the academic world and the exigencies of the practical, one leading American student of science education, David Hawkins, writes as follows:

Those of us who are in the academic world are very much torn. If we get involved in school work at a practical level we come to realize how empty a lot of the theoretical discussion is compared to the practice. We either struggle to express it – some of us are foolish enough to keep on trying to do this – or we acquire a distaste for our own academic ways of functioning. And I know that I myself am very much torn as the result of this. I want on the one hand to do battle with the psychologists and a good many of the American educationists, but that requires that I get into their league and read their papers and books and so on. But then I'm very dissatisfied because they're not talking about things I think are important, and I don't myself quite know how to talk about those things that seem to me to be important.

(1986, p. 1)

The difficulty that Hawkins describes might have much less to do with his inability to use an expressive, artistically influenced and phenomenologically focused language than with his sense that the use of such a language is academically inappropriate. When a senior, distinguished citizen of America's educational elite can express such personal pains, one can only wonder how others, less senior and less vocationally secure, must feel.

The politics of method are not solely rooted in matters of epistemology; they also stem from human frailties. Any method or approach to the world depends upon the exercise of certain skills and dispositions. For example, the ability to employ narrative in an artistic or expressive mode that enables readers to participate in events that can be known only vicariously is a product of skill in seeing and in crafting language. The ability to analyze the variance in a set of statistical distributions and to explain the relationships between them depends upon particular skills in data analysis. As individuals, we are invested with self-interest and we achieve positions of authority because we know how to exercise particular skills. Our methods and our power are intimately related to the games we are adept at playing. When the prospect for a new game arises, we quite naturally assess how good we are at playing it. The prospect of losing competence or sharing turf is not, for most of us, attractive; the familiar is much more comfortable. So we have a tendency to keep the game as it is, particularly if we have been winning. Power, control, and admiration are not easy to share.

To maintain control and to ensure ideological immortality we train acolytes to keep the tradition alive. Our beliefs are passed on to the younger generation through our universities, our journals, and our books. The world we have created through our beliefs seems almost to take on a life of its own. Our interests and our language frequently do not connect with those who actively do the work we say we are trying to influence. Even within the same household, the language of a teacher and the language of a professor of education may have little common ground. Thus, the irony of purporting to develop a knowledge base that will inform practitioners, while creating a language and a professional structure that distances itself from practice.

Now the distance of research from practice may have several utilities for the researcher, not the least of which is the comfort of not having to confront its inadequacy. Distance, even incomprehensibility, can be a source of protection. The rationale, of course, for distancing ourselves from practice is that one needs to be able to see the forest, not only the trees. Getting too close to practice hampers perspective. There is, surely, a grain of truth here. But just as surely the test of theory is how well it enables us to deal with our practical tasks. Theory is a tool, not simply an end within the professional sphere, and tools untested or misunderstood are hardly useful. But the problem might be deeper. Utility might not, after all, be an important criterion for those of us who do educational research. It just might be the case that status among our peers might be more important. We tend, I think, to have cosmopolitan and not simply local aspirations – and so do the institutions in which we work.

## Method and consciousness

Aside from the politics of status, control, and power located in our forms of professional socialization, our social work structures, and our reward systems, the ultimate politics of method is its impact on our view of reality. Neither technique nor technology, whether technology of a physical type or a technology of mind, is epistemologically neutral. The categories we are taught, the sources of evidence that we believe count, the language that we learn to use govern our world-views. How we come to see the world, what we think it means, and eventually what we believe we can do about that world are intimately related to the technologies of mind we have acquired. There is no such thing as a value-neutral approach to the world; language itself, whether the language of the arts or the sciences, is value-laden. To acquire a language or a set of methodological conventions without examining what they leave out as well as what they can contain, is to take the part for the whole. Hence, when I talk about the politics of method, I do not simply mean matters of position, authority, or professional socialization in the narrow sense, but rather the ways in which the mind is shaped and beliefs are fostered. The politics of method ultimately has to do with the politics of experience. Method influences how we think and what we are permitted to feel.

For those of us who have devoted our efforts to thinking about curricular matters, this should come as no surprise. It was, I believe, Basil Bernstein, the British sociologist, who first pointed out (1971) that the curriculum is a mind-altering device. What we teach, whether in the primary school or in the university, is a means for altering the ways in which students think. Our programs are designed to have such effects and, when they fail to change our students' ways of thinking, we regard ourselves as having failed. It is in this sense that education is an enterprise fully political in nature. The methods we espouse, the way we define knowledge, the work we regard as respectable, reflect our conceptions of virtue and the courses we teach, in turn, are designed to help students achieve such virtues.

I have no quarrel with such a view. What I do quarrel with is the effort of some to impose a single version of truth, to prescribe one church and to proscribe all others.[3] What I have even more quarrel with is the view that a scientifically acceptable research method is "objective" or value-free, that it harbors no particular point of view. All methods and all forms of representation are partial and because they are partial, they limit, as well as illuminate what through them we are able to experience.

The views I have expressed in this article are gaining a foothold in the American educational research community. Maxine Greene, Michael Connelly, Philip Jackson, Lee Cronbach, Robert Stake, Michael Apple, William Pinar, Howard Gardner, Fred Erickson, Sara Lightfoot, Madeline Grumet, Egon Guba, Gail McCutcheon, Robert Donmoyer, Tom Barone, Alan Peshkin, and others hold similar views. Their voices have become louder and more articulate during the past decade and a half, and are being heard in wider professional forums. Their messages have won a growing share of the space in the publications and programs of the American Educational Research Association, for example.

The views that have been expressed by some of us have their intellectual roots in continental philosophy, in the work of Cassirer (1945, 1957) and Dilthy (1985), for example, as well as in aspects of Dewey's (1934) work and Langer's (1942). What distinguishes some of our work from that growing from an interest in so-called qualitative research methods is the fact that much of what flies under the flag of qualitative research is a version of anthropology, often referred to as ethnography. Anthropology is more congenial to most as a method of inquiry in education than approaches with roots in the humanities and the arts because anthropology is a member of the family of social sciences: The gap is not too wide.

To promulgate a view of method and knowledge whose justification depends upon unfamiliar criteria is to risk cognitive dissonance. Many deal with such dissonance by rejecting the legitimacy of the approach. However, the ideas that we have been developing are becoming more widely accepted and the emerging climate for educational research in America is increasingly recognizing the primacy of experience. American educational researchers are beginning to go back to the schools, not to conduct commando raids, but to work with teachers as colleagues in a common quest and through such collaboration to rediscover the qualities, the complexities, and the richness of life in classrooms. We are beginning to talk with teachers, not only to teachers.[4] We are beginning to ask ourselves how we can see and describe the minor miracles of stunning teaching instead of prescribing how teachers should go about their work. We are beginning to realize that experiments are being conducted each time a teacher plans a lesson, explains an idea, or encourages a child. Such experiments have more external validity than most of the schemes that are hatched within the halls of ivy.

I have no illusions about how difficult it will be for these developments to succeed as a customary form of educational research practice. University offices and classrooms are comfortable places. Even in California where we don't have to face the cold winter, we find it difficult to leave our pleasant surroundings for our schools. Yet some researchers are making the trip and others are developing working partnerships with teachers. Our views of how we go about our work are beginning to change. My hope is that those of us in the university will be smart enough to learn from what good teachers have to teach us. I hope we will even learn how to see what we are not able to describe in words, much less measure. And, through the consciousness borne of such an attitude, I hope we will be creative enough to invent methods and languages that do justice to what we have seen. Finally, I hope that through such work, through the primacy of experience and the *expansion* of method, our politics will become a liberating force for both understanding and enhancing the educational process.

## Notes

\*   This is an abridged version of a paper given at the University of Oslo, Norway upon receiving an honorary doctorate in September, 1986.
1   Among the first to write about the relationship between language and perception were Edward Sapir and Benjamin Lee Whorf. See, for example, Sapir (1964).
2   Positivism, in all of its varieties, has had a significant impact on how knowledge is defined in educational research. A brief, yet classic statement of this position is found in Ayer (no date).
3   See, for example, Phillips (1983); also see Hospers (1967), especially pp. 143–157. The Hospers volume provides a general overview to a linguistic conception of knowledge.
4   Philip Jackson was among the first to call for such a relationship with teachers. See his most recent book, *The Practice of Teaching*. In the School of Education at Stanford we have created the Stanford Schools Collaborative to foster a partnership with schools in Northern California.

## References

Ayer, A. J. *Language, Truth, and Logic*. New York: Dover, no date.
Barone, T. Things of Use and Things of Beauty. *Daedalus*, 112: 11–13; 1983.
Bernstein, B. On the Classification and Framing of Educational Knowledge. In M. Young (ed.), *Knowledge and Control*. London: Collier-Macmillan, 1971.

Cassirer, E. *An Essay on Man: An Introduction to Human Culture*. New Haven, CT: Yale University Press, 1945.

Cassirer, E. *Philosophy of Symbolic Forms*. New Haven, CT: Yale University Press, 1957.

Collingwood, R. G. *The Principles of Art*. Oxford: Clarendon Press, 1938.

Croce, B. *Aesthetic*. London: Macmillan, 1909.

Dewey, J. *Art as Experience*. New York: Minton, Balch & Co., 1934.

Dilthy, W. *Poetry and Experience*. Princeton, NJ: Princeton University Press, 1985.

Eisner, E. W. *Cognition and Curriculum: A Basis for Deciding What to Teach*. New York: Longman, 1982.

Gardner, H. *Frames of Mind*. New York: Basic Books, 1985.

Goodman, N. *Ways of World-Making*. Indianapolis, IN: Hackett, 1978.

Hawkins, D. *North Dakota Study Group*. Wingspread Conference, (p. 1). Center for Teaching & Learning, University of North Dakota, Grand Forks, 1986.

Hines, C., Cruickshank, D., and Kennedy, J. Teacher Clarity and Its Relationship to Student Achievement. *American Educational Research Journal*, 22: 87–99; 1985.

Hospers, J. *An Introduction to Philosophical Analysis* (2nd edn). London: Routledge and Kegan Paul, 1967.

Jackson, P. *The Practice of Teaching*. New York: Teachers College Press, 1986.

Langer, S. *Philosophy in a New Key*. Cambridge, MA: Harvard University Press, 1942.

Langer, S. *Mind: An Essay on Human Feeling* (Vol. I). Baltimore, MD: Johns Hopkins University Press, 1967.

Langer, S. *Mind: An Essay on Human Feeling* (Vol. II). Baltimore, MD: Johns Hopkins University Press, 1972.

Phillips, D. After the Wake: Post-Positivistic Educational Thought. *Educational Researcher* 12(5): 4–12; 1983.

Polanyi, M. *Personal Knowledge*. Chicago, IL: University of Chicago Press, 1958.

Read, H. *Education through Art*. London: Pantheon Books, 1944.

Sapir, E. *Culture, Language, and Personality*. Berkeley, CA: University of California Press, 1964.

# CHAPTER 13

# SLIPPERY MOVES AND BLIND ALLEYS

## My travels with absolutism and relativism in Curriculum Theory

*Curriculum Inquiry,* 1989, 19(1): 59–65

Hanan Alexander presents the reader with a dazzling array of nonsequiturs and false assumptions upon which to build a case against what he regards as two well-intentioned but misguided positions concerning the nature of liberal education. Without preliminaries I would like to get to the main event.

Alexander's first villain is relativism. He builds his argument by claiming that there are two types of relativism, weak and strong. Although he finds weak relativism unattractive, it is strong relativism that is seriously problematic. Weak relativism implies that knowledge is framework-dependent, but it accepts the notion that framework-dependent knowledge can be criticized by using criteria outside of the framework within which the knowledge was produced. Strong relativism also implies that knowledge is framework-dependent, but holds that knowledge cannot be adequately appraised by criteria outside of the framework within which it was created. It holds further that perception itself is theory-laden.

What troubles Alexander is his belief that if knowledge reflects strong relativism, it is, as he calls it, "critically immune." Further, if perception is, as he says, "determined" by theory, then those operating within different theoretical frameworks will be attending to different phenomena. Since knowledge claims emanating from different percepts are about different phenomena, they are incommensurable; they cannot be criticized outside of the theory that "determined" the perception.

Alexander's second villain is absolutism, that conception that holds that *episteme* – true and certain knowledge – is possible. It is a conception advanced by Plato and which Alexander believes permeates the assumptions, aims, and practices of the Great Books program. Absolutism leads to certainty, and certainty leads to a closed mind. A closed mind is one that does not critically examine anything. Hence absolutism is anathema to education and the Great Books a vivid example of what is wrong with it.

The foregoing claims and theoretical distinctions constitute the core of Alexander's thesis. What follows in his article flows from his views of the weaknesses of relativism in general, but especially what he calls strong relativism, and from the perils of absolutism.

Thus, we have two villains in the piece. Advocates of liberal education who follow Plato blunder because they do not teach the young to look for mistakes. Those who emphasize modes of inquiry blunder because they make mistakes impossible to detect. Hence, the argument that Alexander lays out is intended to display the errors of the two major streams that he believes "dominate contemporary college curricula."

The problems with Alexander's argument are strewn throughout the article. I will identify 12 such problems and discuss them without extensive elaboration.

First, because someone believes that knowledge depends upon the form and framework used to create it, does not mean that one cannot criticize the products of inquiry produced within the form or framework employed. To engage in such criticism one can employ both internal and external criteria, but these criteria must always be relevant to the framework that was used. For example, internal criteria are employed when claims or propositions are examined for internal contradiction. When the product of inquiry is not propositional but qualitative, one makes judgments about coherence, and about what Nelson Goodman (1978) calls "rightness" (p. 19).

External criteria are employed when one asks about the extent to which the theory or form of knowledge produced enables one to see what had not been previously noticed, to anticipate events in the future, or to make sense out of events in the past (Eisner, 1985). There is no reason to assume, as Alexander does, that because there are many different ways in which knowledge is created and represented that there cannot be a critical analysis of what has been created. All one needs to do to check out Alexander's claim about the critical immunity of relativistic criteria is to reflect on the magnitude and diversity of critical material displayed in fields such as cognitive science, literature, behavioral psychology, anthropology, medicine, history, visual art, physics, and others. There is no shortage of critical analyses, even though there is no single set of criteria that is applicable to all in the "objective" and "value-neutral way" that Alexander claims.

Second, Alexander's claim that those working in the liberal arts tradition do not teach students to question what they read is empirically false. On the contrary, there is probably more critical acumen cultivated in liberal arts programs that there is in most university programs that go by another name. One of the important features of the kind of liberal arts program that Robert Maynard Hutchins and Mortimer Adler advocate, among others, is its emphasis on processes requiring the use of reason; what Adler calls *mieutics* and what Hutchins refers to as *dialectics*. Most college programs for undergraduates, particularly in the beginning years, emphasize not dialectics, but didactics. They teach by telling, usually to very large groups. In contrast, at the University of Chicago the standard practice in the College of Liberal Arts was to have 25 students sit around an oval table doing a critical exegesis of a primary source text or testing the validity of the arguments or ideas offered in the text. It was, in my view, a model of the kind of critical rationality that Alexander advocates. It is ironic that he should claim that in such programs a critical attitude is stifled.

Third, Alexander claims that if the polity is introduced to what is regarded as the best art, literature, science, and math that the world has produced it will somehow lead that polity into a life of slavery by being seduced by either charismatic leaders or by the authority of text. This forecast is one that Alexander neither supports by historical evidence nor by a line of argument that I find persuasive. On the contrary, I believe the prospects for cultivating critical rationality and independent thinking are greater when such cognitive skills are honed on the very best of human achievements rather than on lesser material.

Fourth, Alexander's large point that cognitive relativism denies that humans make mistakes is not supported by any quotation from any cognitive relativist in any of the texts that Alexander has used. There is good reason for this. It's simply not true. Who is it that claims that anything goes and that mistakes cannot be made? Such a view is so bizarre that on its face it has no intellectual merit. Yet, this is what Alexander imputes to those with whom he disagrees. It would have been appropriate, to say the least, for him to have displayed the evidence for this claim.

Fifth, Alexander's conviction that there is a super-ordinate set of criteria independent of any framework that is both neutral and objective in character paradoxically leads Alexander to accept what he rejects, namely, absolutism. Since he believes that there are such criteria, that they are not framework-dependent, and that they are both neutral and objective, the least he could have done is to have let us in on what those criteria might be. Nowhere in his argument does he do so. If there is, in fact, a rabbit in the hat, I'm sure we would all like to see it.

Sixth, Alexander worries that if people rely upon their own judgment for determining what is right and what is wrong, what is true and what is false, that "this has the consequence that power *might easily* (italics mine) end up in the hands of a single charismatic individual who would use whatever means available to persuade the majority to accept his or her truth as their own." One of the risks of democracy is that people might make decisions others find repugnant. Madison's Federalist Papers deals with this issue. The US Constitution deals with this issue. But whether one consults Madison's Federalist Papers or the Constitution, there is no guarantee that the majority might not tyrannize the minority. Political democracy is ultimately based upon the faith that rationality and understanding will lead to what is better rather than what is worse, to what is good rather than to what is evil. That is why Jefferson said a people who believe that they can be both ignorant and free, believe in that which never was and never will be.

Seventh, "if ways of knowing are immune from criticism," says Alexander, "then the concept of knowledge becomes meaningless." I concur, but again why the straw man? Who is claiming that knowledge is immune to criticism? Raising claims that have not been made in order to criticize them is a foolish way to proceed with an argument.

Eighth, in addition to nonsequiturs and false assumptions about what other people believe, Alexander also creates false dichotomies. He claims that "Hutchins's 'liberally educated man' understands, comprehends, and knows rather than questioning, puzzling, and challenging." This statement certainly does not represent Hutchins' view. Furthermore, there is no dichotomy between comprehending and questioning. Indeed, it is difficult to see how one could question if one did not understand that one did not understand. Alexander's false dichotomy is set up only to be knocked down.

Ninth, Alexander falsely represents the Great Books orientation to liberal education by claiming that it assumes all people can achieve infallible knowledge. Again, who has asserted this? It is true that Hutchins believed in the existence of knowledge and truth and that education is intended to move people in that direction. Yet, I can locate nothing in his writing that posits the godlike infallibility that Alexander says Hutchins believed all people could attain. Humans are, after all, a little lower than the angels. Someone smart enough to become Chancellor of the University of Chicago at age 29 was smart enough to know that only a few of us could become infallible.

Tenth, in the course of his text Alexander limits knowledge to propositions. It is precisely my argument that knowledge is not limited to propositions. Further, I argue even more radically that propositions are surrogates for what people know and as surrogates both constrain and make possible what can be publicly represented. My argument concerning the cognitive utilities of different forms of representation is that different forms of representation make different kinds of knowledge possible. What we learn about the Holocaust from Elie Weisel's *Night* we are unlikely to learn from a statistical description of the demographics of the Warsaw Ghetto uprising. If we want to know what the Sistine Chapel ceiling looks like we either need to go to Rome or to see a good photograph.

Our biological evolution has provided us with a variety of information pick-up systems through which we experience a multisensory world. Knowledge of what world is as diverse as our ability to use the systems that nature has provided. The forms of representation that our culture makes available makes it possible to represent to ourselves and to others the diversity of experience we have secured. To restrict knowledge to the propositional is to put a corset around human understanding, a corset that might satisfy those verificationists and fallibilists who require a tidy world, but that severely underestimates how and what we come to know. Our actual life and the knowledge that makes it possible is made of sturdier and more complex stuff. It is unfortunate that we have so limited a view of what human knowledge entails and such a restricted conception of the means through which it is secured. My book *Cognition and Curriculum* (Eisner, 1982) was intended to widen our perspective.

Eleventh, Alexander takes issue with the idea that perception is theory-laden. If it were not, much that social scientists do would be unnecessary. Cultural anthropology, for example, is directed precisely at trying to understand how people living in different cultures, with different belief systems and different theories, perceive and make sense of the world. Social science research methodologists work hard at creating the frameworks through which judges can share common perceptions in order to diminish differences across judges. Through attribution theory and perceptual psychology social scientists study the ways in which values and needs influence what people see and attribute to others. The literature is vast in this area and if there is any conclusion that is secure in the field of perceptual psychology it is that believing has as much to do with seeing as seeing has to do with believing.

Somehow Alexander concludes from the fact that perception is theory-laden that claims cannot be criticized. What he apparently forgets is that frameworks and theories can be shared and that human beings have the ability to shift perspectives, to see the world through the eyes of another, to enter into someone else's shoes. One of the marks of maturity according to developmental psychologists is the child's ability to take the place of another. Without it, we fail to understand each other. Only dogmatists who cannot "leave their own skin" are unable to do this. The idea that we could somehow have immaculate perception is an idea whose time has passed.

Twelfth, Alexander goes on to deny the validity of the argument that one needs to be religious to understand religious beliefs. Given his own deep theological commitments this is particularly paradoxical. One can, of course, understand, at some level, Catholicism without being a Catholic. One can, at some level, understand Buddhism without being a Buddhist. One can, at some level, understand Orthodox Judaism without being an Orthodox Jew. But the phrase "at some level" is critical. I can understand, at some level, the Han culture by reading about it in books. But there is an important difference between knowledge of and knowing about. To have knowledge of Han culture I need somehow to participate in that culture, to get at it, as Alexander says, "from the inside."

Again, one of the most difficult tasks anthropologists face is precisely that: to enter into a culture and to grasp it in terms that are as close as possible to those who live it. It is relatively easy to learn *about* how things are. It is a different kind of knowledge to vicariously participate in them. Art is one of the vehicles humans have created that makes such participation possible. That is one of the reasons we prize great writers. They do more than simply titillate; they put us there. Even more, they help us grasp, even beyond the culture itself, those aspects of a culture's life that it shares over time with those who live elsewhere. Between 1948 and 1959

Dostoevsky's *Crime and Punishment* was translated into 19 languages (United Nations Educational, Scientific, and Cultural Organization, 1949–1959). Why? One reason is that works of such quality do indeed help us become insiders.

Clifford Geertz, writing in his most recent books, *Works and Lives: The Anthropologist as Author* (1988), believes the ability to penetrate a culture and to convey that sense in text is so important that it is this feature that distinguishes the most important anthropologists from their lesser colleagues. Geertz writes:

> But perhaps the most intense objection [to attention to form in writing], coming from all quarters, and indeed rather general to intellectual life these days, is that concentrating our gaze on the ways in which knowledge claims are advanced undermines our capacity to take any of those claims seriously. Somehow, attention to such matters as imagery, metaphor, phraseology, or voice is supposed to lead to a corrosive relativism in which everything is but a more or less clever expression of opinion. Ethnography becomes, it is said, a mere game of words, as poems and novels are supposed to be. Exposing how the thing is done is to suggest that, like the lady sawed in half, it isn't done at all....
>
> The ability of anthropologists to get us to take what they say seriously has less to do with either a factual look or an air of conceptual elegance than it has with their capacity to convince us that what they say is a result of their having actually penetrated (or, if you prefer, been penetrated by) another form of life, of having, one way or another, truly "been there." And that, persuading us that this offstage miracle has occurred, is where the writing comes in.
>
> (pp. 2, 4–5)

I could go on, but I think the points I have made thus far indicate the sources of my discontent with Alexander's analysis. No one embracing pluralism or relativism as I do argues that what humans create is immune to criticism. What I do claim is that if I am playing checkers, I do not want to be judged by the rules of chess. If I am playing chess, I do not want to be responsible for the rules of checkers. I do not mind adhering to the rules, I only want the rules to be appropriate to the game I am playing. Without rules there is no game. Without a game there is no inquiry.

Alexander takes us on a tour that is based upon the assumption that there is a single, independent superordinate critical structure that can legitimately be applied to any work of the human mind, regardless of the form it takes or the theoretical framework it employs. Since he knows what that superordinate critical structure is, I'm sure it would be of interest to readers of *Curriculum Inquiry*. Perhaps in his response to this critique Alexander can share with the rest of us that superordinate, neutral, and objective set of criteria through which, regardless of what we have done, we can determine, once and for all, whether we have made a mistake.

## Postscript

After writing my critique of Alexander's article, I read D. C. Phillips's critique. Phillips says, "Furthermore, the relativist would argue that there is no 'superordinate' framework according to which it could *really* be determined whether or not there was a supreme being." Phillips is no relativist. He too believes there is such a framework. Yet, like Alexander, he does not let us in on what that framework is. Why not?

## References

Eisner, E. *Cognition and Curriculum*. New York: Longman, 1982.

Eisner, E. *The Educational Imagination* (2nd edn). New York: Macmillan, 1985.

Geertz, C. *Works and Lives: The Anthropolgist as Author*. Stanford, CA: Stanford University Press, 1988.

Goodman, N. *Ways of Worldmaking*. Indiana: Hackett, 1978.

United Nations Educational, Scientific, and Cultural Organization. *Index Translationum* (Vols 1–10). Paris: UNESCO, 1957.

# CHAPTER 14

# THE MISUNDERSTOOD ROLE OF THE ARTS IN HUMAN DEVELOPMENT

*Phi Delta Kappan,* 1992, 73(8): 591–595

In America 2000 the American people are presented with a reform agenda for their schools in which the arts are absent. Should they be? To provide an intelligent answer, one needs a concept of the arts and a view of the functions of education. What conception of the arts do people who shape education policy have? What image do they have of the aims of education? What kind of culture do they prize? What do they feel contributes to a life worth living? I believe that prevailing conceptions of the arts are based on a massive misunderstanding of the role of the arts in human development and education. This misunderstanding is rooted in ancient conceptions of mind, knowledge, and intelligence. Collectively, these conceptions impoverish the programs of schools and the education of the young.

Make no mistake, the curriculum we prescribe for schools and the time we allocate to subjects show children what adults believe is important for them to learn. There is no more telling indicator of the importance of the subjects students study than the amount of time allocated to them.[1] In American schools, the arts receive about two hours of instructional time per week at the elementary level and are generally not a required subject of study at the secondary level. The allocation of time to what we teach has other consequences as well. The amount of time allocated to a field of study influences the kinds of mental skills children have the opportunity to acquire.

Thus time represents both value and opportunity: value, because it indicates what is considered significant; opportunity, because the school can be thought of as a culture of opportunity. A culture in the biological sense is a place for growing things. Schools, too, are cultures. They are cultures for growing minds, and the direction this growth takes is influenced by the opportunities the school provides. These opportunities are defined by the school's program – its curriculum – and by the artistry with which teachers mediate that program. A school in which the arts are absent or poorly taught is unlikely to provide the genuine opportunities children need to use the arts in the service of their own development.

To speak of mind as developed or, even more pointedly, as grown may seem strange. Yet, in a basic sense, mind is a form of cultural achievement. We are born with brains, but our minds are made, and the shape they take is influenced by the culture in which that development occurs. For children, the school constitutes a primary culture for the development of mind. Therefore, decisions that are made about the school's priorities are also fundamental decisions about the kinds of minds children will have the opportunity to develop. Since our educational priorities are significantly influenced by our conceptions of mind, knowledge, and intelligence and since I believe that prevailing conceptions of the arts misconceive their primary features, I will briefly identify five widely held but fundamentally flawed beliefs about mind, knowledge, and intelligence that give direction to our schools. I will then describe what the arts can contribute to the educational development of the young.

*1. Human conceptual thinking requires the use of language.* Perhaps no belief shapes our understanding of cognition more than the conviction that language plays a necessary role in its operation. Indeed, thinking itself has sometimes been thought of as a kind of subvocalizing, a physical process that accompanies the chain of language activity that best represents the higher mental processes. Language and thought are inseparable.

There are many reasons why this belief will not stand scrutiny. First, to argue that language is a necessary condition for cognition is to conclude that children cannot think until they are able to speak. Yet anyone who has lived with a child knows first-hand how inquisitive a child can be before speech has developed and how intelligent such a child can be in solving problems: a child who cannot think cannot survive.

Second, language as we normally use it is a symbolic device, and symbolic devices that do not have referents do not symbolize. To symbolize, a symbol must be connected to a referent – that is, to an array of qualities one can experience, or that one has experienced, or that one has imagined. To speak meaningfully of baroque music – or of an oak tree or of a jet airplane – requires a conception of these objects and events, and these objects and events exist as qualities in our experience prior to the labels we assign to them. Contrary to popular opinion, in the beginning there was the image. It is the image that gives meaning to the label. The information of the image is a cognitive event.

*2. Sensory experience is low on the hierarchy of intellectual functioning.* The genesis of this belief can be found in Plato's ideas about the nature of human understanding. You will recall that, in the sixth book of *The Republic*, Socrates asks Glaucon to imagine a single, vertical line divided unequally into an upper and a lower segment. The longer upper half of the line represents the intelligible world; the bottom portion, the visible world. The intelligible world is grasped through rational procedures; the visible world, through perception. Rationality is high; perception is low. Plato's hierarchy was not diluted by the expansion of the Roman Empire. It is alive and well in the schools and universities of modern America.

But is it true that the perception of qualities is a low-level cognitive activity? When those qualities are complex and subtle, as they are in the arts, the perception of their relationships and nuances can be daunting. To put this matter in context, listen to Rudolf Arnheim:

> By "cognitive" I mean all mental operations involved in the receiving, storing, and processing of information: sensory perception, memory, thinking, learning. This use of the term conflicts with one to which many psychologists are accustomed and which excludes the activity of the senses from cognition. It reflects the distinction I am trying to eliminate; therefore I must extend the meaning of the terms "cognitive" and "cognition" to include perception. Similarly, I see no way of withholding the name of "thinking" from what goes on in perception. No thought processes seem to exist that cannot be found to operate, at least in principle, in perception. Visual perception is visual thinking.[2]

Ironically, indifference to the refinement of perception and inattention to the development of imagination have limited children's cognitive growth. Since no teacher has direct access to a child's mind, it is the child's ability to see the connections between the example the teacher uses, what the child already knows, and what the teacher hopes he or she will understand that makes the example instrumental to new meaning. In short, understanding depends on the child's ability to think by analogy and to grasp, often through metaphor, what needs to be understood. Poetry may indeed be closer to the most sophisticated forms of cognition than many people suspect.

3. *Intelligence requires the use of logic.* The importance of logic in the exercise of intelligence is clear *if* the form that is to be used to speak to the world is one in which the literal use of propositions is necessary. Mathematics and the sciences place a premium on a certain form of precision: literal statement. Logical consistency in such forms of representation is a condition for meaning. But to regard logic as a necessary condition for the exercise of intelligence is to restrict intelligence to those forms of representation that require its use.[3] The result of such a conception is to banish from the domain of intelligence those forms of representation whose meanings are not conveyed by and do not depend upon the use of logic. Poetry, for example, achieves meaning by employing language in ways that do not depend solely on logic; poetic meaning is often "extra-logical." The meanings conveyed by this extra-logical feature of poetry are what might better be thought of as the product of human rationality, and the same point pertains to the other arts.

Although rationality and logicality have been closely associated, rationality is a broader and more fundamental concept. Logic is one of the ways in which rationality is expressed, but it is not the only way. Individuals who manage human relationships well, those who draw or paint well, those who dance well, those who sing well – all do their thinking *within* the medium in which they work. Writing in 1934, John Dewey recognized that intelligence is usually regarded as the sole property of those whom we regard as intellectuals – especially, but not exclusively, in the academy. For those holding such a view, Dewey said:

> Any idea that ignores the necessary role of intelligence in the production of works of art is based upon identification of thinking with use of one special kind of material, verbal signs and words. To think effectively in terms of relations of qualities is as severe a demand upon thought as to think in terms of symbols, verbal and mathematical. Indeed, since words are easily manipulated in mechanical ways, the production of a work of genuine art probably demands more intelligence than does most of the so-called thinking that goes on among those who pride themselves on being "intellectuals."[4]

4. *Detachment and distance are necessary for true understanding.* Emotion has long been regarded as the enemy of reflective thought: the more we feel, the less we know. Now there certainly is a case to be made that such emotions as rage can radically influence one's perception and judgment. When running rampant, emotions can cloud vision, impair thought, and lead to trouble of all kinds.

But perception without feeling can do the same. Not to be able to feel, say, a human relationship is to miss what may very well be its most critical features. Not to be able to get a sense of history, not to be able to stand with Columbus on the deck of the *Santa Maria* and experience the pounding of the vessel by the relentless sea and the excitement of the first sighting of land is to miss – and perhaps even misunderstand – that aspect of history. And in failing to experience the emotion of such moments, we miss out on an aspect of life that has the potential to inform. Detachment and distance have their virtues, but they are limited resources for understanding, and any conception that assigns them dominion in cognition misconceives the ways in which understanding is fostered.

*5. Scientific method is the only legitimate way to generalize about the world.* The traditional, flawed conception of the arts claims that, when they are about anything, the arts are only about particulars: they yield no generalizations. Their virtues reside in delight rather than insight. They provide nothing that can reasonably be regarded as knowledge or understanding. Since the instrumental value of the products of science is considered greater than the delight derived from the arts (which in any case is usually thought to be merely a matter of personal taste), the value of the arts in comparison to the sciences is set low.

This conception of generalization defines much too narrowly the sources through which generalizations are actually made. The need to generalize is fundamental. Human beings generalized long before either science or statistics were invented. Generalizations are not only scientific and naturalistic; they also emerge from those intense forms of experience that we call the arts: concrete universals they are sometimes called.

Consider the paintings of Francis Bacon, Velàsquez, or Picasso, or consider the novels of John Steinbeck or Cervantes. Even fiction – perhaps especially fiction – can help us grasp the meaning not only of Don Quixote, the particular man, but of what we all share with him as we tilt at our own windmills, struggling to overcome seemingly insurmountable obstacles.[5] Cervantes helps us understand such travails, and, because he succeeds so well, we come away from his work with a new view, a view that enables us to recognize and reflect on one of the important features of our own lives. Through his work, we are also able to recognize these features elsewhere.

My argument thus far has focused on beliefs that have given direction to the educational enterprise. I have contended that the five beliefs I have described – that thought requires language, that sensory experience is a low-level function, that logic is necessary for intelligence, that detachment and distance foster understanding, and that science is the only legitimate way to generalize – create an intellectual climate that marginalizes the arts because what these beliefs celebrate seems to have little to do with what the arts provide. I will now focus on four contributions that I believe are central to all the arts. In doing so, I will not describe the specific contributions that each individual art makes to children of different ages. Instead, my aim is to identify the common, core contributions of the arts and their potential role in furthering the aims of education.

*1. Not all problems have single, correct answers.* One of the important lessons the arts teach is that solutions to problems can take many forms. This lesson from the arts would not be so important were it not for the fact that so much of what is taught in school teaches just the opposite lesson. Almost all of the basic skills taught in the primary grades teach children that there is only one correct answer to any question and only one correct solution to any problem. Spelling, arithmetic, writing, and even reading are pervaded by conventions and rules that, in effect, teach children to be good rule followers.

The arts teach a different lesson. They celebrate imagination, multiple perspectives, and the importance of personal interpretation. The last thing a modern teacher of the arts in America wants is a class full of standardized performances on a given task. The last thing an English teacher wants are idiosyncratic interpretations of how words are spelled. This is as it should be. Creativity in spelling is no virtue. But when the curriculum as a whole is so heavily saturated with tasks and expectations that demand fealty to rule, opportunities to think in unique ways are diminished. When carried to an extreme, the school's program becomes intellectually debilitating.

2. *The form of a thing is part of its content.* We have a tendency in our schools to separate form from content. Form is regarded as the shape something takes, and content is the meaning something conveys. In notational systems, we can live with such a dichotomy. In such systems, attention to form *as such* is largely irrelevant. For example, the number six can be symbolized in many ways, but its meaning is the same as long as one recognizes it as a six. The task is one of categorization. Early reading also emphasizes categorization. And when children learn to assign a form – say, a particular tree – to its category rather than to explore its distinctive features, perception is aborted. As Dewey pointed out, perception ceases when recognition begins. Assigning a label to an entity is an act of categorization, and when entities are assigned to categories, the exploration of their uniqueness stops.

The arts, however, teach the child that the grass is not simply green; it is lavender, grey, gold. And when it is green, its varieties are endless. Furthermore, in the arts and in much of life, the form something takes is very much a part of its content. In fact, what the content *is* often depends on the form it takes. The arts are prime examples of how this marriage of form and content is created and of the effect that it has on our experience.

I have made a special point here of emphasizing the function of the arts in human development. The arts are neglected resources and deserve attention in our schools. But I do not want to give the impression that at least some of the features that the arts possess are not also to be found in the sciences. The products of science have their own aesthetic features: the parsimony of theory, the beauty of conceptual models, the elegance of experiments, and the imagination and insight of interpretation. Indeed, the qualities for which a work of science is cherished are often related as much to its aesthetic appeal as to its explanatory power. A theory, after all, is a perspective about the way the world is. It is a way to secure a coherent view, and coherence is so important that we are often unwilling to give up the views we find attractive, despite contradictory evidence.

My point here is that, although my primary focus is on what may be called the fine arts, some of the features for which the arts are valued are also exhibited by the sciences. At the risk of oversimplifying the differences between the arts and the sciences, let me say that, in the context of creation, a work of science is a work of art.

3. *Having fixed objectives and pursuing clear-cut methods for achieving them are not always the most rational ways of dealing with the world.* There is a tendency in technologically oriented cultures to conceive of rationality as a method for tightly linking means and ends. To be rational, we tell children (and teachers), they must first formulate clear-cut objectives for their work, then use these objectives to define means for their achievement, and finally implement and evaluate the effectiveness and efficiency of the means for achieving the desired objectives.

Of course, there is a sense of sweet reason about such a procedure. Yet we often conceptualize and implement this process in mechanical ways: we give students goals for each lesson, we expect teachers to know exactly where they are headed, and we appraise classrooms and the quality of teaching on the basis of their achievement. We try to create a technology of management so that efficiency in learning and teaching is achieved and public accountability is provided. Our narrow conception of rationality is expressed in our incessant search for "what works"; it supports the belief that there is, in fact, a single best way, that the main task of researchers is to find it, and that the primary obligation of teachers is to use it. The entire effort to standardize educational outcomes is premised on a conviction that efficient and effective systems can be designed that will take luck out of the educational process.

These beliefs not only affect the conditions of teaching, they also create a climate that affects what and how students learn. Moreover, these views are antithetical to what the arts teach. The arts teach that goals need to be flexible and that surprise counts; that chance, as Aristotle wisely remarked, is something that art loves; that being open to the unanticipated opportunities that inevitably emerge in the context of action increases insight; and that purposeful flexibility rather than rigid adherence to prior plans is more likely to yield something of value. No painter, writer, composer, or choreographer can foresee all the twists and turns that his or her work will take. The *work* of art – by which I now mean the *act* of creation – does not follow an unalterable schedule but is a journey that unfolds. The relationship of the maker to the work is not that of lecturer to listener, but a conversation between the worker and the work.

In the context of much of today's schooling, the lessons taught by the arts are much closer to what successful and intelligent corporations do and to what cognitive psychologists are discovering constitute the most sophisticated forms of thinking.[6] These recent psychological discoveries are lessons artists have long understood. What are these lessons? They are that solving complex problems requires attention to wholes, not simply to discrete parts; that most complex problems have no algorithmic solutions; that nuance counts; and that purposes and goals must remain flexible in order to exploit opportunities that one cannot foresee. These newly discovered cognitive virtues are taught in every genuine *work* of art. Yet, ironically, the arts are typically thought of as noncognitive.

What is even more ironic is that, while we say that the function of schooling is to prepare students for life, the problems of life tend not to have the fixed, single correct answers that characterize the problems students encounter in the academic areas of schooling. The problems of life are much more like the problems encountered in the arts. They are problems that seldom have a single correct solution; they are problems that are often subtle, occasionally ambiguous, and sometimes dilemma-like. One would think that schools that wanted to prepare students for life would employ tasks and problems similar to those found outside of schools. This is hardly the case. Life outside of school is seldom like school assignments – and hardly ever like a multiple-choice test.

4. *In addition to their expressive function, the arts perform another function of critical importance.* In all that I have said so far, I have emphasized the contributions that the arts make toward helping students recognize that problems are not restricted to those having single correct answers, that form and content interact, and that purposeful flexibility is a mark of fluid intelligence coping with the vicissitudes of the unpredictable. But I have neglected a contribution that is surely as important. That contribution hinges on a distinction between *expression* and *discovery*. In the arts, students learn that some kinds of meaning may require the expressive forms that the arts make possible. In this sense, the arts expressively represent; they provide the forms through which insight and feeling can emerge in the public world. Indeed, humans invented the arts to serve expressive functions. For most people who have thought about the arts, this particular function is the one most commonly recognized.

But the arts also make discovery possible. Discovery occurs as students learn through adventures in the arts something of the possibilities of human experience. The journeys they take through the patterned sound we call music, through the visual forms we call painting, and through the metaphorical discourse we call poetry and literature are means through which students can discover their potential to respond. In other words, the arts can help students find their individual capacity to feel and imagine.

While such journeys are experienced through the arts, they can also be secured through the ordinary aspects of daily life when it is approached aesthetically. The world outside of art can become something to explore and relish: through the arts students can learn how to discover not only the possibilities the world offers but also their own possibilities. Expression and discovery are two major contributions the arts make to human development.

Just how are such discoveries made? As children learn to manipulate, manage, and monitor the nuances of voice, movement, and visual form, they discover the effects that their own fine-tuning achieves. As form is modulated, so too is feeling. As imagination is given permission to rise, children have the opportunity to enter worlds not tied to the literal, to the concrete, to the practical. Discovery emerges in the appreciation of qualities examined and images pursued. The arts, more than most fields, put a premium on such activities, and those activities can help students discover the special qualities of experience we call aesthetic.

Let me close by returning briefly to my initial claim that prevailing conceptions of the arts are based on a massive misunderstanding of their role in human development. This misconception is reflected in the narrow educational priorities of America 2000. In turn, these priorities are rooted in beliefs that regard mind as fixed rather than developed, that conceive of knowledge as the exclusive property of science, and that consider intelligence as limited to forms of abstract thought dependent on the use of logic. These narrow and misguided conceptions are not ivory tower theories without practical consequences. They influence our educational priorities, shape what we teach, and affect our children's lives. They result in schools that have an antiseptic environment that seldom provides even a nod to our sensuous, poetic, or imaginative sides.

I hope readers realize that my argument here is an optimistic one. What is pessimistic is a fixed view of mind, a conception of knowledge limited to what literal language can convey, and a view of intelligence constrained by the rules of logic. Human intellectual capacity is far wider. The realization of this capacity is surely more likely as we create a richer, more nurturant culture for our students. That culture, as I see it, ought to include significant opportunities for students to experience the arts and to learn to use them to create a life worth living. Indeed, providing a decent place for the arts in our schools may be one of the most important first steps we can take to bring about genuine school reform. Let's hope that, despite the priorities of America 2000, we have the courage and the wit to take it.

## Notes

1   Basil Bernstein, "On the Classification and Framing of Educational Knowledge," in Michael Young (ed.), *Knowledge and Control* (London: Collier, Macmillan, 1971), pp. 47–69.
2   Rudolf Arnheim, *Visual Thinking* (Berkeley, CA: University of California Press, 1969), pp. 13–14.
3   Elliot W. Eisner, *Cognition and Curriculum: A Basis for Deciding What to Teach* (New York: Longman, 1982).
4   John Dewey, *Art as Experience* (New York: Minton, Balch & Co., 1934), p. 46.
5   Nelson Goodman, *Ways of Worldmaking* (Indianapolis, IN: Hackett, 1978).
6   Lauren Resnick, *Toward the Thinking Curriculum: Current Cognitive Research* (Alexandria, VA: Association for Supervision and Curriculum Development, 1989) and James Greeno, "Perspectives on Thinking," *American Psychologist* (1989), 44: 134–141.

## CHAPTER 15

# EDUCATIONAL REFORM AND THE ECOLOGY OF SCHOOLING

*Teachers College Record*, 1992, 93(4): 610–627

The aspiration to reform schools has been a recurrent theme in American education. This aspiration frequently is stimulated by changes outside the United States. For example, the successful launching of *Sputnik I* on October 4, 1957, was sufficiently traumatic to our sense of national security to motivate the Congress of the United States to provide funds for the development of curricula in science and mathematics in order to "catch up with the Russians." During the 1960s over $100,000,000 was spent in building new programs in these fields and in retraining teachers. Despite all the effort and all the money, there is little that now remains in American schools that reflects the aspirations of the curriculum reform movement of the 1960s: Few of the curricula are to be found. *Sputnik I* motivated many, but its educational residue is difficult to find.

Since *Sputnik I*, American schools have been subjected to numerous reform efforts. The latest was initiated at a presidentially sponsored education summit on April 18, 1991, a summit attended by the nation's governors, by the US Secretary of Education, and by educators holding positions of high office, to announce Bush's new plans for educational reform. Yet only a few years earlier another president supported another effort at educational reform. *A Nation at Risk*, a document that enjoyed the highest level of visibility of any American educational policy paper published during this century, caught not only the attention but the enthusiasm of almost everyone.[1] Despite these reform efforts, the major features of schools remain largely as they were. What went wrong? Is there anything to learn from past efforts that might make current efforts more successful? This article first describes some of the conditions that make change in school difficult and then presents a potentially useful framework for developing a more effective agenda for school reform.

## Schools as robust institutions

One thing is clear: it is much easier to change educational policy than to change the ways in which schools function. Schools are robust institutions whose very robustness provides a source of social stability.[2] But what is it about schools that makes them so stable? Consider the following nine factors.

### Internalized images of teachers' roles

The images of what teachers do in classrooms, how they teach and organize children and tasks, are acquired very early in a child's life. In one sense, teaching is the only profession in which professional socialization begins at age five or six – when children begin school. In no other field do children have as much systematic opportunity to learn what a professional does in his or her work. Indeed, many children spend more time with their teachers than with their parents. This fact of early professional socialization should not be underestimated. Many young adults choose teaching because of their image of teachers and this image is not unrelated to what they believe being a teacher entails. Images of teaching and ways of being a teacher are internalized early in a child's life and bringing about significant changes in the ways in which teachers function requires replacing old images with new, more adequate ones. When a university teacher education program tries to promulgate a new image of teaching, but sends its young, would-be teachers back to schools that are essentially like the ones in which they were socialized, the prospects for replacing the old ideals in the all too familiar contexts in which new teachers work is dimmed: the new wine is changed when it is poured into the old bottle.

### Attachment to familiar pedagogical routine

Being a teacher, if it requires any set of skills and understandings, requires the ability to manage a group of children so that the class remains coherent and intact; nothing can be done if the class as such is in a state of disarray. But matters of management are only one part of the equation. The other is having something to teach. Teachers acquire a useful pedagogical repertoire by virtue of their experience in classrooms and that repertoire includes some degree of mastery of both the content they wish to teach and the methods and tactics through which to teach it.[3] This repertoire is extremely important to teachers, for it provides them with a source of security and enables them to cope with pedagogical demands efficiently. If a teacher does not know what to teach or is insecure about a subject, attention must be paid to matters of content. This can exacerbate both problems of management and problems of pedagogy. It is difficult to be pedagogically graceful when you are lost in unfamiliar territory. Teachers are often reluctant to relinquish teaching repertoires that provide an important source of security for them. New content areas might require new pedagogical routines. Given the overload that teachers typically experience in school – large numbers of students and many courses or subjects to teach – economy of effort is an important value.[4] Familiar teaching repertoires provide economy of effort; hence changes in schools that require new content and new repertoires are likely to be met with passive resistance by experienced teachers who have defined for themselves an array of routines they can efficiently employ. To make matters even less promising for school reform, few efforts at reform in the United States have provided time for teachers to develop mastery of new content or the skills required for new forms of teaching. Typically, new expectations for teachers are "add-ons" to already overloaded curricula and very demanding teaching schedules.

### Rigid and enduring standards for appropriate behavior

A third source of school stability resides in the persistence of school norms. Every social occasion from the birthday party to the funeral service is pervaded by social norms that prescribe implicitly, if not always explicitly, ways to be in the world. Schools are no different. What teachers are supposed to be, how children are supposed to behave, what constitutes an appropriate and fair set of expectations for a subject, are defined by the norms of schooling. These norms have been described by Dreeben, Jackson, Lortie, Lightfoot, Powell, and Eisner, and decades earlier by Waller.[5] In the past two decades educational scholars on the political Left such as Apple and Giroux have also examined the ways in which the pervasive and sometimes covert norms of schooling shape attitudes, create inequities, and often reproduce the inequities of the society at large.[6] Undoubtedly some of their observations are correct, but my point here is not so much to make a statement about what Bourdieu has called "cultural reproduction"[7] as to make it plain that if schools are to seriously address matters of intellectual development, the cultivation of sensibility, and the refinement of the imagination, changes must be made in educational priorities. Such changes will require institutional norms different from those now salient in schools.

Norms, after all, reflect values. They adumbrate what we care about. Trying to convert schools from academic institutions – institutions that attempt to transmit what is already known – into intellectual ones – institutions that prize inquiry for its own sake – will require a change in what schools prize. Most efforts at school reform fail to address this challenge. The tack taken in most educational policy papers is typically superficial and the language is technical. The problem is often thought to be solvable by curriculum "installation"; we are to "install" a new curriculum and then "align it" with other curricula. We typically employ a language of change that reveals a shallow and mechanistic conception of what real change requires. Policymakers cannot install new norms in schools any more than they can install new teaching methods. Both need careful cultivation and nurture. By persisting in using inappropriate mechanical metaphors for thinking about the process of school reform, we persist in misconceptualizing the problem and undermining genuine change.

## Teacher isolation

A fourth factor that thwarts school reform is the fact that in the United States, we have structured schools and defined teaching roles in ways that make improved teaching performance difficult to achieve. Consider the ways in which teachers are insulated and isolated from their colleagues. Teaching, by and large, in both elementary and secondary schools is a lonely activity. It is not that teachers have no contact with people; after all, they are with students all day. The point is that they have very little contact with other adults in the context of their classrooms. Some school districts in the United States and some enlightened policies provide teachers with aides and with special assistance by certified professionals, but these human resources are relatively rare. Most teachers spend most of their time in their own classrooms, closed environments, with twenty-five to thirty-five children or adolescents. Of course, there are occasions – lunchtime and the occasional staff meeting, for example – where teachers see each other, but seldom in the context of teaching. Even teachers who have worked in the same school for twenty years are likely to have never seen their colleagues teach.

The result of professional isolation is the difficulty that teachers encounter in learning what they themselves do in their own classrooms when they teach. Classrooms, unlike the rooms in which ballerinas practice their craft, have no mirrors. The only mirrors available to teachers are those they find in their students' eyes, and these mirrors are too small. Hence the teacher, whether elementary or secondary, must learn on his or her own, usually by reflecting on how things went. Such personal reflection is subject to two forms of ignorance, one type remediable, the other not.

The two types of ignorance I speak of are primary and secondary ignorance. Primary ignorance about teaching, or about anything else for that matter, is when you do not know something but you *know* that you do not know it. In such a situation, you can do something about it. Secondary ignorance is when you do not know something but do *not know* you do not know it. In this case, you can do nothing about the problem. The professional isolation of teachers fosters secondary ignorance. How can a teacher learn that he or she is talking too much, not providing sufficient time for student reflection, raising low-order questions, or is simply boring students? Teachers unaware of such features of their own performance are in no position to change them. Educational reform efforts that depend on new and better approaches to teaching yet make it difficult for teachers to learn about their own teaching are destined to have a poor prognosis for success. Despite what seems obvious, we have designed schools both physically and organizationally to restrict the teacher's access to other professionals. Discretionary time for teachers is limited and although the school principal could make the time to provide teachers with useful feedback, he or she often does not have the inclination or the skills or is so preoccupied with other matters of lesser importance that attention to the improvement of teaching become marginalized. As a result, it is not unusual for teachers to feel that no one really cares about the quality of their work.[8]

## Inadequacies of in-service education

In-service education is the major means used in the United States to further the quality of teaching. But in-service education typically means that teachers will attend meetings or conferences to hear experts (often university professors who have had little contact with schools) provide advice on the newest developments in teaching mathematics, social studies, or the language arts. The assumption is that once teachers are exposed to such wisdom, they will implement the practices suggested in their own classrooms. The in-service seminar is one in which the advice-giver typically has never seen the teachers who comprise the audience. The advice-giver does not know the teachers' strengths or their weaknesses. The situation is much like a voice coach giving advice to a singer whom he or she has never heard sing. General recommendations go only so far.

Thus, we try to improve teaching by asking teachers to leave their classrooms so that they can travel to distant locations in order to get general advice from people who have never seen them teach. One does not need to be a specialist in learning theory to know that for complex forms of human action, general advice is of limited utility. Feedback needs to be specific and focused on the actor in context. What we do, however, is to decontextualize in-service education and, as a result, weaken its potential usefulness.

My remarks should not be interpreted to mean that in-service programs for teachers cannot be useful, but that in-service education without some direct observation of teachers in the context of their own classrooms is not likely to be adequate. In this case, as in so many others, we have greatly underestimated what it will take to improve what teachers actually do in their own classrooms.

## Conservative expectations for the function of schools

Another factor that contributes to the robust quality of schools and their resistance to change is that the expectations of both students and parents regarding the function of schools and the forms of practice that are appropriate are usually conservative. What does a good teacher do? What kinds of questions are appropriate for students to ask? How much freedom should teachers provide? What kinds of problems and projects should students be asked to engage in? How should students be evaluated? Should they have any role in their own assessment? Answers to each of the foregoing questions are related to expectations of what schools, classrooms, and teachers should be. The expectations of parents and students are often quite traditional on such matters.

The call for "back to basics" – a return to the educational practices of the past – is regarded by many as the way to save American schools from mediocrity or worse. Familiar practices are not threatening; the past almost always has a rosy glow. Practices that violate tradition are often regarded as subversive of high-quality education. School reform efforts that challenge tradition can be expected to encounter difficulties, especially from the segment of the population that has done well in socioeconomic terms and has the tendency to believe that the kind of schooling that facilitated their success is precisely the kind their own children should receive.

Expectations by students for practices with which they are familiar go beyond general forms of teaching practice; they include expectations for the way in which specific subjects should be taught. For example, students whose experience in art classes has not included learning about the history of art or writing about the qualities of particular works of art may regard such practices as distasteful; for many students reading and writing have no place in an art class. A program in social studies that requires group cooperation on project-centered work can be regarded as inappropriate by students whose concept of social studies is one that is devoted exclusively to individual tasks. Parents whose experience in learning mathematics emphasized drill and practice may regard an arithmetic program oriented toward the practical applications of arithmetic as less intellectual and less rigorous. The point here is that educational consumers can exercise a conservative function in the effort at educational reform. It is difficult for schools to exceed in aim, form, and content what the public is willing to accept.

## Distance between educational reformers and teachers implementing change

Reform efforts in American education are almost always from the top down. For whatever reason, educational policymakers mandate change, often through national or state reports or through new educational legislation that sends the message of changed policies to those "on the front line." The tacit assumption is that once new policies are formulated, a stream of change will begin to flow with little further assistance. When assistance is provided it sometimes comes in the form of new policy papers, curriculum guides, and district conferences. Typically, the structural conditions of schools stay the same. Teachers remain on the receiving end of policy and have little hand in its formation.

The attraction of providing teachers with a hand in shaping educational policy is quite limited if one believes educational practice, at its best, will be uniform across school districts and geographic regions. If one's model of ideal educational practice is one of standardized practice, the way in which an efficient manufacturing plant might function, giving $2\frac{1}{2}$ million American teachers the opportunity to determine what is best for their own school or school district can appear chaotic or even nihilistic. Thus, there is a real tension in the process of school reform. At one end there is the desire to create a uniform and "equitable" program for children and adolescents, regardless of who they are or where they live. This requires centralized decision making. At the other end is the realization that unless teachers feel some commitment to change, they are unlikely to change. To feel such commitment it is important for teachers to have the opportunity to participate in shaping the change process.

Many veteran teachers, those who have seen educational reforms come and go, are skeptical about new reforms and respond with passive resistance: they simply ride out the new policies. This can be done without much difficulty for two reasons. First, educational reform policies come and go about every five or six years, more visible in the media than in the classroom. Second, once the classroom door is closed, the ways in which teachers teach is essentially a private affair. Elementary school principals rarely monitor teaching practice closely, and at the secondary level, they do not have the subject-matter expertise in a wide variety of fields to do so.

The growing desire to engage teachers in the change process has led to the notion of "teacher empowerment." In general, the idea is that, as important stakeholders in what schools do, teachers need to have authority to plan and monitor the quality of the educational process in their schools. The effort, in a sense, is to democratize educational reform by giving teachers a say-so in what happens. This say-so includes defining curricular goals and content, improving teaching practice, and developing ways to assess what children experience during the school day. In some cases, it includes decision making about budget allocations through a process called site-based management.

A practice related to this general thrust of teacher improvement is called *action research*. Action research is intended to encourage teachers to collaborate with other teachers and, at times, with university professors in order to undertake research in their own school or classroom.[9] The aim of the enterprise is to stimulate professional reflection by encouraging teachers to take a more reflective intellectual role in understanding and improving their own teaching practice.

It is not yet clear just how many teachers are interested in being "empowered." It is not yet clear how many teachers want to do educational research. It is not yet clear how many teachers are interested in assuming larger responsibilities such as the formulation of educational policy. Many teachers gain their deepest satisfaction in their own classroom. The classroom is their professional home and they are not particularly interested in collaboration or in doing educational research. As I indicated earlier, conceptions of the teacher's role are acquired early in development and teachers are often comfortable with these conceptions. If a bird has been in a cage for a decade and suddenly finds the door open, it should not be too surprising if the bird does not wish to leave. The familiar is often more comfortable than the uncertainty of the unknown.

Empowering teachers is more complex than I have suggested. When innovative reform policies are formulated or new aims or programs presented, they are often prescribed *in addition* to what teachers are already doing; they are add-ons. Given that the teacher's day is already quite demanding, it should come as no surprise that taking on added responsibilities for the formulation of policy or for monitoring the school should be regarded by some as an extra burden. Put more bluntly, it is unrealistic to expect overworked teachers who have very little discretionary time in the school day to be more active in their school without relief from some of their current responsibilities. To provide relief will require restructuring. Restructuring is likely to require money, something that is in scarce supply in many school districts. As a result, much of the activity in the context of school reform is more at the level of rhetoric than at the level of practice.

As educational reformers have become increasingly aware of the difficulty of bringing about significant change in the ways in which schools function, they have talked about the restructuring of schools.[10] For this term, which to me generates an image of fundamental rather than superficial change, there are almost as many meanings as there are writers. In my discussions with school principals and school superintendents, "restructuring" meant to them changing the ways in which funds were allocated rather than reconceptualizing the organization, content, and aims of schools. Conceptualized in terms of financial resource allocation, the power of the concept was neutralized.

Another complexity regarding teacher empowerment involves the question of authority and responsibility. If teachers are given the authority to change local educational policy in their schools, will they assume responsibility for the consequences of those policies? If so, how will those consequences be determined? What will be the responsibilities of the school district's superintendent and the district's central office staff? Just what is the appropriate balance between authority and responsibility and who is responsible for what when responsibility and authority are localized?

These questions are not yet resolved. The recent interest in giving teachers a genuine role in the reform of schools is seen by many (including me) as salutary, but how lines of authority and responsibility are to be drawn is far from clear. Can genuine school improvement occur without commitment from teachers? It seems unlikely. Just how can such commitment be developed? These questions are on the current agenda of school reform in the United States.

## Artificial barrier between disciplines and between teachers

An eighth factor that impedes school reform pertains to the ways in which the school itself is organized. One of the most problematic features in the organization of schools is the fact that they are *structurally fragmented*, especially at the secondary level. By structurally fragmented I refer to the fact that curricula are divided and organized into distinct subject matters that make it difficult for students to make connections between the subjects they study.[11] In the United States, secondary school students will typically enroll in four to six subjects each semester. As a result, teachers must teach within narrow time blocks. They teach four to seven classes each day, see 130 to 180 students each day; students must move every fifty minutes to another teacher who teaches them another subject. There is no occupation in American society in which workers must change jobs every fifty minutes, move to another location, and work under the direction of a different supervisor. Yet this is precisely what we ask of adolescents, hoping, at the same time, to provide them with a coherent educational program.

Structural fragmentation also pertains to the fact that the form of school organization that we have created isolates teachers. And as I have already indicated, isolation makes it difficult for teachers to receive critical and supportive feedback about their work. Teachers experience little colleagueship in the context of the classroom, and of course it is in the context of a classroom that the real business of education is played out. Unless there is significant change in the way in which teachers and students live and work together, any significant change in schools is illusory.

Because the forms of school organization are cultural rather than natural entities, they need not be regarded as being of necessity; that is, they can be other than the way they are. Moses did not receive instructions about school organization on

Mount Sinai, at least as far as I know. Yet we persist in maintaining school structures that might not be in the best interests of either teachers or students. I can tell you that the organizational structure and the curricular requirements of the secondary school I attended forty years ago are quite like the organizational structure and curricular requirements secondary school students encounter today. How much structural and curricular overlap is there between the secondary school you attended and today's secondary schools?

### Feckless piecemeal efforts at reform

The last factor that impedes significant educational reform is the piecemeal and superficial way in which reformers think about educational reform. Minor efforts at change are eventually swamped by the factors in the school that do not change. Robust systems can withstand minor incursions. Thus the need, I believe, is to think about school reform ecologically, or at least systemically. Aspects of schooling that remain constant militate against those features of schooling that are being changed. For example, efforts to help teachers learn how to teach inductively are not likely to succeed if the evaluation system the school employs rewards other types of teaching. Efforts to encourage teachers to engage in reflective teaching are likely to be feckless if teachers have no time during the school day for reflection. Efforts to create intellectual coherence in the student's understanding are likely to fail if the form that the curriculum takes makes coherence impossible. Improvement in teaching is unlikely as long as teachers get no useful feedback on the work they actually do in their own classrooms.

It is important in educational reform to think big even if one must start small. There needs, I believe, to be an overall conception of what schools are as forms of shared communal life as well as persuasive and attractive visions of what such shared living might become. The next section describes a means for securing a better understanding of what schools are as living organisms. The last section provides a model or framework that identifies important candidates for educational change.

## Schools as living systems

The place to begin school reform is in the effort to understand the ways that schools actually function, what it is they teach both implicitly and explicitly, and how they reward the people who spend so much of their lives there. Unfortunately, the effects of efforts at school reform are based on the results of standardized achievement testing and the results of such testing say little about the processes that lead to them. We cannot know much about the educational quality of schools simply by examining test scores. We need a finer, more refined screen, one that focuses on the processes as well as the outcomes of schooling.

Much recent research in the United States has focused on the quality and process of schooling.[12] Some of these studies have used ethnographic research methods or modifications of such methods.[13] Some studies have been rooted in critical approaches[14] and others in methods derived from the arts and humanities.[15] As a result of this work a number of salient features of schools, many of which are quite common across a variety of schools, have been identified: structural fragmentation, teacher isolation, didactic teaching, treaties between teachers and students, the particular ways in which effective teachers and school administrators relate to students, the emphasis on extrinsic rewards, and the like. How salient are these features? Are there important differences? How can we know?

The only way I know to discover the salient and significant features of schools is to look. The implications of what is found will depend on what is found and on the educational values that give direction to the schools themselves.

To look at schools as I have suggested is not enough. Anyone can look. The trick is to see. Seeing requires an enlightened eye. It requires schemata through which different genres of teaching can be appreciated.[16] It is a mistake to assume that all good teaching has identical characteristics, that one size fits all. Thus, to see what happens in classrooms requires a willingness and a set of sensibilities and schemata that can pick up the distinctive features of particular types of teaching. These types of teaching are not simply generic. They emerge within the constraints and possibilities of particular subject matters – *what* one teaches counts. As Stodolsky says, "the subject matters."[17] Even more than this, any given subject matter – history, for example, or mathematics – can have a wide variety of aims and methods. Perceiving school processes requires an understanding of the types of teaching possible within the subject-matter field and an awareness of the varieties of quality that can be manifested within each.

This article is not the place to describe in detail the forms of perception and description of life in schools I have in mind. Readers interested in what I have called "educational connoisseurship" and "educational criticism" can find the approach described in a variety of articles and particularly in my latest book.[18] The point is that school reform should begin with a decent understanding of the schools themselves, not with old memories of schooling held by middle-aged men and women working in institutions far removed from schools. A major part of the current investment in school reform should be aimed, in my opinion, at trying to understand such processes as how teaching takes place in particular fields, what constitutes the implicit as well as the explicit norms of the school, the sense that students make of what they study, the aims that teachers say are important and the relationship of those aims to what they do in their classrooms. It should also deal with the intellectual quality of what is taught and the procedures that are used in the classroom to motivate and reward students and teachers. The aim of such inquiry is to secure an organic, cultural picture of schools as places to be. The basic questions direct attention to the value of what goes on in them. Such questions are easy to raise but difficult to answer, yet unless they are raised educational reform is likely to be predicated on very partial forms of understanding of what schools are like for teachers and students.

As I have indicated, the kind of study I am suggesting is one that is organic or cultural. To study schools in this way is likely to require an approach to educational research that is *qualitative* in character. It is an approach that pays attention to the processes of schooling and to the context in which those processes occur. I know of no way to find out what schools are like except by going to schools themselves to see, to describe, to interpret, and to evaluate what is occurring. Such an understanding can provide a foundation for reform that addresses what is genuinely important in education.

## Five major dimensions of school reform

In the final section of this article, I identify five dimensions of schooling that I believe must be considered in order to think comprehensively about the reform of schools. I call these dimensions the *intentional*, the *structural*, the *curricular*, the *pedagogical*, and the *evaluative*.

My thesis is that meaningful and educationally significant school reform will require attention to each of these dimensions. Attention to one direction without attention to the others is not likely to lead to change. Where change does occur, it is likely to be temporary and superficial.

*The intentional* refers to what it is that schools are intended to accomplish. What really counts in schools? Defining intentions pertains to both the general aims of schooling and the aims of the particular subject matters being taught. Consider, for example, intentions that are typically *not* given high priority in schools or in reform efforts: fostering a desire to continue learning what schools teach, the development of curiosity, stimulating the ability to think metaphorically, creating a caring attitude toward others, the development of productive idiosyncracy, the ability to define one's own goals and the ability to pursue them, the ability to raise perceptive questions about what one has studied. An argument for each of these intentions could be made that is cogent and relevant to the world in which children live. If such intentions were taken seriously, their ramifications for educational practice would be considerable. My point here is not to advocate such intentions (although I do not reject them) but rather to illustrate the idea that the conventional intentions schools serve are not necessarily the most important ones. What is important will depend on an argued set of educational values and an understanding of the students and society schools serve.

Most efforts at school reform operate on the assumption that the important outcomes of schooling, indeed the primary indices of educational success, are high levels of academic achievement as measured by standardized achievement tests. Just what do scores on academic achievement tests predict? They predict scores on other academic achievement tests. But schools, I would argue, do not exist for the sake of high levels of performance in the context of schools, but in the context of life outside of the school. The significant dependent variables in education are located in the kinds of interests, voluntary activities, levels of thinking and problem solving, that students engage in when they are not in school. In other words, the real test of successful schooling is not what students do in school, but what they do outside of it.

If such intentions were genuinely central in our educational planning, we would probably make other arrangements for teaching, curriculum, and evaluation than those we now employ. Significantly new intentions are likely to require new ways of leading educational lives.

*The structural* aspects of schooling pertain to the ways in which we have organized subjects, time, and roles. I have already alluded to the fact that we structure subjects by type. We use what Bernstein has called a collectiontype curriculum.[19] Each subject is bounded and kept distinct from others. This boundedness is reinforced by how time is allocated, what is taught, and in some secondary schools, where on the school campus a subject matter department is located. In some schools there is a section of the school devoted exclusively to the sciences, another to the fine arts, another to business and computer studies. We emphasize separateness and reinforce that separateness through a departmentalized structure.

Departmentalization might be, in the long run, the most rational way to structure schools, but it is not the only way. My aim here is not to advocate a particular change, but to problematize the structures we have lived with for so long that we come to think about them as natural entities rather than as the results of decisions that could have been otherwise. Is a departmentalized structure the best way to organize schools? It depends on a set of educational values and an exploration of alternative modes of organization. In the United States very few efforts at school reform – open schooling being a vivid exception – have tried to restructure schools. The curriculum reform movement of the 1960s attempted to create curricula designed to fit into existing school structures. Can new messages change the school or will the school change the messages?

The structure of the school also influences the way in which roles are defined. In American schools there are basically two roles for adults: teacher and principal. The teacher spends his or her day with children or adolescents. The principal seldom is responsible for teaching functions and has far more discretionary time than do teachers. If a teacher wants to secure more professional life-space, he or she must leave teaching and become a school administrator. Once such a decision is made, for all practical purposes, there is no return to the classroom – as the caterpillar, once it becomes a butterfly, remains a butterfly until it dies.

Working as an educator in a school need not be limited to two roles, nor must these roles be conceived of as "permanent." Schools can be structured so that teachers who are interested can devote some years or parts of some years to curriculum development, to the design of better evaluation methods for their school, to serving as mentors to beginning teachers. Teachers could create liaisons with community agencies such as museums, hospitals, cultural centers, retirement homes, in order to secure services that could enhance and enrich school programs. Teachers could devote time to research in their own school and assist parents with children who are having difficulty in school. There is a host of possible roles that could make important generic contributions to a school's way of life, but for these contributions to be made, educators need to create school structures that permit them to be developed. American schools, with few exceptions, are structured to inhibit these roles rather than to encourage their formation. The paradigms we have internalized about the nature of schooling – the way time is allocated, the way subjects are defined, the way in which roles are specified – are so strong that efforts at reform are typically conceptualized to fit into the constraints of those structures, thus defining the parameters within which reform efforts are to occur.

*The curricular* is the third dimension that needs attention in any effort to create genuinely significant educational reform. Decisions about curriculum can be made about several of its features. Among the most important are those about the content that is to be provided, about the kind of activities that are to be used to help students experience that content, and the way in which the curriculum itself is to be organized. As I have indicated, most efforts at curriculum reform in the United States have left the organization of curriculum intact: separate subjects separately taught has been the dominant mode of organization, although at the elementary level such organization is less prevalent than at the middle or secondary school levels. Yet in spite of frequent admonitions by educational scholars to reduce curriculum fragmentation,[20] the separation of subject matters persists and is supported by the infrastructure of professional education: testing programs, university admissions criteria, teacher training programs, specialization among subject-matter teachers. This collection-type form of curriculum organization[21] is not the only way in which curriculum can be organized. Whether it is the most appropriate form, given the potential costs of other forms of organization, depends upon our educational intentions. If integration of learning is desired, separation may indeed be problematic. Again, my point here is not to argue for a specific form of curriculum reorganization as much as to urge the careful rethinking of the organization that now prevails.

What is taught in the first place is of primary importance. One way to increase the probability that something *will not be learned* is to ensure that it *will not be taught*, that is, to make a subject matter a part of a *null curriculum*.[22] The fine arts are often relegated to this position. For many citizens the arts are someone else's pleasures. Large and important legacies of culture go unseen, unheard, unread, and as a result, unloved. Schools perpetuate this state of ignorance by withholding from the young important parts of their cultural legacy. The list could be expanded.

Regarding the activities that allow students to grasp or experience what is taught in schools, according to Goodlad, the lecture still dominates at the secondary school level.[23] Students typically have few opportunities to formulate their own questions and to pursue them. They are expected to do what the teacher requests; their role is in the application of means rather than the formulation of ends. They become, says Apple, deskilled, unable to formulate the aims and goals they seek to attain.[24]

The provision of opportunities for students to define at least some of their purposes is arguably an important educational aim and the ability to do so an important educational achievement. To what extent does it occur? Genuine reform of schools will require attention not only to intentions and school structure, but to the content, tasks, and forms of organization of the school curriculum. Which aspects of curricula should receive attention will depend on what is now occurring in schools; the only way to know that is to go to the schools to see.

The fourth dimension needing attention in genuine school reform is *the pedagogical* aspects of educational practice. If the curriculum is the systole of education, teaching is the diastole. No curriculum teaches itself and how it is mediated is crucial. In fact, I find it useful to distinguish between the *intended* curriculum and the *operational* curriculum.[25] What we plan to teach – materials, outlines, projected activities, and goals – constitutes the intended curriculum. The operational curriculum is the curriculum that is played out in the context of classroom life. In this process pedagogy plays a crucial role. When programs call for new teaching skills that teachers do not possess – inductive teaching, for example – teachers understandably use the skills they possess and these may not be adequate to the task.

No intended curriculum can be followed by teachers as a script; the classroom is too uncertain a place for recipes. The professional teacher needs to use the curriculum as a resource, as an amplifier of his or her own ability. Different teachers need different amounts of guidance and specificity. Thus, the pedagogical is a central aspect of school reform. Unless classroom practices change, changes on paper, whether in policy or in curriculum, are not likely to be of much consequence for students.

How can students of education know about the ways in which teaching occurs? What are the strengths teachers possess and what are their weaknesses? Are there important educational consequences on both sides of the ledger? These questions are, of course, easy to pose but difficult to answer. At minimum, qualitative studies of classroom life must be undertaken. Such studies could provide the basis on which effective change strategies could be initiated and could provide a focus for efforts aimed at pedagogical issues. *Both* curriculum and pedagogy need to be seen in context and both need attention for strengthening school reform.

Finally, the fifth dimension needing attention in school reform is *the evaluative*. It makes no sense whatsoever to write policy papers about educational reform and to prepare syllabi and curriculum guides for teachers that advocate a new direction for educational practice and continue to assess the outcomes of schooling on instruments that reflect older, more traditional views. Yet, this is what we often do. Consider the proposition that good schools increase individuality and cultivate productive idiosyncracy. Consider the idea that good schools increase differences among students, not diminish them. If we truly embraced these views, how would we go about evaluating the educational effectiveness of schools? Would commensurability remain an important criterion? What kinds of opportunities could be provided to students to develop what they have learned? To what extent would we use closed-ended examinations?

High-stake assessment procedures symbolically and practically represent what "higher-ups" care about and performance on such procedures significantly affects both the options students have and the professional reputation of teachers. How outcomes are evaluated is a major agent influencing what teachers and school administrators pay attention to. Thus, the redesign of assessment instruments so that they provide information about what teachers and others care about most from an educational perspective is a fundamental aspect of school reform. Schools cannot move in one direction and assess teachers and students using procedures that represent values in quite another direction.

Evaluation, however, should not be conceived of exclusively in terms of outcome assessment. Evaluation, it seems to me, should be regarded as an educational medium. The processes of teaching and the quality of what is taught, as well as their outcomes, are the proper subject matter of an adequate approach to educational evaluation. If the quality of the content being taught is poor, it does not matter much if the quality of teaching is good. Indeed, if the content being taught is pernicious, excellence in teaching is a vice.

Evaluation is an aspect of professional educational practice that should be regarded as one of the major means through which educators can secure information they can use to enhance the quality of their work. Evaluation ought to be an ongoing part of the process of education, one that contributes to its enhancement, not simply a means for scoring students and teachers.

These factors, the *intentional*, the *structural*, the *curricular*, the *pedagogical*, and the *evaluative*, are all important and interacting dimensions of schooling. Collectively they constitute a kind of ecology of schooling. To bring about reform in schools that is more than superficial and short-term requires attention to all of them.

To consider these dimensions not simply as an academic enterprise but as an activity leading to an agenda that can be acted on is the tough test of educational reform efforts. In some way that agenda has to be set. In setting this agenda teachers will need to be involved, as well as school administrators who themselves are not afraid of new forms of practice. The details of this agenda – the role, for example, that universities might play in school reform – cannot be addressed in this article. Yet unless the plan for school reform is comprehensive, it is likely to leave little residue in the long run. We sometimes say in the United States that educational reform is like a pendulum swing – we go back and forth. Pendulums are objects that move without going any place. Recognizing the ecological character of schools and facing up to the magnitude of the task of educational reform are important beginning efforts in dismounting from the pendulum.

## Notes

1  USA Research, *A Nation at Risk: The Full Account* (Cambridge, MA: USA Research, 1984).
2  Larry Cuban, "Reforming Again, Again, and Again," *Educational Researcher*, 19(1) (January–February 1990), 3–13.
3  David Berliner, "In Pursuit of the Expert Pedagogue," *Educational Researcher*, 15(7) (1986), 5–10.

4 D. Flinders, "What Teachers Learn from Teaching: Educational Outcomes of Instructional Adaptation" (PhD dissertation, Stanford University, 1987).

5 Robert Dreeben, *On What Is Learned in School* (New York: Addison-Wesley, 1968); Philip W. Jackson, *Life in Classrooms* (New York: Holt, Rinehart & Winston, 1968); Dan C. Lortie, *School Teacher: A Psychological Study* (Chicago, IL: University of Chicago Press, 1975); Sara Lawrence Lightfoot, *The Good High School: Portraits of Character and Culture* (New York: Basic Books, 1983); Arthur G. Powell, Eleanor Farrar, and David K. Cohen, *The Shopping Mall High School: Winners and Losers in the Educational Marketplace* (Boston, MA: Houghton Mifflin, 1985); Elliot W. Eisner, *What High Schools Are Like: Views from the Inside* (Stanford, CA: Stanford School of Education, 1985); and Willard W. Waller, *The Sociology of Teaching* (New York: John Wiley, 1932).

6 Michael Apple, *Education and Power* (Boston, MA: Routledge & Kegan Paul, 1982); and Henry Giroux, *Critical Pedagogy, the State, and Cultural Struggle* (Albany, NY: University of New York Press, 1989).

7 Pierre Bourdieu, *Reproduction in Education's Society and Culture* (London: Sage Publications, 1977).

8 Eisner, *What High Schools Are Like.*

9 J. M. Atkin, "Can Educational Research Keep Pace with Education Reform?" *Kappan* 71(3) (November 1989), 200–205.

10 *Restructuring California Education: A Design for Public Education in the Twenty-first Century, Recommendations to the California Business Round Table* (Berkeley, CA: B. W. Associates, 1988).

11 Eisner, *What High Schools Are Like.*

12 John I. Goodlad, *A Place Called School: Prospects for the Future* (New York: McGraw-Hill, 1984); Theodore R. Sizer, *Horace's Compromise: The Dilemma of the American High School* (Boston, MA: Houghton Mifflin, 1984); Powell, Farrar, and Cohen, *The Shopping Mall High School*; and Eisner, *What High Schools Are Like.*

13 H. Wolcott, *The Man in the Principal's Office* (Prospect Heights, IL: Waveland Press, 1984).

14 P. Willis, *Learning to Labor* (Lexington, KY: D.C. Heath, 1977).

15 Lightfoot, *The Good High School.*

16 Elliot W. Eisner, *The Enlightened Eye: Qualitative Inquiry and the Enhancement of Educational Practice* (New York: Macmillan, 1991).

17 S. S. Stodolsky, *The Subject Matters* (Chicago, IL: University of Chicago Press, 1988).

18 Eisner, *The Enlightened Eye.*

19 Basil Bernstein, "On the Classification and Framing of Educational Knowledge," in *Knowledge and Control*, M. Young (ed.) (London: Collier-Macmillan, 1971), pp. 47–69.

20 Eisner, *What High Schools Are Like* and Sizer, *Horace's Compromise.*

21 Bernstein, "On the Classification and Framing of Educational Knowledge."

22 Eisner, *What High Schools Are Like.*

23 Goodlad, *A Place Called School.*

24 Apple, *Education and Power.*

25 Eisner, *What High Schools Are Like.*

# CHAPTER 16

# FORMS OF UNDERSTANDING AND THE FUTURE OF EDUCATIONAL RESEARCH*

*Educational Research*, 1993, 22(7): 5–11

My address this afternoon is partly the story of a personal odyssey and partly a confessional. It has three parts. The odyssey, the first part, relates to the journey I have taken to try to understand the development of mind and the forms through which its contents are made public. How my ideas about these matters evolved is a story I want to tell. The confessional, the second part, refers to the dilemmas, uncertainties, and conundrums that the ideas that I embrace have caused me. This presidential address is more about quandaries than certitudes. I intend to display my quandaries. My hope is that at least some of what puzzles me will intrigue you. Indeed, I hope it intrigues you enough to want to join me. Finally, in the third part, I want to say what I think the ideas I have explored might mean for the future of educational research, both how it is pursued and how it is presented.

As some of you know, when I was in my twenties, I was a teacher of art and, before that, a painter. I moved from painting to teaching because I discovered that the children with whom I worked, economically disenfranchised African Americans living on Chicago's West Side, became more important to me than the crafting of images; for some reason I came to believe then, as I believe now, that the process of image-making could help children discover a part of themselves that mostly resides beneath their consciousness. Art was a way of displaying to the children and adolescents with whom I worked dimensions of themselves that I desperately wanted them to discover.

It was my interest in children and my need to clarify my vague convictions about the educational potential of art that led me to the University of Chicago and to an initiation into the social sciences, which were at that time the style of intellectual life that defined doctoral study. The Department of Education at Chicago, while steeped in the social sciences, was also intellectually open, and I was given enough slack not only to sustain, but to pursue my interest in the arts. While no one on the faculty worked in arts education or knew much about it, my intellectual mentors – John Goodlad, Phil Jackson, Joseph Schwab, Ben Bloom, and Bruno Bettelheim – provided support and encouragement. Later I found additional support in the work of Ernst Cassirer, Susanne Langer, Rudolf Arnheim, Michael Polanyi, John Dewey, and Nelson Goodman.

My encounter with the social sciences at Chicago and my long-standing engagement in art, both as a painter and a teacher of art, forced me to confront the tension between my desire to understand and cultivate what is individual and distinctive and my wish to grasp what is patterned and regular.[1] My effort to resolve this tension and my interest in the cognitive character of the arts have been a career-long journey. This journey has been guided by a variety of beliefs.

First among these is the belief that experience is the bedrock upon which meaning is constructed and that experience in significant degree depends on our ability to get in touch with the qualitative world we inhabit. This qualitative world is immediate before it is mediated, presentational before it is representational, sensuous before it is symbolic. This "getting in touch," which is crucial for any artist, I did not regard then nor do I today as a noncognitive, affective event that simply supplies the mind with something to think about. Getting in touch is itself an act of discrimination, a fine-grained, sensitively nuanced selective process in which the mind is fully engaged. I believed then, as I believe now, that the eye is a part of the mind.

Consciousness of the qualitative world as a source of potential experience and the human sensory system as a means through which those potentialities are explored require no sharp distinction between cognition and perception: on the contrary, I came to believe that perception is a cognitive event and that construal, not discovery, is critical.[2] Put another way, I came to believe that humans do not simply have experience; they have a hand in its creation, and the quality of their creation depends upon the ways they employ their minds.

A second idea that has guided my journey is the belief that the use of mind is the most potent means of its development. What we think about matters. What we try to do with what we think about matters. And so it follows, what schools allow children to think about shapes, in ways perhaps more significant than we realize, the kind of minds they come to own. As the English sociologist Basil Bernstein suggests, the curriculum is a mind-altering device (1971). We might extend his observation and say, "Education itself is a mind-making process."

This belief in the constructive character of mind, the critically important role of the senses in its formation, and the contribution of the imagination in defining the limits mind can reach are all consistent with my experience as a painter and as a teacher of art. First, the ability to paint well clearly requires students to de-center their perception, that is, they have to learn how to see relationships among qualities, not just discreet elements.[3] Learning to paint means learning to see how forms fit together, how colors influence each other, how balance and coherence can be achieved. Second, unlike many other school tasks, imagination and individuality are critical to successful production in art. As a teacher of art, I wanted to help students create images that displayed their own personal signature. Individuality of outcome, not conformity to a predetermined common standard, was what I was after. Neither norm-referenced nor criterion-referenced evaluation was an appropriate model for either the aims that mattered or the means through which their realization could be determined.[4] The tasks I pursued in my classroom were both guided by and reinforced by beliefs that only later became more consciously articulated.

One of those beliefs, the third in this journey, has to do with matters of representation. As sensibility is refined, our ability to construct meaning within a domain increases. The refinement of sensibility is no small accomplishment. Hearing, Gilbert Ryle reminds us in *The Concept of Mind* (1949), is an achievement, not simply a task. To *hear* the music, to *see* the landscape, to *feel* the qualities in a bolt of cloth, are not automatic consequences of maturation. Learning how to experience such qualities means learning how to use your mind. But these achievements, as important as they are, are achievements of impression, not expression. Surely there is more. That something more resides in matters of representation.

Representation, as I use the term, is not the mental representation discussed in cognitive science (Shepard, 1982, 1990) but, rather, the process of transforming the contents of consciousness into a public form so that they can be stabilized, inspected, edited, and shared with others. Representation is what confers a publicly social dimension to cognition. Since forms of representation differ, the kinds of experiences they make possible also differ. Different kinds of experience lead to different meanings, which, in turn, make different forms of understanding possible.

This argument, with greater elaboration than I am able to provide here, was the essential line in my John Dewey lecture in 1978 (Eisner, 1982). This lecture was elaborated and published in book form in *Cognition and Curriculum* in 1982. Howard Gardner's *Frames of Mind*, published in 1983, shares a common interest with *Cognition and Curriculum*, yet they differ in significant ways. Gardner is concerned with describing the multiple ways in which people can be smart. He discusses the ways in which different cultures assign different priorities to different kinds of problem solving. He also explores the developmental history of each type of intelligence. I regard his work as among the most influential that have appeared in the field of education in the last decade. My work focuses on matters of meaning, the kinds of meanings that can be made not only through different forms of representation but also through what I refer to as different *modes of treatment*. Different forms of representation can themselves be treated in different ways[5] – both form and mode matter. I will illustrate this point shortly.

How do these ideas about meaning and forms of representation pertain to schools and to what we teach? What relevance do they have for educational practice? As I see it, the curriculum we use in schools defines the opportunities students will have, to learn how to think *within* the media that schools provide.[6] Learning to modulate visual images and learning to logically use language require different forms of thinking. Different forms of thinking lead to different kinds of meaning. By defining the forms of representation that matter within the curriculum, the school significantly influences the kinds of meanings that students can learn to secure and represent.

That meaning is shaped by the form in which it appears is, in many ways, obvious. Humans invented maps to do what narrative could not do as well. The rites and rituals employed in churches and temples, in mosques and in other holy places, are replete with forms of representation that give moment to the occasion. We treat forms in particular ways in order to create the particular meanings we wish to display or experience.

Let's take a look at the way a poem, Tennyson's "Ulysses" (1870, p. 58), shapes our experience when we hear it read, when we listen to its lines spoken in the context of a political speech, and when we experience it in conjunction with an array of visual images.

"Ulysses" was written by Tennyson over a hundred years ago. It's a poem about a pirate-king who went on an incredible 10-year journey to liberate a Greek queen by the name of Helen who was held captive in the city of Troy. It was Ulysses who devised the trick of using a wooden horse – a Trojan horse – to bring Greek warriors into Troy who then opened the gates of the city to the Greek army. [At this point, I showed a 7-minute video to illustrate points in ways I could not do through text alone.]

The "Ulysses" we find in Teddy Kennedy's speech is a Ulysses intended to celebrate his brother's memory and to inspire his disappointed supporters to carry on in the face of his departure as a presidential candidate. Through language, Tennyson provides the image that allows Kennedy to say, paradoxically, what words cannot say.

We exploit different forms of representation to construct meanings that might otherwise elude us. The most prominent modern example of this function is found in the uses of the computer. The development of software and other forms of computer technology, such as computer-aided design, has expanded our capacity to display in graphic form what cannot be displayed in text or number. By virtue of the synchronic characteristic of visual displays, we are able to comprehend, store, retrieve, and act upon information in ways that visualization facilitates. An image gives us information at once. A narrative provides it over time. Synchronicity and diachronicity have their respective virtues. For example, spreadsheets display visual patterns that words or numbers alone cannot as easily reveal. Ross Perot taught us the powerful lesson that even the simplest visual charts can make plain what political language often obscures. Pie charts, histograms, and other diagrammatic material contribute to our understanding of the relationships we seek to grasp. Outliers are obscured in means and variances. Scattergrams make them visible. The limits of our comprehension, it seems, exceed the limits of our language. Or, as Nelson Goodman (1978) has suggested, there are as many worlds as there are ways to describe them.

Well what's the gist of the argument thus far and what are the problems that perplex me about it? First, the argument. Put as succinctly as I can, it goes like this.

Humans are sentient creatures who live in a qualitative world. The sensory system that humans possess provides the means through which the qualities of that world are experienced. Over time, through development, maturation, and acculturation, the human's ability to experience the qualitative environment increases: experience is linked to the process of increased sensory differentiation.

Out of experience, concepts are formed. Concepts are imaginative distillations of the essential features of the experienced world. They can be manipulated and modified and they can be used to generate possibilities that, though never encountered directly in the environment itself – infinity and dragons, quarks and goblins, for example – can have pragmatic and aesthetic value. Our conceptual life, shaped by imagination and the qualities of the world experienced, gives rise to the intentions that direct our activities. Intentions are rooted in the imagination. Intentions depend upon our ability to recognize what is, and yet to imagine what might be.

Experience, however, is private. For experience to become public, we must find some means to represent it. Culture makes available to the developing human an array of forms of representation through which the transformation of consciousness into its public equivalent is created. Schools are culture's agencies for selectively developing competencies in the use of these forms. Once public, the content of consciousness is stabilized, and once stabilized, it can be edited, revised, and shared. But representation is not a one-way street. Since experience can never be displayed in the form in which it initially appeared, the act of representation is also an act of invention: the act of representation provides its own unpredictable options, options that can only emerge in the course of action (Collingwood, 1958).

The meaning that representation carries is both constrained and made possible by the form of representation we employ. Not everything can be "said" with anything. Poetic meaning requires poetic forms of thought and poetically treated form. Visual art requires forms of thought that address the import of visual imagery. How we think is influenced by what we think about and how we choose or are expected to represent its content. By selectively emphasizing some forms of representation over others, schools shape children's thinking skills and in the process privilege some students and handicap others by virtue of the congruence between their aptitudes and the opportunities to use them in school. In this sense, the school is profoundly political.[7]

As tidy as this conception of the sources of meaning, understanding, and representation appears to me, I am vexed by uncertainties and dilemmas I would like to share with you. Some of these uncertainties are theoretical, some practical.

Let's start with the theoretical. Consider the meaning of meaning. We all use the term. It's central to my conception of the aims of education. But just what *meaning* means is not altogether clear. Is it the Peircian (Peirce, 1960) triadic relationship between a sign, an interpretant, and a referent, or can meaning be secured in the direct unsymbolized qualitative encounter? What is the role of context in the construction of meaning? And what about language? Does language require referents to be meaningful?

What shall we do with signs whose referents cannot be identified? Shall we regard stories and poems simply as an array of images that language helps us grasp? Are there meanings that language makes possible that are independent of the referents to which the words refer? Are there ideas that are representable only through language? If so, are they also inconceivable without language? What about Einstein's (Holton, 1982) reference to the muscular and iconic sources of his understanding, and Poincare's (Hadamard, 1945) allusions to visualization? Or how about Barbara McClintock's (Keller, 1983) feeling for the organism? And what about poetic meaning? Don't the meanings of poetry transcend the meaning of words? I worry about such matters because I want to understand the connection between experience and meaning and the contribution that different forms of representation make to each. It seems to me that such matters reside at the heart of any useful theory of education.

Appeals to rationality as an explanation of how meaning is secured are not much of an explanation. In any case, whatever rationality means, I do not want to restrict it to a particular medium of thought. If human rationality can be said to display itself whenever the selection, invention, and organization of elements to form a coherent whole occur, it seems clear that these processes occur in any medium. Why should rational processes be limited to propositional discourse or to number? But then again, why not? And so I return to uncertainty.

Interest in experience, meaning, and understanding ineluctably leads to concerns about knowledge, and so to matters of truth. What shall we do about truth? Should we, as is currently the fashion, give it up altogether – even as a regulative ideal? Frankly, I am reluctant to do so. Should we restrict it to the claims that propositional discourse can make? I think not. To restrict truth to what one can claim is to claim much too little for what we are able to know (Polanyi, 1966). As I said earlier, I believe that our discourse defines neither the scope of our rationality nor the varieties of our understanding. But how do we deal with forms of representation whose referents are at best ambiguous? And if we hold as an ideal for truth matters that aspire to the precision of mathematics, don't we wind up with a conception of truth that is limited by what mathematical forms can reveal? Should we, for example, regard the arts as irrelevant to matters of truth? Aren't they, really, simply sources of pleasure and delight, sensory meals for qualitative gourmets?

I believe there is much too much practical wisdom that tells us that the images created by literature, poetry, the visual arts, dance, and music give us insights that inform us in the special ways that only artistically rendered forms make possible. One example of these ways is found in literature. In the following painful passage Elie Wiesel (1969) recounts his experiences in a Nazi death camp:

> Never shall I forget that night, the first night in camp, which has turned my life into one long night, seven times cursed and seven times sealed. Never shall I forget that smoke. Never shall I forget the little faces of the children, whose bodies I saw turned into wreaths of smoke beneath a silent blue sky.

Never shall I forget those flames which consumed my faith forever.

Never shall I forget that nocturnal silence which deprived me, for all eternity, of the desire to live. Never shall I forget those moments which murdered my God and my soul and turned my dreams to dust. Never shall I forget these things, even if I am condemned to live as long as God Himself. Never.

(p. 44)

One way to understand what Elie Wiesel has achieved through the literary treatment of language is to see it through the conceptual frame that Susanne Langer (1976) has created. In this passage, Langer is talking about the cognitive contributions of art. She says:

A work of art presents feeling for our contemplation, making it visible or audible or in some way perceivable through a symbol, not inferable from a symptom. Artistic form is congruent with the dynamic forms of our direct sensuous, mental, and emotional life; works of art are projections of "felt life," as Henry James called it, into spacial, temporal, and poetic structures. They are images of feeling, that formulate it for our cognition. What is artistically good is whatever articulates and presents feeling to our understanding.

(p. 25)

Although intuitively I find Langer's conceptions compelling, I also know that the arts can be used to persuade people to embrace faulty beliefs, beliefs that mislead. Propaganda and advertising are two such examples. Shall we then restrict our conception of truth only to what science can provide? Again, I think not, even though I cannot demonstrate with the kind of assurance I would like the justification for the views that I hold. But what kind of justification do I seek? Perhaps that is the problem.

Some philosophers, such as Richard Rorty (1979), have put truth on the shelf and have replaced it with what he calls "edification." Making the conversation more interesting, Rorty tells us, is what it's all about. As interested as I am in interesting conversation, it, too, is not enough. How do we avoid the verificationist's constipation of conceptual categories on the one hand and the radical relativist's free-for-all, anything-goes, no-holds-barred nihilism on the other? Or are these really untenable alternatives that nobody really believes? Maybe so. But just what is a better basis? And so I continue to struggle.

In talking about experience and its relationship to the forms of representation that we employ, I am not talking about poetry and pictures, literature and dance, mathematics and literal statement simply as alternative means for displaying what we know. I am talking about the forms of understanding, the unique forms of understanding that poetry and pictures, literature and dance, mathematics and literal language make possible.

What is it to say that we have a poetic form of understanding? Or one rooted in vision or in sound? Just what do we learn when we see Teddy Kennedy's profile, hear his Bostonian accent, experience his sense of personal urgency, rise with him as his voice escalates in his moving acknowledgment of his lost candidacy? What do we grasp when we see a young Chinese student in Tiananmen Square engaged in a waltz, head on, with a Soviet tank? What vision of our nation emerges before us when in 1963 we hear Martin Luther King, in the shadow of the Lincoln Memorial, proclaim to the multitude, "I have a dream," or when, 29 years later, we see Rodney King beaten by police in Los Angeles? "What happens to a dream deferred?" Langston Hughes (1958) asks:

> Does it dry up
> Like a raisin in the sun?
> Or fester like a sore –
> And then run?
> Does it stink like rotten meat?
> Or crust and sugar over –
> Like a syrupy sweet?
> Maybe it just sags
> Like a heavy load.
> *Or does it explode?*
>                         (p. 123)

If there are different ways to understand the world, and if there are different forms that make such understanding possible, then it would seem to follow that any comprehensive effort to understand the processes and outcomes of schooling would profit from a pluralistic rather than a monolithic approach to research. How can such a pluralism be advanced? What would it mean for the way we go about our work?

I hope that questions of these kinds will become an agenda for our research in the future. The battle that once ensued to secure a place for qualitative research in education has largely been won. Although there are still more than a few places where graduate students encounter resistance, the literature is too full and the practice too widespread to go back to older, tidier times. Now the question turns to just what it is that different forms of representation employed within the context of educational research might help us grasp. Are there varieties of human understanding? What is distinctive about them? Just what is poetic insight? What kind of imaginative rationality is made possible through literature? What does the persistent image engender? What sense of life does the fresh metaphor create? Now is the time to search for seas that take us beyond the comforts of old ports.

Let us *suppose* for the time being that the basic notions I have described have merit, that meaning is multiple, and that forms of representation provide the means through which meaning is made. Let us also *suppose* that diversified forms of meaning are related to different forms of understanding and that different forms of understanding have great virtue for knowing how to act in complex circumstances. Given these suppositions, what would the ideas I have been addressing mean for what we do in educational research in the coming few decades? This brings us to the third and final section of my remarks.

If the ideas that I have described were to take hold in the educational research community, we would see an expanding array of research methods being employed in the conduct and display of educational research. In many ways, this diversity has already begun to happen. We now have a growing interest in narrative and in storied approaches to experience. Jerome Bruner's (1990) distinction between paradigmatic and narrative modes of knowing provides a conceptual basis for understanding the differences between scientific and narrativistic ways of dealing with the world.

But stories and narrative by no means exhaust the ways in which the processes of education in and out of schools can be studied or described. Film, video, the multiple displays made possible through computers, and even poetically crafted narrative are waiting in the wings. I believe that we won't have long to wait before they are called to center stage. The exploration of new forms for the presentation of research that this Annual Meeting has made possible is a step in that direction.

The use of visual, narrative, and poetic forms will have consequences for determining who is competent to appraise what they have to say. When research methods are stable and canonized, the rules of the game are relatively clear. With new games, new rules. With new rules, competencies that were appropriate for some forms of research may not necessarily be relevant for others. Furthermore, the ability to make sense of a form of research depends upon one's experience with that form and upon one's conception of what counts as research.[8] These conceptions and abilities will also change. What we need to avoid is political polarization as a result of methodological differentiation. Polarization eventually leads to matters of power and control: there is not only a sociology of knowledge; there is also a sociology of method. I hope we can use the future to achieve complementarity rather than methodological hegemony.

Curriculum development as a form of educational research is also likely to be influenced by an expanding vision of the forms of understanding schools can foster. Film, video, narrative, dance, music, the visual arts, as well as more propositionally formulated descriptions of events all have the potential to reveal aspects of the world we want students to understand. Consider what it might mean for the teaching of history.

How we answer the question of whether history is the text historians write or the past historians write about is crucial to our own view of what history is and, therefore, to what is relevant for helping students understand it. If history is text, then text must continue to be central to the teaching of history: to understand history one has to understand text. But if history is the past about which historians write, then any form of representation that sheds light on the past is a relevant, indeed a useful, way to understand history. In this latter view, music, architecture, film, stories, and the like are not only relevant, they are distinctive; each sheds unique light upon the past. But this requires that we know how to make sense of them.

In a study of the ways in which different forms of representation foster the understanding of history, Marcy Singer (1991) found that the use of a wide array of diverse forms to teach history in the context of social studies had two very interesting consequences. First, high school students had a difficult time regarding anything other than text as a source of knowledge about the past. They regarded the textbook as sacrosanct. What it presented was factual truth.

The forms that Singer studied in her research on the teaching of four decades of the twentieth century – the 1920s, 1930s, 1950s, and 1960s – included Charlie Chaplin's *Modern Times*, the film "Rebel Without a Cause," the music of Scott Joplin, the songs of Pete Seeger, the music of the Beatles, "Eyes on the Prize," *The Autobiography of Malcolm X*, Steinbeck's *Grapes of Wrath*, the Sacco-Vanzetti painting by Ben Shahn, television's "Leave It to Beaver," Chuck Berry, and the paintings of Jackson Pollack. Yet students did not regard these sources as relevant for understanding history.

At the same time, the very ambiguity – or better yet the openness – of such forms made for the best discussions in class. In retrospect, this is not surprising. After all, what is there to discuss when students confront the certainties of the text? When it comes to forms of representation that invite interpretation, interpretation followed. In *The Principles of Psychology* published in 1890, William James asked for what he called "the reinstatement of the vague to its proper place in our mental life" (Gavin, 1986). James recognized then what Singer found about a century later: ambiguity has a more significant cognitive contribution to make to students than the certain facticity of the text.

The use of a wider array of diverse forms in teaching begs for studies of their consequences. At the same time, the problem of determining consequences is notoriously difficult for several reasons. First, the manifestation of consequences requires giving students the opportunity to display what they have learned in forms of representation congenial to both the content of their learning and the nature of their aptitudes. In addition, to be successful in representing such content, students must be skilled in the medium they wish to use. If students do not possess the skills they need, say of producing a video or a film, of writing a poem or creating a visual narrative, the content they wish to represent is simply not likely to emerge. Representation requires the skills needed to treat a material so that it functions as a medium, something that mediates content.

Second, assuming students do possess such skills, the results of their work will differ. This array of differences will play havoc with traditional conceptions of criterion-referenced evaluation. When goals are prespecified, tasks for students are uniform, and the application of standards is procedurally objective, comparisons among student performances is possible. However, I must tell you, I am not sanguine about meaningfully calibrating to a common scale differences among students who use different forms to display what they have learned. I do not say this to dissuade anyone from pursuing it; it is a direction that should be explored. But I can see complexities emerging as I now see them emerging in the use of portfolios and other forms of authentic assessment. Premises about assessment – such as comparability of student performance – may have to change if practices are to change.[9]

Another potential consequence for educational research relates to the education of doctoral students. As the relevance of different forms of representation for understanding schooling grows, schools of education will be pressed to develop programs that help students learn how to use them. Film, for example, will need to be regarded not only as a way of showing pictures but as a way of understanding some aspects of schooling, teaching, and learning that cannot be understood as well in any other way. Furthermore, the artistic features of film are not merely ornamental but essential to the display of particular messages. Thus, the refinement of both artistic and scientific sensibilities, as the theme of this Annual Meeting implies, is relevant for enlarging human understanding.

Another offshoot of this development deals with the features of acceptable dissertations. In the future they are likely to take on forms that only a few now possess. One of my doctoral students once asked me if Stanford's School of Education would accept a novel as a dissertation. At the time she raised this question, about a decade ago, I could only answer in the negative. Today, I am more optimistic, not because all of my Stanford colleagues share my convictions, but because the climate for exploring new forms of research is more generous today than it was then.

Given the ideas I have been developing, a number of questions emerge. Perhaps the most fundamental of these pertains to the notion that humans have the capacity to formulate different kinds of understanding and that these understandings are intimately related to the forms of representation they encounter or employ and the way in which those forms are treated. Discovering, however, how such forms of understanding are secured and the kinds of meanings they make possible is a core theoretical as well as practical problem. It's one thing to speculate about the validity of an idea. It's another to demonstrate it empirically. What kind of empiricism would be required to identify the different ways in which students come to understand aspects of the world? Are there forms of assessment and approaches to curriculum that would make it possible to know, in advance, the probability that some forms of understanding would be engendered if some forms of representation were employed in the course of teaching and learning? Just what is the relationship between student aptitude and the forms that they have access to? Does the fit between the two facilitate comprehension as we would expect? And what does one do to give students not only the opportunity but the skills to display their understanding? Can we translate what is specific and unique to forms other than those in which such understanding is revealed?

I must confess that I do not have answers to the questions I have just posed. I believe, however, that the questions I have posed are crucial for educational practice and research that does justice to the development of human intellectual capacities.

Another issue pertains to the ways in which the research that is done on such matters can be displayed. We are, of course, habituated to text and number. Our journals are, if anything, encomiums to technical language. What would an entirely new array of presentational forms for research look like? What might we learn about a school or a classroom, a teacher or a student, a form of teaching and a style of learning, through an integration of film, text, photo, and poem?

While envisioning such an integration of forms is difficult, it is the exploration of such possibilities, first imaginatively and then practically, that will enable us to invent an agenda for the future. In some ways, through MTV and other such forms, our students are way ahead of us. Sound and image, more than text and number, are the cornerstones of their experience. What do such possibilities hold for a group of scholars steeped in more conservative traditions? In sum, I am asking us to do what we don't know how to do. I am asking us to recognize the limits of our comfortable past, but not to discard it. As I said, I am asking us to bypass familiar ports and to explore the new seas that we might sail. I think we have already made a wonderful beginning on that journey.

It's not only the conventional canon that's being questioned; it's deeper. It's how we think about mind, the enlargement of human understanding, and what counts as meaningful. From the feminist critique of science by a Sandra Harding (1991) to the reappearance of the Windelbandian distinction between the ideographic and the nomothetic (von Wright, 1971) from the postmodern constructions of a Paul Ricoeur (1981) and a Roland Barth (1985) to the phenomenological perspectives of a Merleau-Ponty (1962) and a Maxine Greene (1988), the times they are a-changing. And we are also changing.

\* \* \*

Virtually everything that I have said pertains to the theoretical matters that continue to puzzle me and to their practical relevance for the conduct of research, the careers of researchers, and the preparation of those who will do research. But I would be remiss if I left this podium leaving the impression that the advancement of research, or the careers of researchers, or the satisfactions that come from the reduction of puzzlement constitute the major aim of the common enterprise in which we are engaged. The major aim, we must not forget, has to do with the African American children with whom I worked on Chicago's West Side at the beginning of my career. It has to do with the improvement of educational practice so that the lives of those who teach and learn are themselves enhanced. Put more succinctly, we do research to understand. We try to understand in order to make our schools better places for both the children and the adults who share their lives there. That aim, from my perspective, needs to remain as frontlets between our eyes. We should fix them as signposts upon our gates. In the end, our work lives its ultimate life in the lives that it enables others to lead. Although we are making headway toward that end, there will continue to be difficulties and uncertainties, frustrations and obstacles. Working at the edge of incompetence takes courage. When the doubts emerge and the safe road beckons, it might be well to remember Tennyson's lines. And so I close my comments with them:

> Tho' much is taken, much abides; and tho'
> We are not now that strength which in old days
> Moved heaven and earth; that which we are, we are;
> One equal temper of heroic hearts,
> Made weak by time and fate, but strong in will
> To strive, to seek, to find, and not to yield.

## Acknowledgments

While I was preparing this address, I benefited from the good advice of several colleagues and friends. I am pleased to acknowledge their contributions here: David Ecker, Howard Gardner, Lisa Goldstein, Alan Peshkin, Richard Snow, and Lesley Taylor.

## Notes

\*   This article was the presidential address at the AERA Annual Meeting in April 1993.
1   This tension is described as residing within the idiographic and the nomothetic, that is, between efforts to understand the particular and efforts to grasp the general. See von Wright's (1971) *Explanation and Understanding* for further discussion.
2   The cognitive character of perception is given a special force in the writings of Rudolf Arnheim and Ulric Neisser. See Arnheim's (1969) *Visual Thinking* and Neisser's (1976) *Cognition and Reality*. For a philosophical interpretation of the relationship between perception and cognition, see Hanson's (1971) *Observation and Explanation: A Guide to the Philosophy of Science*.
3   The concept of de-centering perception is embedded in the works of Jean Piaget and Rudolf Arnheim. Arnheim calls the focus on particulars in the act of drawing "local solutions," referring to the fact that children are so focused or centered on the object they wish to draw that they neglect its relationship to the context in which it appears.
4   Both norm-referenced and criterion-referenced evaluation are predicated on the need to compare. In norm-referenced evaluation, the comparison is made between one student's performance and the performances of others within some relevant population. In criterion-referenced evaluation, the comparison is made between the student's performance and a known criterion or model. Neither of these conceptions is wholly adequate for evaluation in the arts since in artistic activity a premium is placed upon surprise and the generation of creative solutions that, by definition, are not predictable. Appropriate assessment practice in the arts requires the use of what Robert Stake calls responsive evaluation and what I have referred to as expressive outcomes (see, e.g. Stake, 1975 and Eisner, 1969).
5   In *Cognition and Curriculum* (Eisner, 1982), I identified three ways in which forms of representation can be treated: through mimesis, through expressiveness, and through convention. Mimesis provides an imitation of the world to be represented, as, for example, in onomatopoeia, in efforts at visual realism, and in program music. The expressive treatment of form is found in works whose features evoke responses congruent with the deep structure of what they represent: for example, the images of Edvard Münch, the overtures of Richard Wagner, and the poetry of e. e. cummings. Conventional forms, like the Red Cross or the American flag, reflect social agreements to use the form to refer

to "specific" meanings. These meanings cannot, of course, be entirely specified. Nevertheless, there is usually enough congruence within a culture to enable its members to achieve commonality of meaning.

6   In his book *Art as Experience* (1934), John Dewey makes the following point regarding the relationship of mode of thought to medium: "Those who are called artists have for their subject matter the qualities of things of direct experience; 'intellectual' inquiries deal with those qualities at one remove, through the medium of symbols that stand for qualities but are not significant in their immediate presence" (p. 73).

7   The fact that schools both withhold and provide opportunities for students to succeed by virtue of the agenda that they make available to students makes them profoundly political. Students whose aptitudes are not given an opportunity to emerge within the context of schools are often handicapped. Significantly, universities often discount or disregard the grades that students receive in the fine arts when considering a candidate for admission. Even when schools make certain kinds of performances possible for students, and even when those performances are graded by the schools, there is no assurance that the quality of student performance will be taken into account by tertiary institutions. This practice, utterly unconscionable from my perspective, has a profound influence on what college-bound students believe they can afford to study in school.

8   One of the most significant shifts that is likely to occur in the educational research community is the broadening of its conception of what counts as educational research. This increased breadth is not a license for "anything goes," but a recognition that the roads to understanding are many and that a narrow view of method is likely to lead to a limited understanding of how schools work.

9   Educational evaluation and measurement have been predicated on the need to compare students with each other or with a known criterion. As I indicated earlier, such a premise is not a necessary condition for any kind of evaluation. As our premises change so that we are open to forms that are distinctive, we will be in a much better position to develop evaluation practices that recognize the cultivation of productive idiosyncrasy as an important educational outcome and thus to honor it in assessment.

# References

Arnheim, R. *Visual Thinking*. Berkeley, CA: University of California Press, 1969.

Barth, R. *The Responsibility of Forms*. New York: Hill & Wang, 1985.

Bernstein, B. "On the Classification and Framing of Educational Knowledge." In M. Young (ed.), *Knowledge and Control*. London, England: Collier Macmillan, 1971, pp. 47–69.

Bruner, J. *Acts of Meaning*. Cambridge, MA: Harvard University Press, 1990.

Collingwood, R. G. *The Principles of Art*. New York: Oxford University Press, 1958.

Dewey, J. *Art as Experience*. New York: Balch, 1934.

Eisner, E. "Instructional and Expressive Educational Objectives: Their Formulation and Use in Curriculum". In W. James Popham, E. Eisner, H. Sullivan, and L. Tyler (eds) *Instructional Objectives* (American Educational Research Association Monograph Series on Curriculum Evaluation). Chicago, IL: McNally & Co., 1969, pp. 1–18.

Eisner, E. *Cognition and Curriculum: A Basis for Deciding What to Teach*. New York: Longman, 1982.

Gardner, H. *Frames of Mind*. New York: Basic Books, 1983.

Gavin, W. *William James and the Need to Preserve "the Vague"* [Speech]. Portland, OR: University of Southern Maine, 1986.

Goodman, N. *Ways of Worldmaking*. Indianapolis, IN: Hackett, 1978.

Greene, M. *The Dialectic of Freedom*. New York: Teachers College Press, 1988.

Hadamard, J. *An Essay on the Psychology of Invention in the Mathematical Field*. Princeton, NJ: Princeton University Press, 1945.

Hanson, N. R. *Observation and Explanation: A Guide to Philosophy of Science*. New York: Harper & Row, 1971.

Harding, S. *Whose Science? Whose Knowledge?* Ithaca, NY: Cornell University Press, 1991.

Holton, G. J. *Albert Einstein: Historical and Cultural Perspectives*. Princeton, NJ: Princeton University Press, 1982.

Hughes, L. *The Langston Hughes Reader*. New York: Braziller, 1958.

James, W. *The Principles of Psychology*. New York: Holt, 1890.

Keller, E. F. *A Feeling For the Organism*. San Francisco, CA: Freedman, 1983.

Langer, S. *Problems of Art*. New York: Scribners, 1976.

Merleau-Ponty, M. *Phenomenology of Perception*. New York: Humanities Press, 1962.

Neisser, U. *Cognition and Reality*. Ithaca, NY: Cornell University Press, 1976.

Peirce, C. S. *Collected Papers* (C. Hartshorn and P. Weiss, eds), 8 Vols. Cambridge, MA: Harvard University Press, 1931–1958.

Polanyi, M. *The Tacit Dimension*. Garden City, NJ: Doubleday, 1966.

Ricoeur, P. *Hermeneutics and the Human Sciences*. New York: Cambridge University Press, 1981.

Rorty, R. *Philosophy and the Mirror of Nature*. Princeton, NJ: Princeton University Press, 1979.

Ryle, G. *The Concept of Mind*. London, England: Hutchinson's University Library, 1949

Shepard, R. *Mental Images and Their Transformation*. Cambridge, MA: MIT Press, 1982.

Shepard, R. *Mind Sights*. New York: Freeman, 1990.

Singer, M. "Sound, Image, and Word in the Curriculum: The Making of Historical Sense." Unpublished doctoral dissertation, Stanford University, 1991.

Stake, R. *Evaluating the Arts in Education: A Responsive Approach*. Columbus, OH: Merrill, 1975.

Tennyson, A. *The Poetical Works of Alfred Tennyson*. New York: Harper, 1870.

von Wright, H. *Explanation and Understanding*. Ithaca, NY: Cornell University Press, 1971.

Wiesel, E. *Night*. New York: Avon, 1969.

# CHAPTER 17

# STANDARDS FOR AMERICAN SCHOOLS*
## Help or hindrance?

*Phi Delta Kappan*, 1995, 76(10): 758–764

Efforts to reform American schools are not exactly a novel enterprise. When the Soviet Union sent Sputnik circling the globe in 1957 the US Congress looked to the schools to recover what we had thought we had: leadership in space. The curriculum reform movement of the 1960s was intended, in part, to help us regain our technological superiority in the Cold War. In the 1970s "accountability" became the central concept around which our education reform efforts turned. If only we could identify the expected outcomes of instruction and invent means to describe their presence, school administrators and teachers could be held accountable for the quality of their work.

In April 1983 *A Nation at Risk* was published. In its memorable opening passage the impact of the schools on US society was likened to a foreign invasion. By the late 1980s *A Nation at Risk*, one of the most prominent reform publications of the century, seemed to have faded, and its passing set the stage for America 2000 – the reform agenda of the Bush Administration, now signed on to by the Clinton Administration. America 2000 was intended to do what the curriculum reform movement of the 1960s, the accountability movement of the 1970s, and *A Nation at Risk* and the "excellence movement" of the 1980s had been unable to accomplish.

We now have in Goals 2000 (the Clinton version of America 2000) an approach to education reform that uses standards as the linchpin of its efforts. Standards are being formulated for the certification of teachers, for the content of curricula, and for the outcomes of teaching. Virtually every subject-matter field in education has formulated or is in the process of formulating or revising national standards that describe what students should know and be able to do.

If anyone detects a slight echo of the past in today's reform efforts, let me assure you that you are not alone. We seem to latch on to approaches to reform that are replays of past efforts that themselves failed to come to grips with what it is that makes school practices so robust and resistant to change.

Consider, for example, the concept of standards. The term is attractive. Who among us, at first blush at least, would claim that schools – or any other institution for that matter – should be without them? Standards imply high expectations, rigor, things of substance. To be without standards is not to know what to expect or how to determine if expectations have been realized – or so it seems.

Yet once we get past the illusions that the concept invites – once we think hard about the meaning of the term – the picture becomes more complex. To begin with, the meaning of the term is not as self-evident as many seem to believe. A standard meal, for example, is a meal that I think we would agree is nothing to rave about – and the same could be said of a standard hotel room or a standard reply to a question. A standard can also be a banner, something that trumpets one's identity and commitment. A standard can represent a value that people have cared enough about to die for. Standards can also refer to units of measure. The National Bureau of Standards employs standards to measure the quality of manufactured products. Electrical appliances, for example, must achieve a certain standard to get the UL seal of approval.

Which conception of standards do we embrace in the reform movement? Surely we do not mean by standards a typical level of performance, since that is what we already have without an iota of intervention. As for standards that represent beliefs or values, we already have mission statements and position papers in abundance, but they do not have the level of specificity that reformers believe is needed for standards to be useful.

The third conception of standards – as units of measure that make it possible to quantify the performance of students, teachers, and schools – seems closer to what we have in mind. We live in a culture that admires technology and efficiency and believes in the possibility of objectivity. The idea of measurement provides us with a procedure that is closely associated with such values. Measurement makes it possible to describe quantity in ways that allow as little space as possible for subjectivity.[1] For example, the objectivity of an objective test is not a function of the way in which the test items were selected, but of the way in which the test is scored. Objective tests can be scored by machine, with no need for judgment.

Standards in education, as we now idealize them, are to have such features. They are to be objective and, whenever possible, measurable. Once a technology of assessment is invented that will objectively quantify the relationship of student performance to a measurable ideal, we will be able to determine without ambiguity the discrepancy between the former and the latter, and thus we will have a meaningful standard.

Those who have been working in education for 20 or so years or who know the history of American education will also know that the vision I have just described is a recapitulation of older ideals. I refer to the curriculum reform movement of the 1960s. It was an important event in the history of American education, but it was not the only significant movement of that period. You will also remember that it was in the 1960s that American educators became infatuated with "behavioral objectives." Everyone was to have them. The idea then, like the notion of standards today, was to define our educational goals operationally in terms that were sufficiently specific to determine without ambiguity whether or not the student had achieved them.

The specifics of the procedures, given prominence by Robert Mager's 1962 book. *Preparing Instructional Objectives*, required that student behavior be identified, that the conditions in which it was to be displayed be described, and that a criterion be specified that made it possible to measure the student's behavior in relation to the criterion.[2] For Mager a behavioral objective might be stated as follows: "At the end of the instructional period, when asked to do so, the student will be able to write a 200-word essay with no more than two spelling errors, one error in punctuation, and no errors in grammar."

It all seemed very neat. What people discovered as they tried to implement the idea was that to have behaviorally defined instructional objectives that met the criteria that Mager specified required the construction of *hundreds* of specific objectives. Heaven knows, school districts tried. But it soon became apparent that teachers would be bogged down with such a load. And even so ardent a supporter of behavioral objectives as James Popham eventually realized that teachers would be better off with just a few such objectives.[3] The quest for certainty, which high-level specificity and precision implied, was soon recognized as counterproductive.

Those who know the history of American education will also know that the desire to specify expected outcomes and to prescribe the most efficient means for achieving them was itself the dominant strain of what has come to be called the "efficiency movement" in education.[4] The efficiency movement, which began in 1913 and lasted until the early 1930s, was designed to apply the principles of scientific management to schools. Its progenitor, Frederick Taylor, the inventor of time-and-motion study, was a management consultant hired by industrialists to make their plants more efficient and hence more profitable. By specifying in detail the desired outcomes of a worker's efforts and by eliminating "wasted motion," output would increase, profits would soar, wages would rise, and everyone would benefit.

American school administrators thought that in Taylor's approach to the management of industrial plants they had found a surefire method for producing efficient schools. Moreover, Taylor's approach was based on "science." The prescription of expected outcomes, of the manner of performance, and of the content in which competence is to be displayed is a not-too-distant cousin of the teacher performance standards and curriculum content standards that accompany today's discussions of standards for student performance.

School administrators caught up in the efficiency movement gradually learned that the basic conception and the expectations that flowed from it – namely, that one could mechanize and routinize teaching and learning – did not work. Even if it were possible to give teachers scripts for their performance, it was not possible to give students scripts. There was no "one best method," and there was no way to "teacher-proof" instruction.

My point thus far is that what we are seeing in American education today is a well-intentioned but conceptually shallow effort to improve our schools. My point thus far is to make it plain that the current effort in which we are enmeshed is no novelty; we have been here before. My point thus far is to suggest that successful efforts at school reform will entail a substantially deeper analysis of schools and their relationships to communities and teachers than has thus far been undertaken.

To try to do justice to the aspirations of the national education reform movement, I will try to make a sympathetic presentation of its arguments. I start with the acknowledgment that there is a sense of sweet reason to the arguments that the reformers have made. After all, with standards we will know where we are headed. We can return rigor to schooling; we can inform students, parents, and teachers of what we expect; we can have a common basis for appraising student performance; and we can, at last, employ a potent lever for education reform. Without standards, we are condemned to an unbroken journey into an abyss of mediocrity; we will remain a nation at risk.

In addition, the task of formulating standards is salutary for teachers and others involved in curriculum planning. By establishing national goals for each subject that schools teach, we will be able to achieve professional consensus that will give us a unified and educationally solid view of what students are expected to learn. By trying to define standards for each field, a single vision of a subject will be created, teachers will have an opportunity to profit from the goals and standards formulated by their peers, and ambiguity will be diminished because teachers will know not only the direction their efforts are to take, but also the specific destinations toward which their students are headed. Furthermore, teachers will have something of a timetable to help determine not only whether, but when, they have arrived.

As if they had just taken a cold shower, a population of sometimes lethargic and burned-out teachers will be reawakened and will become alert. Our nation will, at last, have a national educational agenda, something that it has never possessed. Ultimately, such resources and the approach to education that those resources reflect will help us regain our competitive edge in a global economy. Parents will be satisfied, students will know what is expected of them, and the business community will have the employees it needs for America to become number one by the year 2000, not only in science and in math but in other fields as well. Our students and our schools will go for and get the gold at the educational Olympics in which we are competing. Our schools will become "world class."

An attractive vision? It seems so, yet a number of questions arise. You will recall that the standards about which reformers speak are national standards. The organizations – and there are dozens – that are engaged in formulating standards are doing so for the nation as a whole, not for some specific locality. Put another way, in a nation in which 45 million students in 50 states go to approximately 108,000 schools overseen by some 15,000 school boards and in which 2.5 million teachers teach, there is the presumption that it makes good educational sense for there to be uniform expectations with respect to goals, content, and levels of student achievement. I regard this assumption as questionable on at least two counts.

First, the educational uses of subjects are not singular. The social studies can be used to help students understand history, to help create a socially active citizenry, or to help students recognize the connection between culture and ideas. Biology can be used to help students learn to think like biologists, to understand the balance of nature, to appreciate the limits of science in establishing social policy, or to gain an appreciation of life. The language arts can be used to develop poetic forms of thought, to learn to appreciate great works of literary art, to acquire the mechanics of written and spoken language, to learn to appreciate forms of life that require literary rather than literal understanding. Mathematics can be taught to help students learn to compute, to understand the structure of mathematics, to solve mathematical problems, to cultivate forms of mathematical cognition, and to help students appreciate the beauty of structures in space. Where is it written that every subject has to be taught for the same reasons to 45 million students? Despite the effort to achieve professional consensus about the educational agendas of specific subjects, the virtue of uniformity is, to my mind, questionable.

Uniformity in curriculum content is a virtue *if* one's aim is to be able to compare students in one part of the country with students in others. Uniformity is a virtue when the aspiration is to compare the performance of American students with students in Korea, Japan, and Germany. But why should we wish to make such comparisons? To give up the idea that there needs to be one standard for all students in each field of study is not to give up the aspiration to seek high levels of educational quality in both pedagogical practices and educational outcomes. Together, the desire to compare and the recognition of individuality create one of the dilemmas of a social meritocracy: the richness of a culture rests not only on the prospect of cultivating a set of common commitments, but also on the prospect of cultivating those individual talents through which the culture at large is enriched.

A second problematic feature of the aspiration to adopt a common set of standards for all is a failure to recognize differences among the students with whom we work. I am well aware of the fact that deleterious self-fulfilling prophecies can be generated when the judgments educators make about individuals are based on a limited appreciation of the potentialities of the students. This is a danger that requires our constant vigilance. However, the reality of differences – in region, in aptitude, in interests, and in goals – suggests that it is reasonable that there be differences in programs.

The framers of the US Constitution implicitly recognized the need for the localities they called states to develop educational programs that addressed the values and features of the populations in those states. We do not need the US equivalent of a French Ministry of Education, prescribing a one-size-fits-all program. Ironically, at a time when the culture at large is recognizing the uniqueness of us all and cultivating our productive differences, the education reform movement, in its anxiety about quality, wants to rein in our diversity, to reduce local discretion, and to give everybody the same target at which to aim.

Thus, with respect to aspiration, I think there are fundamental problems with the concept of standards as applied to the nation as a whole. But there are other problems as well, and these problems relate to the concept of standards as it applies to the process of education and to what we know about normal patterns of human development.

You will remember that I referred to standards as units of measure that make possible the "objective" description of quantitative relationships. But there are qualitative standards as well. To have a *qualitative* standard you must create or select an icon, prototype, or what is sometimes called a benchmark against which the performance or products of students are matched. To have a *quantitative* standard you must specify the number or percentage of correct answers needed to pass a test or the number of allowable errors in a performance or product and to use that specification as the standard.

In each case, there is a fixed and relatively unambiguous unit of measurement. In the qualitative case, the task for both judge and performer is one of matching a performance with a model. This kind of matching is precisely what occurs in the Olympics. Olympic judges know what a particular dive should look like, and they compare a diver's performance to the model. The diver, too, knows what the model looks like and does his or her best to replicate the model.

With respect to the quantitative case, the application of a standard occurs in two different ways. The first has to do with determining the correctness of any individual response. An item response is judged correct if the appropriate bubble is filled in, or if the appropriate selection is made, or if some other indication is given that the student has hit a prespecified mark. The prespecified correct response serves as a standard for each item. Once these item responses are summed, a determination is made as to whether the total number of correct responses meets a second standard, the standard specified as a passing grade by the test-maker or by some policy-making body.

Notice that in both cases innovation in response is not called for. The diver replicates a known model. The test-maker determines whether a student's score is acceptable, not by exercising judgment, but by counting which bubbles have been filled in and comparing the number of correct responses to a fixed predetermined standard.

There are, we must acknowledge, a number of important tasks that students must learn in school in which innovation is not useful. Learning how to spell correctly means knowing how to replicate the known. The same holds true for much of what is taught in early arithmetic and in the language arts. There are many important tasks and skills that students need to learn – i.e. conventions – that are necessary for doing more important work and that educational programs should help them learn. The more important work that I speak of is the work that makes it possible for students to think imaginatively about problems that matter to them, tasks that give them the opportunity to affix their own personal signature to their work, occasions to explore ideas and questions that have no correct answers, and projects in which they can reason and express their own ideas.

Learning to replicate known conventions is an important part of the *tactical outcomes* of education, but it is not adequate for achieving the *strategic aspirations* that we hold. These strategic aspirations require curricula and assessment policies that invite students to exercise judgment and to create outcomes that are not identical with those of their peers. Again, the cultivation of productive idiosyncrasy ought to be one of the aims that matter in American schools, and, to my way of thinking, we ought to build programs that make the realization of such an outcome possible, even if it means that we will not find it easy to compare students. When we seek to measure such outcomes, we will not be able to use a fixed standard for scoring the work students have produced. We will have to rely on that most exquisite of human capacities – judgment.

Paradoxically, many of the groups that have been working diligently to formulate standards are not really formulating standards at all. They are formulating goals. Consider the following, all of which purport to be standards.

• "Accomplished teachers work with families to achieve common goals for the education of their children" (Board for Professional Teaching Standards, 1994).
• "Construct Personal Meaning from Nontraditional Dramatic Performances" (National Standards for Arts Education, 1994).
• "How Progressives and Others Addressed Problems of Industrial Capitalism, Urbanization, and Political Corruption" (United States History: Exploring the American Experience, 1994).
• "Folklore and Other Cultural Contributions from Various Regions of the United States and How They Help to Form a National Heritage" (United States History: Exploring the American Experience, 1994).

Such broad, general statements are aspirations that can function as criteria with which to interrogate the work students produce. But criteria are not the same as standards. John Dewey described the difference in *Art as Experience*, one of his most important books, which is largely unread by educators. In a telling chapter on the relationship of art criticism to perception, written when he was 75 years old, Dewey said that, in assessing works of art, standards are inappropriate; criteria are needed. Standards fix expectations; criteria are guidelines that enable one to search more efficiently for the qualities that might matter in any individual work. Describing the features of a standard, Dewey wrote:

> There are three characteristics of a standard. It is a particular physical thing existing under specified physical conditions; it is *not* a value. The yard is a yard-stick, and the meter is a bar deposited in Paris. In the second place, standards are measures of definite things, of lengths, weights, capacities. The things measured are not values, although it is of great social value to be able to measure them, since the properties of things in the way of size, volume, weight, are important for commercial exchange. Finally, as standards of measure, standards define things with respect to quantity.[5]

Later, he went on to argue:

> Yet it does not follow because of absence of an uniform and publicly determined external object [a standard], that objective criticism of art is impossible. What follows is that criticism is judgment; that like every judgment it involves

a venture, a hypothetical element; that it is directed to qualities which are nevertheless qualities of an *object*; and that it is concerned with an individual object, not with making comparisons by means of an external preestablished rule between different things.[6]

To say that by the end of a course students will be able to write a convincing essay on the competing interests of environmentalists and industrialists that marshals good arguments supported by relevant facts is to identify criteria that can be used to appraise the essay; it is not to provide a standard for measuring it. Regarding the meaning of criteria, Dewey wrote:

> If there are no standards for works of art and hence none for criticism (in the sense in which there are standards of measurement), there are nevertheless criteria in judgment.... But such criteria are not rules or prescriptions. They are the result of an endeavor to find out what a work of art is as an experience, the kind of experience which constitutes it.[7]

One might wonder whether it is appropriate to think about the appraisal of work produced by students at the elementary and secondary school level as being comparable to the assessment of works of art. Aren't artworks objects in a different category? Criteria may be appropriate for paintings and poetry, but schoolwork requires the application of standards.

As plausible as this might seem at first glance, things are not so simple. The creation of conditions that allow students to display their creative and reasoning abilities in ways that are unique to their temperaments, their experience, and their aims is of fundamental importance in any educational enterprise – in contrast to one concerned with training. And because such features are important, it is criteria that must be salient in our assessment.

Standards are appropriate for some kinds of tasks, but, as I argued above, those tasks are instrumental to larger and more important educational aims. We really don't need to erect a complex school system to teach the young how to read utility bills, how to do simple computation, or how to spell; they will learn those skills on their own. What we do need to teach them is how to engage in higher-order thinking, how to pose telling questions, how to solve complex problems that have more than one answer. When the concept of standards becomes salient in our discourse about educational expectations, it colors our view of what education can be and dilutes our conception of education's potential. Language matters, and the language of standards is by and large a limiting rather than a liberating language.

The qualities that define inventive work of any kind are qualities that by definition have both unique and useful features. The particular form those features take and what it is that makes them useful are not necessarily predictable, but sensitive critics – and sensitive teachers – are able to discover such properties in the work. Teachers who know the students they teach recognize the unique qualities in students' comments, in their paintings, in the essays they write, in the ways in which they relate to their peers. The challenge in teaching is to provide the conditions that will foster the growth of those personal characteristics that are socially important and, at the same time, personally satisfying to the student. The aim of education is not to train an army that marches to the same drummer, at the same pace, toward the same destination. Such an aim may be appropriate for totalitarian societies, but it is incompatible with democratic ideals.

If one used only philosophical grounds to raise questions about the appropriateness of uniform national standards for students in American schools, there would still be questions enough to give one pause. But there are developmental grounds as well. The graded American public school system was built on an organizational theory that has little to do with the developmental characteristics of growing children. In the mid-nineteenth century we thought it made very good sense for the school to be organized into grades and for there to be a body of content assigned to each grade.[8] Each grade was to be related to a specific age. The task of the student was to master the content taught at that grade as a precondition for promotion to the next grade. At the end of an 8- or 12-year period, it was assumed that, if the school and the teacher had done their jobs, everyone would come out at roughly the same place.

If you examine the patterns of human development for children from age 5 to age 18, you will find that, as children grow older, their rate of development is increasingly variable. Thus the range of variation among children of the same age increases with time.

For example, for ordinary, nonhomogeneous classes, the average range of reading achievement is roughly equal to the grade level: at the second grade there is, on average, a two-year spread in reading achievement. Some second-graders are reading at the first-grade level, and others are reading at the third-grade level. At the fourth grade the spread is about four years, and at the sixth grade, about six years. In the seventh grade the range is about seven years: some children are reading at the fourth-grade level, and some are reading at the tenth-grade level.

What this means is that children develop at their own distinctive pace. The tidy structure that was invented in the nineteenth century to rationalize school organization may look wonderful on paper, but it belies what we know about the course of human development. Because we still operate with a developmentally insensitive organizational structure in our schools, the appeal of uniform standards by grade level or by outcome seems reasonable. It is not. Variability, not uniformity, is the hallmark of the human condition.

I do not want to overstate the idea. To be sure, humans are like all other humans, humans are like some other humans, and humans are like no other humans. All three claims are true. But we have become so preoccupied with remedying the perceived weaknesses of American schools that we have underestimated the diversity and hence the complexity that exists.

The varieties of unappreciated complexity are large. Let me suggest only a few. When evaluating students in the context of the classroom, the teacher – the person who has the widest variety of information about any particular student – takes into consideration much more than the specific features of a student's particular product. The age, grade, and developmental level of the student; the amount of progress a student has made; the degree of effort that the student has expended; the amount of experience a student has had in a domain are all educationally relevant considerations that professionally competent teachers take into account in making judgments about a student's progress. Experienced teachers know in their bones that the student's work constitutes only one item in an array of educational values and that these values sometimes compete. There are times when it may be more important educationally for a teacher to publicly acknowledge the quality of a student's work than to criticize it, even when that work is below the class average.

Beyond the details of the classroom, there are more general questions having to do with the bases on which educational standards are formulated. Should educational standards be derived from the average level of performance of students in a school, in a school district, in a state, in a nation, *in the world*? How much talk have we heard of "*world class*" standards?

If national policy dictates that there will be uniform national standards for student performance, will there also be uniform national standards for the resources available to schools? To teachers? To administrators? Will the differences in performance between students living in well-heeled, upper-class suburbs and those living on the cusp of poverty in the nation's inner cities demonstrate the existing inequities in American education? Will they not merely confirm what we already know?

The socioeconomic level of the students and the resources available to them and their teachers in a school or school district do make a difference. If those urging standards on us believe that the use of standards will demonstrate inequities – and hence serve to alleviate them – why haven't these already painfully vivid inequities been effective in creating more equitable schools?

And, one might wonder, what would happen to standards in education if by some magic all students achieved them? Surely the standards would be considered too low. At first blush this doesn't sound like a bad thing. Shouldn't the bar always be higher than we can reach? Sounds reasonable. Yet such a view of the function of standards will ineluctably create groups of winners and losers. Can our education system flourish without losers? Is it possible for us to frame conceptions of education and society that rest on more generous assumptions? And consider the opposite. What will we do with those students who fail to meet the standards? Then what?

Perhaps one of the most important consequences of the preoccupation with national standards in education is that it distracts us from the deeper, seemingly intractable problems that beset our schools. It distracts us from paying attention to the importance of building a culture of schooling that is genuinely intellectual in character, that values questions and ideas at least as much as getting right answers. It distracts us from trying to understand how we can provide teachers the kind of professional opportunities that will afford the best among them opportunities to continue to grow through a lifetime of work. It distracts us from attending to the inevitable array of interactions between teaching, curriculum, evaluation, school organization, and the often deleterious expectations and pressures from universities.

How should these matters be addressed? Can schools and teachers and administrators afford the kind of risk-taking and exploratory activity that genuine inquiry in education requires?

Vitality within any organization is more likely when there are opportunities to pursue fresh possibilities, to exercise imagination, to try things out, and to relinquish the quest for certainty in either pedagogical method or educational outcome. Indeed, one of the important aims of education is to free the mind from the confines of certainty. Satisfaction, our children must learn, can come from the uncertainty of the journey, not just from the clarity of the destination.

I am not sure that American society is willing at this time to embrace so soft a set of values as I have described. We have become a tough-minded lot. We believe that we can solve the problems of crime by reopening the doors to the gas chamber and by building more prisons. But it's never been that simple. Nor is solving the problems of schooling as simple as having national education standards.

And so I believe that we must invite our communities to join us in a conversation that deepens our understanding of the educational process and advances our appreciation of its possibilities. Genuine education reform is not about shallow efforts that inevitably fade into oblivion. It is about vision, conversation, and action designed to create a genuine and evolving educational culture. I hope we can resist the lure of slogans and the glitter of bandwagons and begin to talk seriously about education. That is one conversation in which we must play a leading role.

## Notes

*   Elliot W. Eisner wishes to thank Joby Gardner for helpful comments on and assistance with this article.
1   The presence of subjectivity in scientific work has long been regarded as a source of bias. Most measurement procedures aspire to what is called "procedural objectivity," which represents a process in which the exercise of judgment is minimized. A competent 10-year-old can do as well as a Nobel Prize winner in measuring a room. Tasks that can be accomplished without appealing to human judgment can also be done by machine. Optical scanners can score multiple test forms more quickly and more accurately than humans. Some idealizations of science aspire to a pristine quantitative descriptive state that does not depend on human judgment or interpretation at all. For an extended discussion of the concept of "procedural objectivity," see Elliot W. Eisner, *The Enlightened Eye: Qualitative Inquiry and the Enhancement of Educational Practice* (New York: Macmillan, 1991).
2   Robert Mager, *Preparing Instructional Objectives* (Palo Alto, CA: Fearon Publishers, 1962).
3   W. James Popham, "Must All Objectives Be Behavioral?," *Educational Leadership* (April 1972), pp. 605–608.
4   Raymond Callahan, *Education and the Cult of Efficiency* (Chicago, IL: University of Chicago Press, 1962).
5   John Dewey, *Art as Experience* (New York: Minton, Balch & Co., 1934), p. 307.
6   Ibid., p. 308.
7   Ibid., p. 309.
8   John I. Goodlad and Robert Anderson, *The Nongraded Elementary School*, rev. edn. (New York: Teachers College Press, 1987).

# CHAPTER 18

# THE PROMISE AND PERILS OF ALTERNATIVE FORMS OF DATA REPRESENTATION*

*Educational Researcher, 1997, 26(6): 4–10*

"Come to the edge," he said.
They said, "We are afraid."
"Come to the edge," he said.
They came.
He pushed them
And they flew.

                    Apollinaire

The theme of this article – alternative forms of data representation – resides on the cutting edge of inquiry in research methodology. One of the basic questions scholars are now raising is how we perform the magical feat of transforming the contents of our consciousness into a public form that others can understand. The assumption that the languages of social science – propositional language and number – are the exclusive agents of meaning is becoming increasingly problematic, and as a result, we are exploring the potential of other forms of representation for illuminating the educational worlds we wish to understand.

The motives for such concerns emanate from the growing discontent with traditional conceptions of knowledge, conceptions that for many – especially younger scholars – have been regarded on one hand as too restrictive to encompass and convey all that is important about education and on the other hand as preserving the status quo and the power of the methodologically enfranchised (Eisner, 1988). Indeed, the form this article takes, originally prepared for an address, has been retained because I believe form and content cannot be disaggregated: how one writes shapes what one says. I want to retain the spoken quality of what I have to say.

The desire to open up new ways of seeing and saying has been motivated by both epistemological and political impulses. As a result of these impulses, we find ourselves on the edge of methodological inquiry. Edges can be treacherous, but they can also be exciting. And, in any case, edges are not a bad location if one is a university professor – especially one with tenure. Universities, after all, should be places with big erasers on their pencils, or if that image is antediluvian, they should be places with big delete keys. Yet, it's not a bad idea to be aware of the potential problems and pitfalls of new ideas and practices as well as their promise. My aim here is to explore both the promise and the perils of alternative forms of data representation. I also wish to put our interests in this matter in an historical context, and I want to make some projections as to where I hope our interests might lead.

First, it is right to acknowledge that, methodologically speaking, the field of educational research has come a long way since the late 1960s and the early 1970s. Those who were around then will remember that it was in 1966 that the Campbell and Stanley (1966) monograph on quasi-experimental and experimental research design was published. For a time, the Campbell and Stanley monograph represented a methodological ideal for educational research. If you could, the true experiment was the model to use. In the 1960s, qualitative research in the field of education had little saliency, though there were some exceptions. Interestingly, many of the most influential exceptions came from those who worked in a quantitative tradition. Lee Cronbach (1975) and Donald Campbell (1978), two traditional researchers, raised fundamental questions about time-honored assumptions in doing research. Egon Guba (1978), another former quantitative researcher, was beginning to explore what he called "naturalistic methods." Philip Jackson (1968), someone who studied with Irving Lorge, a psychometrician at Teachers College, explored life in classrooms while Harry Wolcott (1973) studied the man [*sic*] in the principal's office.

Today the picture looks quite different. Since the late eighties, qualitative research as a category in AERA programs has been the fifth or sixth largest classification for papers presented at its annual meetings. At Stanford, the institution in which I work, what was once viewed with skepticism among some faculty and dismay among others, methodologically speaking, is now the favored approach for doing educational research among doctoral students. But these changes did not come easily.

In the early seventies, when I turned to the arts and humanities as sources of research method and my students and I started to do research using educational connoiseurship and educational criticism, we were expected by most of my colleagues to write extensive justifications for so personal an approach. Times have changed – although I must confess there are still some faculty holdouts. The difference is that while in earlier times I could not ignore them, today I can. The climate has changed.

In 1975, I was asked to give an invited address to Division B of AERA (Eisner, 1977). In that address, I closed my remarks by expressing the hope that someday there would be journals in education devoted to the publication of qualitative studies, that programs in universities would prepare researchers to do such research, and that conferences devoted to its examination would be available. Today, over 20 years later, the field has two journals devoted to qualitative research[1] and many more that publish such research. As for training programs and conferences, we now have both. In less than a quarter of a century, the field has come a long way.

But my aim is neither to praise the achievements of qualitative researchers nor to talk about the changing status of qualitative research. My aim is to provide context. One part of that context is the fact that until quite recently discussions of qualitative research methods almost always were reduced to doing ethnography; to do qualitative research for many in our field was to do ethnography. It is not difficult to understand why ethnography was a safe haven for researchers. Ethnography is a subset of cultural anthropology, and cultural anthropology is a division of the social sciences. It is, one might say, a member of the same church. In addition, ethnography, some people believed, had a teachable and learnable "method," it had a technical language, and most important, it had scholarly standards. It was a recognized discipline.

What became clear – slowly, to be sure – was that qualitative research methods were not the monopoly of ethnographers. Qualitative methods were used by sociologists (Goffman, 1962), clinical psychologists (Sullivan, 1953), historians

(Tuchman, 1962), and writers of all kinds (Capote, 1965). Indeed, the arts and humanities were bastions of qualitative research, and for artists of all persuasions, qualitative inquiry was at the heart of their enterprise. Over time, the concept of research itself was broadened, and science was recognized as *one* among several of its species.

The emergence of this insight – namely, that research did not belong to science alone – represents for me a defining moment. Once it became clear that qualitative research was more than a species of a social science applied to education, the door was opened to questions about what constitutes legitimate forms of inquiry in education and of those forms of inquiry, what should count as research (Eisner *et al.*, 1996). This question – what should count as research – leads to a very deep agenda. It is also an agenda with high stakes for it pertains to matters of legitimacy, authority, and ultimately to who possesses the power to publish and promote. Issues of epistemology have political ramifications as well as intellectual ones (Eisner, 1988). Yet from a purely intellectual perspective, the exploration of alternative forms of data representation is simply a symptom of a fertile imagination seeking to discover its limits.

The title of this article signals both an interest in the possibilities of representation and, at the same time, a recognition of the limits of the forms of representation that are conventionally employed. When we talk about alternative forms of data representation, I assume we mean forms whose limits differ from those imposed by propositional discourse and number. In other words, we are exploring forms of communication that we do not normally use to represent what we have learned about the educational world. How do we make such representations? What forms can they take?

If we reflect on the culture at large and ask how we convey what we know, a large number of forms for doing so come immediately to mind. First, we tell stories. Stories have particular features. Stories instruct, they reveal, they inform in special ways. We also use pictures. Pictures depict. They do many things; among the most important is the obvious: they show us what things, places, and people look like.

People have also been known to make diagrams that display relationships that otherwise would be impossible to grasp. And, of course, people make maps to stand for much more than what we are able to see directly. In fact, we have all kinds of maps, from Mercator projections to globes, to displays of population density, climate, and terrain, all designed to represent what we think we know (Tufte, 1997). In addition to maps, we have theater that, after all, is a frame for expanding our awareness of those forms of life that are best portrayed within the proscenium arch. In addition to stories, pictures, diagrams, maps, and theater, we use demonstrations, often unencumbered by language, to show to others how something is done. And, perhaps above all, we have poetry, that linguistic achievement whose meanings are paradoxically non-linguistic: poetry was invented to say what words can never say. Poetry transcends the limits of language and evokes what cannot be articulated.

What is clear is that the forms we use to inform, the forms that display what we make of what we have chosen to call "data" are as old as the hills; they may be new in the context of educational research, but they have been around forever. In the educational research community, the full array of such forms has been limited. Not all forms of data representation have been considered legitimate in the context of research. That's why the conversation about these matters is so important. That conversation is not only about the use, say, of film as a form of data display; at a more fundamental level, it is about what it means to do research.

There is an intimate relationship between our conception of what the products of research are to look like and the way we go about doing research. What we think it means to do research has to do with our conception of meaning, our view of cognition, and our beliefs about the forms of consciousness that we are willing to say advance human understanding – an aim, I take it, that defines the primary mission of research. What succeeds in deepening meaning, expanding awareness, and enlarging understanding is, in the end, a community decision. Conversation and publication are, in part, aimed at testing ideas in that community.

There are two other points I wish to make about alternative forms of data representation. One is that when AERA decided to encourage its members to propose experimental sessions by inventing new ways to present the results of their research at its annual meeting, when it finally realized that the talking head – indeed, in the typical AERA session there were four to six talking heads – was not necessarily an optimal way of enlarging the understanding of its members, it too displayed an interest in alternative forms of data representation.

Second, it is important to realize that the issues I have identified are not issues restricted to scholars in the field of education. Scholars in the social sciences are now and have been coping with similar issues in their fields. It's in the air. You see it in the work of Clifford Geertz (1983) when he writes about "blurred genres" and "thick description" or when Nelson Goodman (1978) writes about "ways of world making" or when Richard Rorty (1979) writes that pragmatism views science as "one genre of literature" or when George Lakoff and Mark Turner (1989) write that mind is "more than cool reason" or when Jerome Bruner (1986) distinguishes between paradigmatic and narrative ways of knowing or when Michael Polanyi (1966) says simply that man [sic] knows more than he can tell. There is no better collection of essays in the field of anthropology that address what some have called "the crisis of representation" than Clifford and Marcus's (1986) *Writing Culture*, whose subtitle, *The Poetics and Politics of Ethnography* is especially revealing. As I said, it's in the air.

In the field of education, we find these issues addressed in the work of Kathy Carter (1993), Robert Stake (1995), Connelly and Clandinin (1990), and in the pioneering work of Philip Jackson (1968) and Lou Smith (1968). These scholars are a part of a larger community exploring the assumptions employed in the conduct of science, the usefulness of distinctions between objectivity and subjectivity, the functions of voice in writing, the relationship of the general to the particular, and the utilities and limits of quantification. Again, the edges are being explored.

Although it is important to have a climate that supports the growth of the ideas I have been addressing, climates are not enough to ensure their healthy development. We need to nurture them ourselves. That is best achieved when we are critically reflective about what we are doing. That is best achieved when we ask why we are interested in alternative forms of data representation. What functions do such forms serve? Do we really need them? What are we trying to accomplish with these excursions onto the edges I spoke about earlier? And what is a particular form of representation unlikely to do?

Questions such as these bring me to the core of my remarks. One way to get into that core is for me to describe short segments from two films.[2] The first is a segment from *Dead Poets Society* (Haft *et al.*, 1989) and the second from a film about Berkeley High in Berkeley, California. I have selected film simply as one example of data representation. Film and video have much to recommend them. They contain dialogue and plot, they display image, and they can use sound, particularly music, to augment image and word. Put another way, film can teach.

With film, we can ask: what does the soundtrack tell you, the expressions on the faces of those portrayed, the visual features of the setting? Put another way, *how* do these films inform? What did the filmmakers do to make this happen? We start with the introductory segment of *Dead Poets Society*.

What we see early on in this film are two boys, one wearing a beanie and the other wearing a straw boater a tad too big, preparing for some kind of ceremony. The oversized boater makes the boy look something like a miniature adult. It provides a foretaste of what he will someday become. At the same time, the boater symbolizes both class and tradition. The images we see bespeak of hallowed halls, the moneyed east, Princeton, the Ivy League. As we will soon learn, this is no working-class school. The straw boater and the Gothic interior that the boy and the others are soon to enter, banners raised, stepping in a single-file procession to the strains of a bagpipe, exude a sense of tradition and history. The quickness with which the boys respond to the urgent command, "Raise banners!," says the ceremony we are about to witness is serious business.

They enter a long aisle bisecting a chapel-like interior crowded with waiting adults and an all-White student body. Leading the procession is the boy in the beanie followed by the boy in the boater, who in turn are followed by an old man whose trembling hands hold a lit candle. It is the light of knowledge that he passes to a young student sitting in the first row. This young student smiles and nods with gratitude and respect as he receives it. We are at Welton Academy, a venerable institution that, according to its headmaster, is the best preparatory school in America, a school about which we learn that "more than 75% of its students went on to the Ivy Leagues!" But this is not all that we learn.

The filmmakers have created a visual narrative that displays an array of values, not by describing them, but by depicting them. We are drawn into the culture of Welton, almost enveloped by it in only a matter of minutes. In this brief segment, we are given a glimpse of what seems to be an authentic place. We see the well-scrubbed faces of its blazer-jacketed students, the tweedy dress of their parents, the academic regalia of the faculty, the cocky self-assurance of the medaled headmaster. When the boys rise to respond in unison to the question, "Gentlemen, what are the four pillars?" "Tradition, honor, discipline, excellence!," we feel the elite character of a venerable school supported by wealthy parents, designed to give their sons all that they need to preserve their class and to realize their destinies. Without being didactic, the filmmakers give us what we need to make sense out of what we see and hear. In less than four minutes' running time, we are introduced to a place we can read, an array of values we can recognize, and a setting we might even grudgingly admire. And if we cannot admire, we think we can understand.

Now, literally speaking, Welton Academy does not exist. This film is fiction. Yet schools like Welton do exist. Just where is the line to be drawn between fact and fiction? Is it between truth and falsehood, reality and its imitation? Assume that the filmmakers are all qualitative researchers. Assume for a moment that they decided to create this film to share what they had learned from their research regarding the common features of several privileged preparatory schools. Would such a work count as a legitimate form of data representation? It provides no theoretical analysis of what it depicts. Its methods – if that term does not seem too mechanical – do not seem replicable. Does this matter? If we insist that a work has to be theoretical to count as research, do we also assume that theory and replicability are necessary conditions for doing research, even if we collectively agree that the film does advance our understanding of places like Welton Academy? And even if we cannot know if places like Welton Academy are indeed like Welton Academy, would this film help us determine if the culture and the values the film depicts can be found in other preparatory schools? Put another way, does the film streamline our search? Does it sensitize us to the possible? Does it offer us an anticipatory set with which to seek and find? Yet, can fiction count as a form of data display? Can fiction count in doing research? Might not the desire to realize artistic values mislead, as they apparently have in Oliver Stone's *Nixon?* Questions such as these have been pondered and discussed by narratologists (Mitchell, 1986) and anthropologists (Clifford and Marcus, 1986). The debates lead us once again to the edges of discourse about cognition and representation (Eisner *et al.*, 1996).

Just what is at stake here in this discussion of this film and other alternative forms of data representation? A great deal. What we are dealing with is a conception of how meaning is made and what shall count as knowledge or, to use a more felicitous phrase, how understanding is enlarged. If there are different ways of knowing, what way is this?

The way we usually do research is to reduce what we have learned to text and number. Our official text is propositional; we try to put our experience into claims that propositions can carry. We also try to quantify the qualitative features of our experience – an effort that began, according to Dewey, with Galileo. Dewey writes:

> The work of Galileo was not a development, but a revolution. It marked a change from the qualitative to the quantitative or metric; from the heterogenous to the homogeneous; from intrinsic forms to relations; from esthetic harmonies to mathematical formulae; from contemplative enjoyment to active manipulation and control; from rest to change; from eternal objects to temporal sequence.
>
> (1929, pp. 94–95)

Put another way, we report the temperature even when we are interested in the heat; we expect a reader to be able to transform the numbers representing the former into the experience that constitutes the latter. New forms of data representation signify our growing interest in inventing ways to represent the heat.

There are, of course, good reasons why text – or more precisely, propositions – should be so central to our traditional view of knowledge. For one, our view of knowledge is tied up with matters of verification, and verification is tied up with matters of truth. Truth is related to claims, and claims cannot be made without making assertions. Assertions, in turn, require propositions, and propositions return us to text.

Philosophers whose epistemologies travel the route I have just described will have no truck with the non-propositional as a source of knowledge (Ayer, 1952). They regard the non-propositional as imprecise and subjective. Non-propositional forms undermine verifiability, compromise truth, and invite ambiguity; such is not the stuff of knowledge. Concerns for verification, truth, and precision have led us away from an experiential conception of understanding and toward a verificationist conception of knowledge – something that can be tested, packaged, imparted, and sent like bricks across country to build knowledge structures that are said to accumulate. In fact, we often talk about knowledge as if it consisted of measurable units, as in the often-heard claim that knowledge doubles every 20 years. One can only wonder what constitutes a unit of knowledge. We have – to mix metaphors – concretized our view of what it means to know. We prefer our knowledge solid and like our data hard. It makes for a firm foundation, a secure place on which to stand. Knowledge as process, a temporary state, is scary to many.

The concept of alternative forms of data representation presents another image. It is an image that acknowledges the variety of ways through which our experience is coded. It is about the ways in which the transformation of experience from the personal to the public can occur. It is about what we can learn from each of these transformations. It is about the trade-offs that are inevitable in the selection of any option. It is about exploring the edges and reexamining the meaning of research.

In emphasizing, as I have, the output side of the issue – that is, how we go about the magical task of reducing the multimedia world of our experience to a form of representation – I have, I'm afraid, given the impression that trade-offs occur only in the transformation of what is inside of consciousness into what can be carried outside. This conclusion, if you drew it, would be only half right. The selection of a form of representation – or, as some people call it – a symbol system (Solomon, 1997) is a selection of not only what can be conveyed but of what is likely to be noticed. The selection of a form of representation, whether by mindless habit or by reflective choice, affects what we see. As E. H. Gombrich was said to have quipped, "Artists do not paint what they see, they see what they know how to paint." Gombrich's point is that perception is selective and that the motives for selection are influenced by the tools one has or knows how to use: we tend to seek what we know how to find.

Let's consider the contents of another film, this one is about Berkeley High. The title of the film is *School Colors* (Andrews *et al.*, n.d.). It was made by both the students of Berkeley High and by professional filmmakers. It is an example of cinema verité. Berkeley High is a school with a racially diverse student population. It is also a school struggling with racial conflict. Again, the question we are asking is, what do the filmmakers make it possible for us to learn?

Assume you are trying to understand racial segregation in high school. Assume you want to know something about the conflicts, the resistance to integration, the dilemmas that racial minorities experience, and the struggles that teachers experience dealing with students who must cope every day with stigma. What does *School Colors* help you understand, and how does it do so? What do the scenes have to say that a traditional quantitative rendering of Berkeley High would be likely to leave out? And what would a traditional rendering reveal that *School Colors* omits? Put another way, what do we get and what do we give up? What gets revealed and what gets concealed?

What do we feel when we see Louis Farrakhan on TV in *School Colors?* What do the students feel? How do we know? How do we interpret the relationship displayed on film between the Black studies teacher and his students? What do we make of his arm around his student's shoulder as they leave his classroom?

And what about the White students in the film, the student who says he's "real White" and who quickly follows up with, "I'm just trying to survive"? What does the expression on his face tell us? Does material of this kind enlarge our understanding? If so, how?

The students who produced this film were inquiring into the culture of their school. More than likely, they knew that culture very well and used the opportunity to reveal what they took it to be. Is the visual collage they created a sample of educational research? It is interpretive. As a matter of fact, deciding what to shoot, what to keep, and how to compose the segments is inherently interpretive. How shall we regard such a form of data display, and once again, is it research? My conception of research is broad. I will count as research reflective efforts to study the world and to create ways to share what we have learned about it. Research can take the forms that echo the forms of the arts and humanities or those of the natural and social sciences. Its forms of data representation are open to invention. Ultimately its value as research is determined by the judgment of a critical community. What is your conception of research?

I raise these questions because I think they ought to be pondered. Those of us who think we need new forms of data representation need to be able to explain why. I have partially described some of the features of two examples of visual forms of representation. These examples should be regarded as illustrative of only a small portion of what is possible. I have not talked about readers' theater, still photography, or the use of journals or narratives. I have not spoken of multimedia resources. I have presented only a general picture of some of what I think film and video make possible. Now, let me indicate what I believe to be the promise and the perils of alternative forms of data representation.

First, it is clear that all of the forms of representation I have identified are used to shape experience and to enlarge understanding. Whether you use a story, create a film, employ a diagram, or construct a chart, what such tools have in common is the purpose of illuminating rather than obscuring the message. One reason for selecting one tool rather than another is because it does the job that you want done better than the others. What kind of jobs need to be done?

One job that scholars increasingly want done is engendering a sense of empathy for the lives of the people they wish us to know. Why empathy? Because we have begun to realize that human feeling does not pollute understanding. In fact, understanding others and the situations they face may well require it. Forms of data representation that contribute to empathic participation in the lives of others are necessary for having one kind of access to their lives. Artistically crafted narrative, including the crafting of film, comes into play here. Facts described literally are unlikely to have the power to evoke in the reader what the reader needs to experience to know the person someone portrays. Alternative forms of data representation can make empathy possible when work on those forms are treated as works of art.

Second, alternative forms of data representation can, as in the case of both Welton Academy and Berkeley High, provide a sense of particularity that abstractions cannot render. We come to see the place, to know each individual character. When done well, the situation and the people take on their own distinctive qualities. They acquire dimension. Particularity and dimensionality are conditions of something being "real." One function of all forms of data representation is to confer a sense that what is being portrayed is real. Authenticity is not a bad quality for research of any kind to have.

Third, alternative forms of data representation can provide what might be called "productive ambiguity." By productive ambiguity, I mean that the material presented is more evocative than denotative, and in its evocation, it generates insight and invites attention to complexity. Unlike the traditional ideal of conventional research, some alternative forms of data representation result in less closure and more plausible interpretations of the meaning of the situation. I provided one interpretation of a small section of *Dead Poets Society;* how many other plausible interpretations are possible? The open texture of the form increases the probability that multiple perspectives will emerge. Multiple perspectives make our engagement with the phenomena more complex. Ironically, good research often complicates our lives.

Fourth, alternative forms of data representation promise to increase the variety of questions that we can ask about the educational situations we study. A student who recently learned how to calculate Pearson product moment correlations is likely to look for things to correlate. A student who recently learned how to use a video camera is likely to look for things to shoot. As the use of alternative forms of data representation increases, we can expect new ways of seeing things, new settings for their display, and new problems to tackle. The invention of time-lapse and slow-motion photography has enabled us to see what is otherwise invisible to the naked eye. The invention of the telescope and the microscope has made possible the formation of questions that were unaskable before their presence. Put another way, our capacity to wonder is stimulated by the possibilities that new forms of representation suggest. As we learn to think within the medium we choose to use, we also become more able to raise questions that the media themselves suggest; tools, among other things, are also heuristics.

Finally, the presence of alternative forms of data representation allows us to exploit individual aptitudes. Neither the literal nor the quantitative are everybody's cup of tea. Individuals who shine at the creation of a film or story might have little competence using the modes of thought and the forms of representation used in conventional types of research. If intelligence can be defined, as Olson (1988) suggested, as skill in a medium, then the use of different media for the creation of research is a way to activate wider varieties of human intelligence. This, I take it, would not be a bad thing.

If the virtues I have described are the positive side of alternative forms of data representation, what are the perils?

Consider the matter of referential precision. One of the ideals of conventional social science is to reduce ambiguity and increase precision: what one seeks are claims and explanations that give as little space as possible to competing explanations, rival hypotheses, or personal judgment. The operational definition and the objective test stand as encomia to such aspirations.

Many alternative forms of data representation do not provide that kind of precision. The visual display of a scene in a classroom or a school can be seen from multiple perspectives. Is it important for the viewer to know the perspective taken by the researcher, or is it not necessary? What will count as a misinterpretation? You will remember that I identified ambiguity as a potential source of insight, a way of keeping the door open for fresh insights and multiple interpretations. Yet ambiguity is not without its perils. One peril of ambiguity is the Rorschach syndrome: everyone confers his or her own idiosyncratic meaning to the data. No consensus is possible. The data mean whatever anyone wants them to mean; or worse, no one knows what they mean.

Clearly, there is a trade-off here. How much precision do we need? When is precision constraining? How shall we test – if that's the right word – the validity of the data or their meaning. How shall we know if we are advancing the conversation? Those questions need to be addressed.

A second peril has to do not with a problem inherent in the use of alternative forms of data representation, but in a potential backlash from their use. I have no doubt that there will be presentations of research that more than a few in the educational research community will consider bizarre. Their amazement is not a good reason for not exploring the edges of possibility, but it is a reason to recognize the need for interpretation, especially for those who sail by other stars. It is a good reason for describing the context in which the results of research are to be presented. A genre of work can stand alone without an interpretive context when those reading, seeing, or hearing it bring that context with them. When they do not, they are likely to be lost. Few people like to be lost. When the terrain is new, we need context. We also need to be sure, if we can be, that we are not substituting novelty and cleverness for substance. In other words, we need to be our own toughest critics.

Third, consider the constraints imposed by our publication system on material that does not take printed form. Where, for example, will the video segments so central to a presentation appear? Give the practical need of establishing a publication record, not to mention our need to share what we have learned, the current constraints on the use of alternative forms of representation are not insignificant.

There is promise, however. That promise may reside in the use of the computer and in the creation of multimedia displays for capturing the meanings new forms of data representation make possible. It is not beyond our practical capabilities to provide material that combines text and image, image and music, music and measurement. The computer may make possible what our pictureless journals find impossible to provide. The current constraints may be temporary.

Let me return to where I started. How do we display what we have learned? What forms can we trust? What modes are legitimate? How shall we know? Those questions and how we explore them can help redefine what educational research means, how it is pursued, and what we can learn from it. It can enlarge our discourse and widen our conceptions.

I cannot think of a more important agenda. We are, in a sense, looking for new stars. We are also looking for new seas. We are, as I said earlier, exploring the edges. There is, I think, no better place from which to see the stars and no better position from which to discover new seas than the view one gets from the edge.

> "Come to the edge," he said.
> They said, "We are afraid."
> "Come to the edge," he said.
> They came.
> He pushed them
> And they flew.
>                                    Apollinaire

## Notes

\*   This article was delivered as a keynote address at the 1996 Conference on Qualitative Research in Education at the University of Georgia. I want to express my gratitude to Mike Atkin and Alan Peshkin for their very helpful comments while I was preparing this article. Because the form an article takes is part of its content, I chose to retain the form in which this article was originally prepared, that of an oral delivery.

1   See, for example, *Qualitative Inquiry* and *The International Journal of Qualitative Studies in Education*.

2   I am unable to include the films from which the descriptions to follow were derived – which is exactly my point about the limits of our journals and traditions.

## References

Andrews, S., Olsson, S., and Robinson-Odom, I. M. (Producers). *School Colors* (Frontline Special Edition) [Videotape]. Washington, DC: Corporation for Public Broadcasting, n.d.

Ayer, A. J. *Language, Truth and Logic*. New York: Dover Publications, 1952.

Bruner, J. Two Modes of Thought. *Actual Minds, Possible Worlds* (pp. 11–43). Cambridge, MA: Harvard University Press, 1986.

Campbell, D. Qualitative Knowing in Action Research. In M. Brenner and M. Marsh (eds), *The Social Contexts of Method* (pp. 184–209). London: Croon Helm, 1978.

Campbell, D. and Stanley, J. *Experimental and Quasi-Experimental Designs for Research*. Chicago, IL: McNally & Co., 1966.

Capote, T. *In Cold Blood*. New York: Random House, 1965.

Carter, K. The Place of Story and the Study of Teaching and Teacher Education. *Educational Researcher* 22(1): 5–12; 1993.

Clifford, J. and Marcus, G. (eds). *Writing Culture: The Poetics and Politics of Ethnography.* Berkeley, CA: University of California Press, 1986.

Connelly, F. M. and Clandinin, D. J. Stories of Experience and Narrative Inquiry. *Educational Researcher* 19(5): 2–14; 1990.

Cronbach, L. Beyond the Two Disciplines of Scientific Psychology. *American Psychologist* 30(2): 116–127; 1975.

Dewey, J. *The Quest for Certainty.* New York: Minton, Balch & Co., 1929.

Eisner, E. On the Use of Educational Connoiseurship and Educational Criticism for Evaluating Classroom Life. *Teachers College Record* 78(3): 345–358; 1977.

Eisner, E. The Primacy of Experience and the Politics of Method. *Educational Researcher* 17(5): 15–20; 1988.

Eisner, E., Gardner, H., Cizek, G. J., Gough, N., Tillman, L., Stotsky, S., and Wasley, P. Should Novels Count as Dissertations in Education? *Research in the Teaching of English* 30(4): 403–427; 1996.

Geertz, C. Blurred Genres: The Refiguration of Social Thought. In C. Geertz (ed.), *Local Knowledge: Further Essays in Interpretive Anthropology* (pp. 19–35). New York: Basic Books, 1983.

Goffman, E. *Asylums.* Chicago, IL: Aldine Publications Co., 1962.

Goodman, N. *Ways of Worldmaking.* Indianapolis, IN: Hackett Publishing Co., 1978.

Guba, E. *Toward a Methodology of Naturalistic Inquiry in Educational Evaluation.* Los Angeles, CA: UCLA Graduate School of Education, University of California Center for the Study of Evaluation, 1978.

Haft, S., Witt, P. J., and Thomas, T. (Producers), and Weir, P. (Director). *Dead Poets Society* [Videotape]. Burbank, CA: Vista Home Video, 1989.

Jackson, P. *Life in Classrooms.* New York: Holt, Rinehart and Winston, 1968.

Lakoff, G. and Turner, M. *More than Cool Reason.* Chicago, IL: University of Chicago Press, 1989.

Mitchell, W. *Iconology: Image, Text and Ideology.* Chicago, IL: University of Chicago Press, 1986.

Olson, D. *Developing Theories of Mind.* Cambridge, MA: Cambridge University Press, 1988.

Polanyi, M. *The Tacit Dimension.* London: Routledge and Kegan Paul, 1966.

Rorty, R. *Philosophy and the Mirror of Nature.* Princeton, NJ: Princeton University Press, 1979.

Smith, L. *The Complexities of an Urban Classroom.* New York: Holt, Rinehart and Winston, 1968.

Solomon, G. Of Mind and Media: How Culture's Symbolic Forms Affect Learning and Thinking. *Phi Delta Kappan* 78(5): 375–380; 1997.

Stake, R. *The Art of Case Study Research.* Thousand Oaks, CA: Sage Publications, 1995.

Sullivan, H. *The Interpersonal Theory of Psychiatry.* New York: Norton, 1953.

Tuchman, B. *The Guns of August.* New York: Macmillan, 1962.

Tufte, E. *Visual Explanations.* Cheshire, CT: Graphics Press. 1997.

Wolcott, H. *The Man in the Principal's Office.* New York: Holt, Rinehart and Winston, 1973.

# CHAPTER 19

# WHAT DOES IT MEAN TO SAY A SCHOOL IS DOING WELL?*

*Phi Delta Kappan*, 2001, 82(5): 367–372

Driven by discontent with the performance of our schools, we are, once again, in the midst of education reform, as we were in 1983 with *A Nation at Risk*, in 1987 with America 2000, and a few years later with Goals 2000. Each of these reform efforts was intended to rationalize the practice and performance of our schools. Each was designed to work out and install a system of measurable goals and evaluation practices that would ensure that our nation would be first in science and mathematics by the year 2000, that all our children would come to school ready to learn, and that each school would be drug-free, safe, and nonviolent.[1]

The formulation of standards and the measurement of performance were intended to tidy up a messy system and to make teachers and school administrators truly accountable. The aim was then, and is today, to systematize and standardize so that the public will know which schools are performing well and which are not. There were to be then, and there are today, payments and penalties for performance.

America is one of the few nations in which responsibility for schools is not under the aegis of a national ministry of education. Although we have a federal agency, the US Department of Education, the 10th Amendment to the US Constitution indicates that those responsibilities that the Constitution does not assign explicitly to the federal government belong to the states (or to the people). And since the Constitution makes no mention of education, it is a responsibility of the states.

As a result, we have 50 departments of education, one for each state, overseeing some 16,000 school districts that serve 52 million students in more than 100,000 schools. In addition, each school district has latitude for shaping education policy. Given the complexity of the way education is organized in the United States, it is understandable that from one perspective the view looks pretty messy and not altogether rational. Furthermore, more than a few believe that we have a national problem in American education and that national problems require national solutions. The use of highly rationalized procedures for improving schools is a part of the solution.

I mention the concept of rationalization because I am trying to describe the ethos being created in our schools. I am trying to reveal a world view that shapes our conception of education and the direction we take for making our schools better.

Rationalization as a concept has a number of features. First, it depends on a clear specification of intended outcomes.[2] That is what standards and rubrics are supposed to do. We are supposed to know what the outcomes of educational practice are to be, and rubrics are to exemplify those outcomes. Standards are more general statements intended to proclaim our values. One argument for the use of standards and rubrics is that they are necessary if we are to function rationally. As the saying goes, if you don't know where you're headed, you will not know where you have arrived. In fact, it's more than knowing where you're headed; it's also knowing the precise destination. Thus the specification of intended outcomes has become one of the primary practices in the process of rationalizing school reform efforts. Holding people accountable for the results is another.

Second, rationalization typically uses measurement as a means through which the quality of a product or performance is assessed and represented. Measurement, of course, is *one* way to describe the world. Measurement has to do with determining matters of magnitude, and it deals with matters of magnitude through the specification of units. In the United States, the unit for weight is pounds. In Sweden or the Netherlands, it is kilograms. It's kilometers in Europe; it's miles in the United States. It really doesn't matter what unit you use, as long as everyone agrees what the unit is.[3]

Quantification is believed to be a way to increase objectivity, secure rigor, and advance precision in assessment. For describing some features of the world, including the educational world, it is indispensable. But it is not good for everything, and the limitations of quantification are increasingly being recognized. For example, although initial discussions about standards emphasized the need for them to be *measurable*, as standards have become increasingly general and ideological, measurability has become less salient.

Third, the rationalization of practice is predicated on the ability to control and predict. We assume that we can know the specific effects of our interventions, an assumption that is questionable.

Fourth, rationalization downplays interactions. Interactions take into account not simply the conditions that are to be introduced in classrooms or schools but also the kinds of personal qualities, expectations, orientations, ideas, and temperaments that interact with those conditions. Philosophical constructivists have pointed out that what something means comes both from the features of the phenomenon to be addressed and from the way those features are interpreted or experienced by individuals.[4] Such idiosyncratic considerations always complicate assessment. They complicate efforts to rationalize education as well. Prediction is not easy when what the outcome is going to be is a function not only of what is introduced in the situation but also of what a student makes of what has been introduced.

Fifth, rationalization promotes comparison, and comparison requires what is called "commensurability." Commensurability is possible only if you know what the programs were in which the youngsters participated in the schools being compared. If youngsters are in schools that have different curricula or that allocate differing amounts of time to different areas of the curriculum, comparing the outcomes of those schools without taking into account their differences is extremely questionable. Making comparisons between the math performance of youngsters in Japan and those in the United States without taking into account cultural differences, different allocations of time for instruction, or different approaches to teaching makes it impossible to account for differences in student performance or to consider the side effects or opportunity costs associated with different programs in different cultures. The same principle holds in comparing student performance across school districts in the United States.

Sixth, rationalization relies upon extrinsic incentives to motivate action; that's what vouchers are intended to do. Schools are likened to businesses, and the survival of the fittest is the principle that determines which ones survive. If schools don't produce effective results on tests, they go out of business.

In California and in some other parts of the country, principals and superintendents are often paid a bonus if their students perform well on standardized tests: payment by results. And, of course, such a reward system has consequences for a school's priorities. Are test scores the criteria that we want to use to reward professional performance?

The features that I have just described are a legacy of the Enlightenment. We believe our rational abilities can be used to discover the regularities of the universe and, once we've found them, to implement, as my colleague David Tyack titled his book, "the one best system."[5] We have a faith in our ability to discover what the US Department of Education once described as "what works." The result is an approach to reform that leaves little room for surprise, for imagination, for improvisation, or for the cultivation of productive idiosyncrasy. Our reform efforts are closer in spirit to the ideas of René Descartes and August Compte than to those of William Blake. They are efforts that use league tables to compare schools and that regard test scores as valid proxies for the quality of education our children receive.[6] And they constitute an approach to reform that has given us three major educationally feckless reform efforts in the past 20 years. Are we going to have another?

What are the consequences of the approach to reform that we have taken and what should we pay attention to in order to tell when a school is doing well? First, one of the consequences of our approach to reform is that the curriculum gets narrowed as school district policies make it clear that what is to be tested is what is to be taught. Tests come to define our priorities. And now we have legitimated those priorities by talking about "core subjects." The introduction of the concept of core subjects explicitly marginalizes subjects that are not part of the core. One of the areas that we marginalize is the arts, an area that when well taught offers substantial benefits to students. Our idea of core subjects is related to our assessment practices and the tests we use to determine whether or not schools are doing well.

Because those of us in education take test scores seriously, the public is reinforced in its view that test scores are good proxies for the quality of education a school provides. Yet what test scores predict best are other test scores. If we are going to use proxies that have predictive validity, we need proxies that predict performances that matter outside the context of school. The function of schooling is not to enable students to do better in school. The function of schooling is to enable students to do better in life. What students learn in school ought to exceed in relevance the limits of the school's program.

As we focus on standards, rubrics, and measurement, the deeper problems of schooling go unattended. What are some of the deeper problems of schooling? One has to do with the quality of conversation in classrooms. We need to provide opportunities for youngsters and adolescents to engage in challenging kinds of conversation, and we need to help them learn how to do so. Such conversation is all too rare in schools. I use "conversation" seriously, for challenging conversation is an intellectual affair. It has to do with thinking about what people have said and responding reflectively, analytically, and imaginatively to that process. The practice of conversation is almost a lost art. We turn to talk shows to experience what we cannot do very well or very often.

The deeper problems of schooling have to do with teacher isolation and the fact that teachers don't often have access to other people who know what they're doing when they teach and who can help them do it better.[7] Although there are many issues that need attention in schooling, we search for the silver bullet and believe that, if we get our standards straight and our rubrics right and make our tests tough enough, we will have an improved school system. I am not so sure.

The message that we send to students is that what really matters in their education are their test scores. As a result, students in high-stakes testing programs find ways to cut corners – and so do some teachers. We read increasingly often not only about students who are cheating but also about teachers who are unfairly helping students get higher scores on the tests.[8] It's a pressure that undermines the kind of experience that students ought to have in schools.

Perhaps the major consequence of the approach we have taken to rationalize our schools is that it ineluctably colors the school climate. It promotes an orientation to practice that emphasizes extrinsically defined attainment targets that have a specified quantitative value. This, in turn, leads students to want to know just what it is they need to do to earn a particular grade. Even at Stanford, I sometimes get requests from graduate students who want to know precisely, or as precisely as I can put it, what they need to do in order to get an A in the class.

Now from one angle such a request sounds reasonable. After all, it is a means/ ends approach to educational planning. Students are, it can be said, rationally planning their education. But such planning has very little to do with intellectual life, where risk-taking, exploration, uncertainty, and speculation are what it's about. And if you create a culture of schooling in which a narrow means/ends orientation is promoted, that culture can undermine the development of intellectual dispositions. By intellectual dispositions I mean a curiosity and interest in engaging and challenging ideas.

What the field has not provided is an efficient alternative to the testing procedures we now use. And for good reason. The good reason is that there are no efficient alternatives. Educationally useful evaluation takes time, it's labor intensive and complex, and it's subtle, particularly if evaluation is used not simply to score children or adults but to provide information to improve the process of teaching and learning.

The price one pays for providing many ways for students to demonstrate what has been learned is a reduction of commensurability. Commensurability decreases when attention to individuality increases. John Dewey commented about comparisons in a book that he wrote in 1934 when he was 76 years old. The book is *Art as Experience*. He observed that nothing is more odious than comparisons in the arts.[9] What he was getting at was that attention to or appreciation of an art form requires attention to and appreciation of its distinctive features. It was individuality that Dewey was emphasizing, and it is the description of individuality we would do well to think about in our assessment practices. We should be trying to discover where a youngster is, where his or her strengths are, where additional work is warranted. Commensurability is possible when everybody is on the same track, when there are common assessment practices, and when there is a common curriculum. But when students work on different kinds of problems, and when there is concern with the development of an individual's thumbprint, so to speak, commensurability is an inappropriate aim.

What have been the consequences of the rationalized approach to education reform that we have embraced? Only this: in our desire to improve our schools, education has become a casualty. That is, in the process of rationalization, education – always a delicate, complex, and subtle process having to do with both cultural transmission and self-actualization – has become a commodity. Education has evolved from a form of human development serving personal and civic needs into a product our nation produces to compete in a global economy. Schools have become places to mass produce this product.

Let us assume that we impose a moratorium on standardized testing for a five-year period. What might we pay attention to in schools in order to say that a school is doing well? If it is not higher test scores that we are looking for, what is it? Let me suggest the kind of data we might seek by raising some questions that might guide our search.

What kinds of problems and activities do students engage in? What kind of thinking do these activities invite? Are students encouraged to wonder and to raise questions about what they have studied? Perhaps we should be less concerned with whether they can answer our questions than with whether they can ask their own. The most significant intellectual achievement is not so much in problem solving, but in question posing. What if we took that idea seriously and concluded units of study by looking for the sorts of questions that youngsters are able to raise as a result of being immersed in a domain of study? What would that practice teach youngsters about inquiry?

What is the intellectual significance of the ideas that youngsters encounter? (I have a maxim that I work with: if it's not worth teaching, it's not worth teaching well.) Are the ideas they encounter important? Are they ideas that have legs? Do they go someplace?

Are students introduced to multiple perspectives? Are they asked to provide multiple perspectives on an issue or a set of ideas? The implications of such an expectation for curriculum development are extraordinary. To develop such an ability and habit of mind, we would need to invent activities that encourage students to practice, refine, and develop certain modes of thought. Taking multiple perspectives is just one such mode.

In 1950 the American psychologist J. P. Guilford developed what he called "the structure of intellect," in which 130 different kinds of cognitive processes were identified.[10] What if we used that kind of structure to promote various forms of thinking? My point is that the activities in which youngsters participate in classes are the means through which their thinking is promoted. When youngsters have no reason to raise questions, the processes that enable them to learn how to discover intellectual problems go undeveloped.

The ability to raise telling questions is not an automatic consequence of maturation. Do you know what's the biggest problem that Stanford students have in the course of their doctoral work? It is not getting good grades in courses; they all get good grades in courses. Their biggest obstacle is in framing a dissertation problem. We can do something about that before students get to the doctoral level. In a school that is doing well, opportunities for the kind of thinking that yields good questions would be promoted.

What connections are students helped to make between what they study in class and the world outside of school? A major aim of education has to do with what psychologists refer to as "transfer of learning." Can students apply what they have learned or what they have learned how to learn? Can they engage in the kind of learning they will need in order to deal with problems and issues outside of the classroom? If what students are learning is simply used as a means to increase their scores on the next test, we may win the battle and lose the war. In such a context, school learning becomes a hurdle to jump over. We need to determine whether students can use what they have learned. But even being able to use what has been learned is no indication that it will be used. There is a difference between what a student can do and what a student will do.

The really important dependent variables in education are not located in classrooms. Nor are they located in schools. The really important dependent variables are located outside schools. Our assessment practices haven't even begun to scratch that surface. It's what students do with what they learn when they can do what they want to do that is the real measure of educational achievement.

What opportunities do youngsters have to become literate in the use of different representational forms? By representational forms, I mean the various symbol systems through which humans shape experience and give it meaning.[11] Different forms of human meaning are expressed in different forms of representation. The kinds of meaning one secures from poetry are not the kinds of meaning one secures from propositional signs. The kinds of meanings expressed in music are not the meanings experienced in the visual arts. To be able to secure any of those meanings, you have to know how to "read" them. Seeing is a reading. Hearing is a reading. They are processes of interpreting and *construing* meaning from the material encountered; reading text is not only a process of decoding, it is also a process of encoding. We *make* sense of what we read.

What opportunities do students have to formulate their own purposes and to design ways to achieve them? Can a school provide the conditions for youngsters, as they mature, to have increased opportunity to set their own goals and to design ways to realize them? Plato once defined a slave as someone who executes the purposes of another. I would say that, in a free democratic state, at least a part of the role of education is to help youngsters learn how to define their own purposes.

What opportunities do students have to work cooperatively to address problems that they believe to be important? Can we design schools so that we create communities of learners who know how to work with one another? Can we design schools and classrooms in which cooperating with others is part of what it means to be a student?

Do students have the opportunity to serve the community in ways that are not limited to their own personal interests? Can we define a part of the school's role as establishing or helping students establish projects in which they do something beyond their own self-interest? I want to know that in order to know how well a school is doing.

To what extent are students given the opportunity to work in depth in domains that relate to their aptitudes? Is personal talent cultivated? Can we arrange the time for youngsters to work together on the basis of interest rather than on the basis of age grading? Youngsters who are interested in ceramics might work in depth in ceramics; those interested in science might work in depth in science. To make these possibilities a reality, we would need, of course, to address the practical problems of allocating time and responsibility. But without a conception of what is important, we will never even ask questions about allocating time. A vision of what is educationally important must come first.

Do students participate in the assessment of their own work? If so, how? It is important for teachers to understand what students themselves think of their own work. Can we design assessment practices in which students can help us?

To what degree are students genuinely engaged in what they do in school? Do they find satisfaction in the intellectual journey? How many students come to school early and how many would like to stay late? The motives for such choices have to do with the "locus of satisfactions." Satisfactions generate reasons for doing something. Basically, there are three reasons for doing anything. One reason for doing something is that you like what it feels like and you like who you are when you do it. Sex, play, and art fall into this category. They are intrinsically satisfying activities.

A second reason for doing something is not because you like doing it, but because you like the results of having done it. You might like a clean kitchen, but you might not enjoy cleaning your kitchen. The process is not a source of enjoyment, but the outcome is.

A third reason for doing something is not because you like the process or even the outcome, but because you like the rewards. You like the grades you earn. You like the paycheck you receive. That's what Hannah Arendt described as labor.[12] There is too much labor in our schools – and not enough work. Work is effort from which you derive satisfaction. We ought to be paying attention to the joy of the journey. This is easy to say but difficult and challenging to do. Nevertheless, we ought to keep our minds focused on it as a goal.

Are teachers given the time to observe and work with one another? To what degree is professional discourse an important aspect of what being a teacher means in the school? Is the school a resource, a center for the teacher's own development? Is the school a center for teacher education? The center for teacher education is not the university; it is the school in which the teacher works. Professional growth should be promoted during the 25 years that a teacher works in a school – not just during the year and a half that he or she spends in a teacher education program. Can we create schools that take the professional development of teachers seriously? And what would they look like? Schools will not be better for students than they are for the professionals who work in them.

All of us who teach develop repertoires. We all have routines. We all get by. We get by without serious problems, but getting by is not good enough. We need to get better. And to get better, we have to think about school in ways that address teachers' real needs. And when I say, "addressing teachers' real needs," I don't mean sending them out every 6,000 miles to get "inserviced" by a stranger.

Are parents helped to understand what their child has accomplished in class? Do they come to understand the educational import of what is going on? Very often children's artwork is displayed in the school, with the only information provided being the student's name, the grade, and the teacher's name, all in the lower right-hand corner. Then the best student work is posted more formally. What we do, in effect, is use a gallery model of exhibition. We take the best work, and we display it. What we need to create is an educationally interpretive exhibition that explains to viewers what problems the youngsters were addressing and how they resolved them.[13] This can be done by looking at prior work and comparing it with present work – that is, by looking at what students have accomplished over time. I am talking about interpretation. I am talking about getting people to focus not so much on what the grade is, but on what process led to the outcome.

What is my point? All my arguments have had to do with creating an educationally informed community. We need to ask better questions.

Can we widen what parents and others believe to be important in judging the quality of our schools? Can we widen and diversify what they think matters? Can those of us who teach think about public education not only as the education of the public in the schools (i.e. our students), but also as the education of the public outside of our schools (i.e. parents and community members)? Can a more substantial and complex understanding of what constitutes good schooling contribute to better, more enlightened support for our schools?

Can a more informed conception of what constitutes quality in education lead to greater equity for students and ultimately for the culture? Educational equity is much more than just allowing students to cross the threshold of the school. It has to do with what students find after they do so. We ought to be providing environments that enable each youngster in our schools to find a place in the educational sun. But when we narrow the program so that there is only a limited array of areas in which assessment occurs and performance is honored, youngsters whose aptitudes and interests lie elsewhere are going to be marginalized in our schools. The more we diversify those opportunities, the more equity we are going to have because we are going to provide wider opportunities for youngsters to find what it is that they are good at.

And that leads me to the observation that, in our push for attaining standards, we have tended to focus on outcomes that are standard for all youngsters. We want youngsters to arrive at the same place at about the same time. I would argue that really good schools increase variance in student performance. Really good schools increase the variance *and* raise the mean. The reason I say that is because, when youngsters can play to their strengths, those whose aptitudes are in, say, mathematics are going to go faster and further in that area than youngsters whose aptitudes are in some other field. But in those other fields, those youngsters would go faster and further than those whose aptitudes are in math. Merely by conceiving of a system of educational organization that regards productive variance as something to be valued and pursued, we undermine the expectation that everybody should be moving in lockstep through a series of 10-month years in a standardized system and coming out at pretty much the same place by age 18.

Part of our press toward standardization has to do with what is inherent in our age-graded school system. Age-graded systems work on the assumption that children remain more alike than different over time and that we should be teaching within the general expectations for any particular grade. Yet, if you examine reading performance, for example, the average range of reading ability in an ordinary classroom approximates the grade level. Thus at the second grade, there is a two-year spread; at the third grade, a three-year range: at the fourth grade, a four-year range. Consider how various the picture would be if performance in four or five different fields of study were examined. Children become more different as they get older, and we ought to be promoting those differences and at the same time working to escalate the mean.

Does a more enlightened grasp of what matters in schools put us in a better position to improve them? I hope so. What I have argued here is intended to divert our focus away from what we normally use to make judgments about the quality of schools and redirect it instead toward the processes, conditions, and culture that are closer to the heart of education. I am unabashedly endorsing the promotion of improvisation, surprise, and diversity of outcomes as educational virtues that we ought to try to realize through our teaching.

The point of the questions I have raised is to provide something better than the blinkered vision of school quality that now gets front-page coverage in our newspapers. Perhaps this vision serves best those in positions of privilege. Perhaps our society needs losers so it can have winners. Whatever the case, I believe that those of us who wish to exercise leadership in education must do more than simply accept the inadequate criteria that are now used to determine how well our schools are doing.

We need a fresh and humane vision of what schools might become because what our schools become has everything to do with what our children and our culture will become. I have suggested some of the features and some of the questions that I believe matter educationally. We need reform efforts that are better than those we now have. The vision of education implicit in what I have described here is just a beginning.

## Notes

\* A version of this article was presented as the Boisi Lecture at Boston College, April 2000.

1 The document that most directly expresses this view is National Commission on Excellence in Education. *A Nation at Risk: The Imperative for Educational Reform* (Washington, DC: US Government Printing Office, 1983).

2 Donald Schön describes the process of rationalization of behavior as "technical rationality." See Donald Schön, *The Reflective Practitioner: How Professionals Think in Action* (New York: Basic Books, 1983). Nor is this the first time technically rational approaches to planning and assessment have dominated schooling. The efficiency movement in American schools – from about 1913 to about 1930 – is one example. The behavioral objectives and accountability movements of the 1960s and 1970s are two more.

3 For a discussion of issues pertaining to the quantification and use of standards, see Elliot W. Eisner, "Standards for American Schools: Help or Hindrance?," *Phi Delta Kappan*, June 1995, pp. 758–764.

4 One of the foremost philosophical constructivists is John Dewey. The concept of interaction was a central notion in his philosophy of mind and in his conception of the educational process. For a succinct view of his ideas pertaining to education, see John Dewey, *Experience and Education* (New York: Macmillan, 1938).

5 David Tyack, *The One Best System* (Cambridge, MA: Harvard University Press, 1974).

6 League tables not only affect the priorities of the school, they are a major influence on real estate values. The value of houses is influenced significantly by perceptions of the quality of the schools in a neighborhood, and test scores are the indices used to determine such quality.

7 For a full discussion of the processes of observation and disclosure as they pertain to teaching and its improvement, see my book *The Enlightened Eye: Qualitative Inquiry and the Enhancement of Educational Practice* (New York: Macmillan, 1991).

8 For an insightful and lucid discussion of the pressures secondary school students experience in the high-stakes environment that we have created in schools, see Denise Pope, "Doing School" (Doctoral dissertation, Stanford University, 1998).

9 John Dewey, *Art as Experience* (New York: Minton, Balch & Co., 1934), especially chapter 13.

10 J. P. Guilford, *The Nature of Human Intelligence* (New York: McGraw-Hill, 1967).

11 Elliot W. Eisner, "Forms of Understanding and the Future of Educational Research," *Educational Researcher*, October 1993, pp. 5–11. Also see my book *Cognition and Curriculum Reconsidered* (New York: Teachers College Press, 1994).

12 Hannah Arendt, *The Human Condition* (Chicago, IL: University of Chicago Press, 1958).

13 For a discussion and illustration of what I call educationally interpretive exhibitions, see Elliot W. Eisner, Kelly Bass, Teresa Cotner, Tom Yacoe, and Lee Hanson, *The Educationally Interpretive Exhibition: Rethinking the Display of Student Art* (Reston, VA: National Art Education Association, 1997).

# CHAPTER 20

# FROM EPISTEME TO PHRONESIS TO ARTISTRY IN THE STUDY AND IMPROVEMENT OF TEACHING

*Teaching and Teacher Education,* 2002, 18: 375–385

This paper is about change. It is about changes in the way we think about knowledge and the kinds of knowledge teachers need to teach well. The change I will address is the shift from episteme to phronesis and from phronesis to artistry. Episteme is a term that represented, for the ancient Greeks, the discovery of knowledge; but not just any kind of knowledge. Episteme refers to what Greek philosophers regarded as true and certain knowledge. For the Greeks, to have episteme, what one believed to be the case needed to actually be the case. Put another way, if you knew something, that is, if you *really* knew something, it had to be true. False knowledge was for the Greeks an oxymoron.

Phronesis, on the other hand, refers to wise practical reasoning. Knowledge as a form of episteme in the sphere of practical life was not an option. The practical domain had a subject matter that was contingent rather than necessary. In the world of the practical, things did not, by nature, need to be the way they were; they could be otherwise. Practical matters required practical reasoning. They required phronesis. Practical reasoning is deliberative, it takes into account local circumstances, it weighs tradeoffs, it is riddled with uncertainties, it depends upon judgment, profits from wisdom, addresses particulars, it deals with contingencies, is iterative and shifts aims in process when necessary. Practical reasoning is the stuff of practical life. It is not the stuff of theoretical science. It is not enduring and it is not foundational. Its aim is to arrive at good but imperfect decisions with respect to particular circumstances.

The search for the enduring, the foundational, the really solid, in sum, the search for episteme, has been a long-standing aspiration for those seeking to build a positive science of education. Science is a prestigious practice and education has historically been a field that has suffered somewhat from its absence. Creating a form of practice built upon what is both solid and prestigious has an undeniable appeal. Today, however, our confidence in episteme is less secure that it once was. The reasons are several. Pluralism has become more salient in our approach to knowledge. We are, in general, less confident about finding the one best way, even though in some circles this ambition still lingers.

For a look back into time to learn how it once was viewed, consider the prognostications of one of the two giants of American education, Edward L. Thorndike. Writing in 1910 as the first editor of *The Journal of Educational Psychology*, Thorndike (1910) projects his vision of the promise of a science of psychology.

Thorndike (1910) writes:

> A complete science of psychology would tell every fact about everyone's intellect
> and character and behavior, would tell the cause of every change in human
> nature, would tell the result every educational force – every act of every person
> that changed any other or the person himself – would have. It would aid us to
> use human beings for the world's welfare with the same surety of the result
> that we now have when we use falling bodies or chemical elements. In pro-
> portion as we get such a science we shall become the masters of our own souls
> as we now are masters of heat and light. Progress toward such a science is
> being made.
>
> (p. 6)

Thorndike was caught up in the euphoria of the times. The social sciences were
still new and it is not uncommon for the utility of new tools to be initially over-
estimated. Today, I think, we have become more realistic, at least I hope so.

But just what are the traditional assumptions that we have made about the conditions of knowledge? What have been the consequences of those assumptions?
How have beliefs about the conditions of knowledge changed and, most importantly, what do those changes mean for the theory, practice, and improvement of
education? Put another way, where have we been, where are we now, and what
does the present mean for the future, particularly, what does it mean for reflecting
on the role of artistry in teaching? These questions will constitute our agenda.

Let me start by describing five assumptions about the conditions of knowledge
that have long served as a foundation for research and practice in education.

First, we have regarded knowledge as having beliefs about the world that correspond to the world as it truly is. It is like putting up a mirror to nature. Given this
view, what we want to know is the way things are that are *really* the way they are
and not simply our beliefs or opinions – what the Greeks called *doxa* – about the
way they are. We seek the mirror that Rorty (1979) rejects in his book *Philosophy
and the Mirror of Nature*.

The aspiration to know the world as it truly is, is as humanly understandable as
it is intuitively reasonable. We prize the truth in all matters great or small – yet we
have learned, as Rorty and others have taught us, that we can never know that our
views correspond to anything. The correspondence theory of truth falters in the
need to know, if one is to know about correspondence, two things not one. We
would need to know the world as it truly is if we are to know if our view of it cor-
responds. And if we knew the former, we would not need to know the latter. What
we do have, as Popper (1962) suggested, is conjecture and refutation. The history
of science is, if anything, a history of changed minds. That, I believe, is an index of
its strength, not its weakness.

Second, we think about knowledge as being about what is regular and patterned and therefore predictable, not about what is unique. Knowledge production
is a nomothetic not an ideographic enterprise. This was not always the case.
During the Renaissance, interest in the particularities of the qualitative was high
but with the Enlightenment came a desire to discover the orderly, the recurrent and
to create the formalisms that described the empirical patterns of nature as abstractions in the form of ratios. Toulmin (1990), philosopher of science and historian,
describes the shift in the focus of philosophy this way:

> for Descartes and his successors, timely questions were no concern of philoso-
> phy: Instead their concern was to bring to light permanent structures underlying

all the changeable phenomena of Nature... These four changes of mind [that occurred during the Enlightenment] – from the oral to written, local to general, particular to universal, timely to timeless – were distinct: but, taken in a historical context, they had much in common, and their joint outcome exceeded what any of them would have produced by itself. All of them reflected a historical shift from *practical* philosophy, whose issues arose out of clinical medicine, juridical procedure, moral case analysis, or the rhetorical force of oral reasoning, to a *theoretical* conception of philosophy: the effects of this shift were so deep and long lasting that the revival of practical philosophy in our own day has taken many people by surprise.

(p. 34)

There is a grandness in the general, in abstraction, in theory, in the ability to tame complexity and chaos through mathematical abstractions that efficiently reduce them to theoretical essences, purified of the particularities that contaminate what is essential. It is not difficult to see why such an image appealed.

Related to the assumption that knowledge consisted of what is regular and patterned is a third assumption, namely, that genuine knowledge, episteme, is universal not local. If knowledge of the way the world works is really knowledge, the relationships one comes to know are neither fugitive nor restricted to a small corner of the world. The free fall of an object in vacuum is the same in Beijing as it is in San Francisco. When one penetrates the surface structure of appearance to get at its deep underlying mechanisms, these mechanisms are identical; they are independent of time and space. Given this view there is no such thing as local knowledge. The laws of learning, if they are laws, apply universally.

Fourth, knowledge as we have traditionally conceived of it is thought to be a value neutral description of a state of affairs. The reason is quite clear: if knowledge is a true description of what is, whatever is, is. The *is* is separated from the *ought*. In this view science does not prescribe, it does not express values, it provides an accurate picture or analysis of what is the case; fact and value reside in different mansions and the intrusion into the former by the latter can only lead to problems.

This conception of values as choices independent of those that science makes neglects, of course, the value consequences of this view itself. The idea that the method one uses, the choice of instruments, beliefs about the nature of warrant are all the result of value decisions was not considered relevant to the argument. It was almost as if someone could stand outside of a value-saturated world, that he or she could rise above the smog of daily life in order to see forever.

Fifth, knowledge was to be regarded as warranted assertion; knowledge was declarative. To know something you needed to be able to put it into propositions, something that was testable. The verifiability of belief was critical as a certification of genuine knowledge, and as a way to expose impostors. Looked at another way, the limits of cognition were very much defined by the limits of language and this view led some to conclude that thinking itself was, of necessity, made possible by language. This, in turn, led to the even stranger notion that what you could not say, you could not know – so much for tacit knowledge (Polanyi, 1966), like knowing how to ride a bicycle, or knowing that you loved someone, or knowing what autumn feels like when the weather is crisp and the scent of burning leaves perfumes the air.

The centrality of language to knowledge was made most explicit by the language analysts of the Oxford school in the 1940s and 1950s. Alfred Jules Ayer's doctoral thesis, *Language, Truth, and Logic* (n.d.) made the case about as well as any philosophical work. Although in his more mature years he acknowledged that almost all of what he had written about these matters in his earlier days was wrong, Ayers set the pace and helped define a climate that did and still does shape our conception of what it means to know. Episteme is with us still, not as strong as it once was but not dead either.

Well, what have these five assumptions about knowledge, that is, about the possibility of episteme, meant for education? What have been the practical and conceptual consequences of the belief that knowledge was not the same as belief, that knowledge reveals regularities not uniqueness, that knowledge was universal, not local, that knowledge was separable from values, and that knowledge depended on language for its very existence? Let me describe a few of those consequences and then go on to talk about the changes that have been taking place, changes that provide a place for phronesis – and more, for artistry.

## The consequences of assumptions about knowledge for education

Consider the consequences for the practice of research. One of those consequences was rooted in the model that educational research was to emulate. The model selected was experimental physics. Experimental physics was attractive for several reasons. It depended upon measurement and thus could claim to be objective. It was experimental and therefore could make things happen, something that educators wanted to do. It put a premium on control so that explanation was possible, something that was believed important if there was to be a genuine science of education and not merely a set of routines that might work in school but whose effects were not understood. Finally, physics was high-status science, an example of naturwischenschaft, not geisteswischenschaft; the natural sciences, not the arts and humanities provided the methodological ideal.

A second consequence of this model was to regard the university as the place where knowledge was discovered and the school as the place where it was applied. The university would be the location for discovery, these discoveries would then be passed on to educational extension workers, who like agricultural extension workers, would bring them to eager teachers who would, with alacrity, use the suggested practices in their classrooms. Or so it seems.

This relationship between the work of professors and the work of teachers reflects the distinction Glazer (Schon, 1983) makes between major and minor professions. Major professions generate theory or are governed by it. Teaching, like social work and other practical fields whose aims are ambiguous, is a minor profession. Education, especially in the university, is low status.

A third consequence was to regard what Guba (personal communication) calls the *true experiment* as a methodological ideal for discovering the laws of learning. The true experiment was an effort to create an experiment having both internal and external validity. To do this subjects in the experimental and control groups had to be matched or randomly assigned and all sources of confounding needed to be controlled, while at the same time experimental conditions prescribed by the theory from which they were derived were employed, thus serving as a test of the theory.

It became clear that even if such controls were achieved in the experiment, they would be unlikely to be replicated in the school or classroom; classrooms and schools simply were messy and unpredictable. Raising kids and raising corn were not the same and the vacuums that were possible in the physics laboratory had no counterpart in schools. The model itself was problematic. Furthermore, context differences, differences in what was being taught, differences in aptitude and interest among students, in their prior experience and innumerable other factors, produced such significant interactions that assumptions about additivity – the assumption that an experimental treatment had an equal effect on each student – were themselves doubtful.

Related to the aspiration to create, for education, a true experiment was the image that science proceeds brick by brick and that eventually when every brick is in place an edifice of knowledge will have been constructed. The brick metaphor is telling. Bricks are modular units. They can be wrapped and stored and shipped. They are interchangeable. Knowledge framed in the image of a brick is material, it is an object, a noun, something that can be sent and delivered something countable, it is an image that allows us to say as we do so often that knowledge doubles every 20 years. A unit is eminently countable. But is knowledge a unit – really? Not for Kuhn (1962), who regards significant progress in science as the result of seeing the world in new ways and therefore being able to ask new questions. What changes are not the number of bricks, but the character of paradigms.

The saliency of a physical science oriented social science gave pride of place to theory and to the holders of theory; professors, not grade school teachers. Teachers were led to believe that if they only understood the theory everything would be all right. And if they could not understand the theory, there was, as Tyack (1974) points out, a single best method that they could use. From 1913 to the early 1930s, scientific management (Callahan, 1962) provided one putative solution to the problem of creating effective schools; the theory laden classes of professors of education provided the other. In these classes little to no attention was paid to the use of practical examples that illustrated through video, films, and case studies the application of the theoretical ideas that were being taught. The assumption, at least the tacit assumption, was that theory would do it all and that the application from the theoretical to the practical would pretty much take care of itself. This assumption and this practice still typifies many classrooms in teacher preparation.

Related to the saliency of the theoretical was the image of the teacher as a scientific problem-solver. The teacher was, it seems, at his or her professional best, engaged in scientific problem solving. The professional teacher was someone who was to exude a technical rationality (Schon, 1983); little or no attention was devoted towards exploration of the artistic or the aesthetic features of teaching. The model of human rationality was the scientist, not the artist.

Given the idealized state of science, it is not surprising that researchers looked for the one best method. If teaching could, as they say, be gotten down to a science, both efficiency and effectiveness would be achieved. Cool rationality would prevail.

It is important to note that the cool rationality and search for the one best method was a caricature of science. The practice of science is itself an art pervaded by passion, dependent upon imagination, filled with uncertainty, and often motivated by the challenge and joy of the journey. It is not the application of sanitized routines that teachers were to use as a way to carry on in the classroom.

Looking back, the pursuit of episteme – the search for true and certain knowledge – has had a number of consequences for the study and improvement of education. First was an inveterate reliance upon theory in a field in which theory is limited and a belief that once the laws of teaching and learning were discovered, improved practice would follow. Second, educational reform efforts were to come from the research efforts of university professors who at that time had ready access to elementary and secondary classrooms. Third, the image of what it meant to be a professional teacher was analogized to that of a professional pilot. Teaching was seen as a process of knowing what routines to use when needed and these routines were the routines that research provided. Fourth, the idea that teachers had what Atkin (1992) calls insider knowledge, that could not be translated into scientific language, and that scientific psychology was of limited use in teaching was seldom taken into account except by a few scholars – James (1958) in his talks to teachers being one. Most of those voices were located at the margins of the field.

## What has changed and what it means for education

What has changed? And what do these changes mean? Let me describe some of the more important changes and then go on to discuss their meaning for education. First, the tidy distinction between knowledge as episteme and belief as *doxa* is a lot less clear than it used to be. Episteme in the Greek sense as true and certain knowledge, writes Toulmin (Eisner, 1991), was always an unrealistic aspiration. But let him speak for himself. Toulmin writes:

> All of our scientific explanations and critical readings start from, embody, and imply some interpretive standpoint, conceptual framework, or theoretical perspective. The relevance and adequacy of our explanations can never be demonstrated with Platonic rigor of geometric necessity. (Not to mince matters, episteme was always too much to ask.) Instead, the operative question is, which of our positions are rationally warranted, reasonable, or defensible – that is, well founded rather than groundless opinions, sound *doxai* rather than shaky ones?
>
> (p. 51)

The implications of this shift from the search for immutable Truth to a conception of knowledge that recognizes that all we will ever have are ideas about the world whose truth value is itself dependent upon the opinions of others – the critical communities to which our ideas are sent through conversations, journals, books, and speeches – makes our ideas about the world more tentative. It should also make us more modest. This realization should, in addition, help us realize that mind and matter cannot be uncoupled. What we make of a classroom, a school, or a teacher's work is what *we* make of it. As Jackson (1992) reminds us, the perception of classrooms is a reading, an interpretation. We *make* meaning.

This should not be interpreted to mean that any making is as good as any other. It does mean that how good a making is subject to debate and that at present the criteria for goodness have become more diversified than they once were.

This diversification is itself due to a growing realization that science, as wonderful as it is, has no monopoly on knowledge. In about 350 BC Aristotle pointed out in his Physics that there were different kinds of knowledge – theoretical, practical, and productive – each defined by the nature of the subject matter it addresses. Aristotle, unlike Plato who put knowledge on a continuum, called our attention to a pluralistic conception of what it means to know, a conception that is represented in modern times by the work of philosophers such as Cassirer (1961), Langer (1976), Polanyi (1966), and Goodman (1978).

The realization that there are many ways in which human understanding is enlarged gives emphasis to the constructed character of knowledge. Indeed, constructivism, among the most important and widely held philosophic views among educators, specifically recognizes the interactive nature of all human experience.

What we have learned is that knowledge is the creation of an inventive mind interacting with a universe which itself is a part of what humans construe in the process of interaction. This view has double-edged consequences. First, it confers a sense of freedom upon us as inquirers to invent forms of explanation that satisfy our rationality; in a sense, we become creators. Second, the price we pay for freedom is the loss of security that a foundationalist conception of knowledge makes possible. With a belief in the possibility of finding immutable laws of one kind or another comes a kind of reassurance that there is something really solid, as Goodman (1978) says, underneath. To say none of these laws exist save those we ourselves fashion is to gain freedom, but also to give up the comforts of the nearly certain. From my perspective, the quest for certainty is long gone.

We have also learned that the choice of symbolic forms, what I have called in my own writing forms of representation (Eisner, 1993), influences more than we have previously realized, not only what one is able to say, but also what one is able to see. We seek what we are able to find. This realization is especially important for those who do case study. Narrative, for example, makes use of a form of language in which *how* something is said influences what Saussure (1974) calls the said, that is, the meaning beneath the saying. Thus narrative, or film, or drama, or video, or combinations of the foregoing make possible meanings that can expand our understanding of what we seek to comprehend. Images in the hands of an artist make it possible for us to apprehend what we wish to comprehend. Put as simply as I can, permission to use new tools and new forms of representation enables us to look for different things and to ask new questions (Eisner, 1993).

What is also changed is the realization that the general also resides within the particular and that the process of generalizing takes more than one form. We generalize all the time without random selection; we engage in what Stake (1980) and Donmoyer (1990) call naturalistic generalization. What we have learned is that we can treat the lessons learned from case studies as anticipatory schemata that facilitate our search processes, for a case is not only about itself but an example of things like it. Put into a more literary form, Steinbeck's (1945) *Grapes of Wrath* is about much more than the American depression in the 1930s, Macbeth (Shakespeare, 1958) is about more than the travails of the thane of Glamis who lived in Scotland in 1606, and *Street Corner Society* (Whyte, 1993) is about far more than the Italians in Boston in the 1940s. What we have learned is that there is more than one way to find out about the educational world, that the forms through which that world is described are not passive, that no particular method or family of methods owns the ways in which understanding can be advanced. We have learned that research itself is an umbrella concept and that science is *one* of its species.

These developments upon which the growing interest in case study rests have complicated our methodological lives and have created both tensions and uncertainties regarding the meaning and utility of different forms of research; indeed, the meaning of research itself is in a process of reconstruction. Questions propagate. When foundationalism is lost, what do we do with the notion of objectivity? When paradigms proliferate, what do we do with relativism? When warranted assertability is regarded as but one way in which our understanding can be revealed, what do we do with verification procedures? How shall we know if we are wrong? When literary forms and narrative are permissible, what do we do with threats to referential precision? When the constructed character of knowledge is recognized, how shall we deal with distinctions between fact and fiction? And given all of this diversity, who is competent to judge the quality of the research? What criteria should be used?

Despite these uncertainties there is little appetite to go back to more secure days; the prospects ahead are too exciting, the methods now possible too appealing. The social balance has changed. Teachers, for example, are not regarded now as those who implement the prescriptions of others but as those most intimate with life in classrooms; partnerships with professors are possible, but the professor is no longer the boss. Teachers are collaborators in knowledge construction and bring to the table of deliberation a kind of insider knowledge, say, of the second grade, that most professors do not possess. Teachers have what some call lived experience (Connolly and Clandinin, 1988). The body is now considered a source of understanding: some things you can understand only through your ability to feel. Knowledge, at least a species of knowledge, has become embodied. It is intimate. To know has taken on a biblical meaning.

The ability to deal with what might be called the dynamics of practical situations, as I have indicated, is what the Greeks called phronesis. Phronesis is a kind of morally pervaded practical wisdom. It could be acquired by a phronimos, a practically wise person, through experience. But experience takes time. Phronesis could not be taught like geometry. It did not submit to didactic procedures. Phronesis addresses the particularity of things and situations, it addresses their distinctive conditions so that someone could decide how to move in a morally framed direction.

What is important for educational theory, in general, and the improvement of teaching, in particular, regarding phronesis is the recognition of the importance of particularity. Educational research, like other scientific efforts, has attempted to draw conclusions that held up across contexts. With the advent of Schwab's (1969) important essay on the practical, the ground shifted. Those interested in curriculum matters and in teaching began to recognize that the conditions teachers addressed were each distinctive. As a result, abstract theory about general relationships would be of limited value. Each child needed to be known individually, at least as far as possible. Each situation, even in the same classroom, was unique. It was a grasp of these distinctive features that the teacher needed, not in order to produce knowledge about teaching but, rather, to make good decisions in the classroom. Aristotle writes,

> Now each man judges well the things he knows, and of these he is a good judge. And so the man who has been educated in a subject is a good judge of that subject, and the man who has received an all-round education is a good judge in general. Hence a young man is not a proper hearer of lectures on political science; for he is inexperienced in the actions that occur in life, but its discussions start from these and are about these; and, further, since he tends to follow his passions, his study will be vain and unprofitable, because the end aimed at is not knowledge but action. And it makes no difference whether he is young in years or youthful in character; the defect does not depend on time, but on his living, and pursuing each successive object, as passion directs. For to such persons, as to the incontinent, knowledge brings no profit; but to those who desire and act in accordance with a rational principal knowledge about such matters will be of great benefit.
>
> (McKeon, 1941, pp. 936–937)

Aristotle tells us that time and experience are required. But what kind of experience and how is it acquired? How does one learn to become a phronimos? If phronesis cannot be taught explicitly, how is it secured? A part of the answer is through deliberation with others. Practical problems are vexing. They traffic in trade-offs. They are riddled with a variety of possible solutions, each of which is likely to create other problems. Deliberation is a way of exploring meta-cognitively those possibilities and their likely consequences. The current interest in teachers deliberating with teachers is an example of a professional practice that can refine phronesis. It can do so by creating a context where multiple interpretations and analyses are likely. Such contexts liberate one from a monocular perspective and a single interpretation. In addition, in the process teachers can strengthen their sense of community by joint deliberation.

When particularity becomes salient and the aims of the teacher become differentiated from the aims of the researcher – the researcher seeks to know theoretically, the teacher seeks to make good choices – a new frame emerges for reflecting on the role of the practical in the locations in which phronesis lives. In a sense, with the recognition of the importance of the practical we became a bit more modest in our ambitions; it is not likely we will have a break-through of the kind produced in physics in the social sciences and certainly not in the field of education. Perhaps, some ponder, we need a new conception, one more congenial to the phenomena with which we in education are concerned.

As important as this new conception was in reframing what was intellectually relevant for those who needed to act, not even phronesis is adequate for achieving excellence in teaching. The missing ingredient pertains to the *crafting* of action, to the rhetorical features of language, to the skill displayed in guiding interactions, to the selection and description of an apt example. In short, what is missing is artistry. One might be able to assess a situation quite well and still be inept at execution. Teaching profits from – no, requires at its best – artistry. Artistry requires sensibility, imagination, technique, and the ability to make judgments about the feel and significance of the particular. Interestingly, in the seven and a half pound *Third Handbook of Research on Teaching* (Wittrock, 1986), amidst hundreds of pages and several hundred references, not one is directed to artistry in teaching.

What has also changed is that teaching is no longer seen as a kind of applied social science, although there may be such applications in it. Good teaching depends upon artistry and aesthetic considerations. It is increasingly recognized that teaching in many ways is more like playing in a jazz quartet than following the score of a marching band. Knowing when to come in and take the lead, knowing when to bow out, knowing when to improvise are all aspects of teaching that follow no rule, they need to be felt. Much of good teaching is like that.

There is another sense in which artistry is important in teaching and that sense has to do with the place of aesthetic experience in its pursuit. To understand what teachers do, one needs to understand where they receive their satisfactions, what gives them their highs in teaching. Teachers craft experience by shaping the environment that both students and teachers share. This environment, in turn, shapes how teachers and students interact. The quality of that interaction is influenced, in the main, by the moves the teacher makes, by the plans the teacher designs, and by matters of timing, manner, and tone. All of these are qualitative matters that are informed in part by theory, but in the context of action played out also by feel, in real time on the spot. When it goes well, we call it aesthetic. There is a sense of pride in craft.

As you have probably realized, the quality of life and the sources of action I am describing now have moved from phronesis to artistry, a concept related to what Aristotle referred to as productive, as contrasted with practical knowledge. Productive *knowledge* refers to knowing how to make something. I want to extend the process of making from the making of physical objects to the making of ideas and to the way they are expressed.

Practical knowledge is deliberative and reflective. It can be personal, as in a conversation with one's self, or it can be social, something engaged in with others. The image of the practical and the meditative features of the deliberative are surely fitting for much of teaching. Reflection and deliberation suggest the comparison of alternative courses of action and the estimation of their potential costs and benefits. Practical reasoning is iterative, there is a sense of action and correction, of trying things out, of making choices and engaging in tradeoffs. Phronesis is riddled with the deliberative. Its aim is to make wise decisions.

As fitting as this conception seems for a part of what teachers do, it surely is not all that they do. Teaching is also the making of something – clear explanations, the motivation of children, knowing when and how to change the subject, for example. These actions are typically made in flight. They are more immediate than deliberative. These in-flight actions of the teacher are matters of artistry, of acting on the sense of rightness – rightness of fit, Goodman (1978) calls it. No conception of teaching can be adequate without attention to the ways in which such processes function and no teacher education program will be optimally effective that neglects their cultivation. How such forms of action might be developed brings me to the final section of my remarks.

As is apparent, my discussion has moved from the field's interest in the discovery of the bricks of knowledge from which pedagogical routines could be deduced, to a view of teaching based upon practical reasoning, to a conception of human action rooted in artistry and guided by the feel, the aesthetics of experience. The first orientation, episteme, seeks to discover the regularities of nature as they truly are. These discovered regularities are believed to yield science-based "best practices." The second, phronesis, seeks to prepare practitioners who can use their professional wisdom in local and always unique circumstances, and the third, the productive, treats teaching as a making and holds that anything made can be made well and that making things well constitutes the central aims of an art. The implications of the first view leads, at its most powerful, to what has been called teacher-proof methods, the implications of the second to the preparation of reflective practitioners. But what of the third? What does it imply for teaching, its improvement, and indeed for the study of practice?

At least one implication seems clear: when artistry in teaching becomes an ideal towards which teachers strive, the conditions used to enhance artistry in other fields become relevant resources for thinking about the improvement of teaching. What does this mean practically? It means that teachers will be able to discuss with others their performance as teachers. It means that those who discuss their teaching with them will have the skills needed to see what is subtle and significant about the teaching they observe. It means that those who engage in such discussions will need to have a language to talk about what they see. It means that the school will have the institutional norms to make such professional relationships a routine part of the way in which professionals work. This means, in turn, that schools will have teaching studios, one-way glass, and time for consultation. It means that teacher education institutions will need to provide opportunities for students to learn how to participate in sessions that provide critiques of their work. And it means that we should expect that, like every other art, each teacher would confer his or her own distinctive signature to the art of teaching. It means that different teachers will be good at different things in different ways. It means that the metaphor of the studio is at least as appropriate for the preparation of teachers as the laboratory.

These consequences are a far cry from current approaches to school reform, what is sometimes referred to as "Standards-Driven Reform."

How to sum up? Let me do it this way. Episteme was not only an unrealistic aim, it also limited what could be studied. Phronesis, the development of wise practical reasoning, is better suited to what teachers do and need. But even phronesis, as reasonable and relevant as it is, does not give us all that we need to know to understand and promote excellence in teaching. We also need to understand artistry, that is, how people learn to make things well. Artistry is most likely when we acknowledge its relevance to teaching and create the conditions in schools in which teachers can learn to think like artists.

This agenda is a formidable one. Current institutional norms often make it difficult to have access to classrooms. The professional isolation to which many teachers have become accustomed will need to change. To change these conditions both those who work in the schools and those who work in universities must come to realize that the long-term heart of teacher education is not primarily the university, it is the workplace, the school, the place in which teachers spend the better part of their lives. The college and university have an important role to play in teacher education, but it cannot be the long-term heart of teacher education. We need a changed view of schooling. Such a changed view is something of a revolution. It is a revolution in assumptions and practice.

If the change in assumptions about what schools might become represents revolution, the creation of schools in which the growth of teachers is taken seriously will require evolution: it will take time to learn how to create them. To create such places a new kind of school culture will have to be crafted, a culture that cares as much about the growth of teachers as the growth of students. I mentioned the word culture. You know what a culture is. A culture in the biological sense is a medium for growing things. A culture in the anthropological sense is a shared way of life. Schools need to create a shared way of life that provides a medium for growing teachers, for ultimately the growth of students will go no farther than the growth of those who teach them.

## References

Atkin, M. Teaching as Research: An Essay. *Teaching and Teacher Education* 8(4): 381–390; 1992.

Callahan, R. *Education and the Cult of Efficiency*. Chicago, IL: University of Chicago Press, 1962.

Cassirer, E. *The Philosophy of Symbolic Forms*. New Haven, CT: Yale University Press, 1961.

Connolly, M. and Clandinin, D. J. *Teachers as Curriculum Planners: Narratives of Experience*. New York: Teachers College Press, 1988.

Donmoyer, R. Generalizations and the Single Case Study. In E. Eisner and A. Peshkin (eds), *Qualitative Inquiry in Education*. New York: Teachers College Press, 1990.

Eisner, E. *The Enlightened Eye: Qualitative Inquiry and the Enhancement of Educational Practice*. Columbus, OH: Merrill-Prentice Hall, 1991.

Eisner, E. Forms of Understanding and the Future of Educational Research. *Educational Researcher* 22(7): 5–11; 1993.

Goodman, N. *Ways of World Making*. Indianapolis, IN: Hackett Publishing, 1978.

Jackson, P. *Untaught Lessons*. New York: Teachers College Press, 1992.

James, W. *Talks to Teachers on Psychology and to Students on Life's Ideals*. New York: Norton Publishing, 1958.

Kuhn, T. *The Structure of Scientific Revolutions*. Chicago, IL: The University of Chicago Press, 1962.

Langer, S. *Problems of Art*. New York: Scribner's Sons, 1976.

McKeon, R. *The Basic Works of Aristotle*. New York: Random House, 1941.

Polanyi, M. *The Tacit Dimension*. New York: Doubleday and Co., 1966.

Popper, K. *Conjectures and Refutations: The Growth of Scientific Knowledge*. New York: Basic Books, 1962.

Rorty, R. *Philosophy and the Mirror of Nature*. Princeton, NJ: Princeton University Press, 1979.

Saussure, F. *Course in General Linguistics*. London: Fontana, 1974.

Schon, D. *The Reflective Practitioner: How Professionals Think in Action*. New York: Basic Books, 1983.

Schwab, J. The Practical: A Language for Curriculum. *School Review* 78(5): 1–24; 1969.

Shakespeare, W. *Macbeth*. New York: Dell Publishing, 1958.

Stake, R. *Generalizations*. A paper presented at meetings of the American Educational Research Association, 1980.

Steinbeck, J. *Grapes of Wrath*. New York: Bantam Books, 1945.

Thorndike, E. L. The Contributions of Psychology to Education. *Journal of Educational Psychology* 1: 5–12; 1910.

Toulmin, S. *Cosmopolis: The Hidden Agenda of Modernity*. New York: The Free Press, 1990.

Tyack, D. *The One Best System*. Cambridge, MA: Harvard University Press, 1974.

Wittrock, M. C. (ed.) *Handbook of Research on Teaching,* 3rd edn. New York: Macmillan, 1986.

Whyte, W. F. *Street Corner Society*. Chicago, IL: The University of Chicago Press, 1993.

# CHAPTER 21

# WHAT CAN EDUCATION LEARN FROM THE ARTS ABOUT THE PRACTICE OF EDUCATION?*

*Journal of Curriculum and Supervision*, 2002, 18(1): 4–16

Before I begin my remarks, I want to express my gratitude to the Dewey Society for inviting me to deliver this address. It's the third time I have been asked to do so. The first invitation came from the University of Chicago in 1976, the second from the Dewey Society in 1979, and the third this year. I regard the invitation as both a pleasure and a privilege. For both the pleasure and the privilege I thank you.

I want to talk with you today about what education might learn from the arts about the practice of education. In many ways the idea that education has something to learn from the arts cuts across the grain of our traditional beliefs about how to improve educational practice.

Our field, the field of education, has predicated its practices on a platform of scientifically grounded knowledge, at least as an aspiration. The arts and artistry as sources of improved educational practice are considered, at best, a fallback position, a court of last resort, something you retreat to when there is no science to provide guidance. It is widely believed that no field seeking professional respectability can depend on such an undependable source.

Despite prevailing doubts, I intend to examine what a conception of practice rooted in the arts might contribute to the improvement of both the means and ends of education. What I want to do is to foreshadow the grounds for a view of education that differs in fundamental ways from the one that now prevails. To do this I will be describing the forms of thinking the arts evoke and their relevance for reframing our conception of what education might try to accomplish. To secure a perspective for the analysis, let's first look at the historical context within which our current assumptions about reliable and effective practice have been based.

As we know, when, in the fourth quarter of the nineteenth century, education was coming into its own as a field of study, it received its initial guidance from psychology. It was the early psychologists who were interested in making psychology a scientific enterprise, one that emulated the work done in the so-called hard sciences. Their aim was to develop a physics of psychology – what they called psychophysics – and, consistent with their mission, they made laboratories rather than studios the venues for their work.[1] People like Galton in England and Helmholtz and Fechner in Germany were among its leaders, and even William James, Charles Spearman, and G. Stanley Hall made passage to Europe to learn the secrets and methods of those seeking to create a science of the mind. One example of the faith placed in a science of psychology can be found in Edward L. Thorndike's 1910 lead article in the *Journal of Educational Psychology*.

He writes:

> A complete science of psychology would tell every fact about everyone's intellect and character and behavior, would tell the cause of every change in human nature, would tell the result every educational force – every act of every person that changed any other or the person himself – would have. It would aid us to use human beings for the world's welfare with the same surety of the result that we now have when we use falling bodies or chemical elements. In proportion as we get such a science we shall become the masters of our own souls as we now are masters of heat and light. Progress toward such a science is being made.[2]

Thorndike's optimism was not shared by all. James and Dewey, for example, had reservations regarding what science could provide to so artful an enterprise as teaching. Nevertheless, by the end of the first quarter of the twentieth century, the die was cast. Except for some independent schools, Thorndike won and Dewey lost.[3] Metaphorically speaking, schools were to become effective and efficient manufacturing plants. Indeed, the language of manufacture was a part of the active vocabulary of Thorndike, Taylor, Cubberly, and others in the social efficiency movement. In their vision of education, students were raw material to be processed according to specifications prescribed by supervisors trained in Fredrick Taylor's time and motion study.[4]

I suspect that even teachers working during the first quarter of the twentieth century could not be coaxed into employing wholeheartedly the Taylorisms that were prescribed. Yet for many, especially for those in school administration, the managed and hyper-rationalized educational world that Fredrick Taylor envisioned became the methodological ideal needed to create effective and efficient schools.[5]

The influence of psychology on education had another fallout. In the process, science and art became estranged. Science was considered dependable; the artistic process was not. Science was cognitive; the arts were emotional. Science was teachable; the arts required talent. Science was testable; the arts were matters of preference. Science was useful; the arts were ornamental. It was clear to many then, as it is to many today, which side of the coin mattered. As I said, one relied on art when there was no science to provide guidance. Art was a fallback position.

These beliefs and the vision of education they adumbrate are not altogether alien to the contemporary scene. We live at a time that puts a premium on the measurement of outcomes, on the ability to predict them, and on the need to be absolutely clear about what we want to accomplish. To aspire for less is to court professional irresponsibility. We like our data hard and our methods stiff – we call it rigor.

From a social perspective, it is understandable why tight controls, accountability in terms of high-stakes testing, and the pre-specification of intended outcomes – standards, they are called – should have such attractiveness. When the public is concerned about the educational productivity of its schools, the tendency – and it is a strong one – is to tighten up, to mandate, to measure, and to manage. The teacher's ability to exercise professional discretion is likely to be constrained when the public has lost confidence in its schools.

It does not require a great leap of imagination or profound insight to recognize that the values and visions that have driven education during the first quarter of the twentieth century are reappearing with a vengeance today. We look for "best methods" as if they were independent of context; we do more testing than any nation on earth; we seek curriculum uniformity so parents can compare their schools with other schools, as if test scores were good proxies for the quality of education. We would like nothing more than to get teaching down to a science even though the conception of science being employed has little to do with what science is about. What we are now doing is creating an industrial culture in our schools, one whose values are brittle and whose conception of what's important narrow. We flirt with payment by results, we pay practically no attention to the idea that engagement in school can and should provide intrinsic satisfactions, and we exacerbate the importance of extrinsic rewards by creating policies that encourage children to become point collectors. Achievement has triumphed over inquiry. I think our children deserve more.

The technically rationalized industrial culture I speak of did not begin with psychology; it began with the Enlightenment. The move by Galileo from attention to the qualitative to a focus on the quantification of relationships was, as Dewey points out, not merely a modification in method; it was a conceptual revolution.[6] It represented a fundamental shift in the way the world was viewed and represented. According to philosopher and historian of science Stephen Toulmin, the shift was from attention to the timely to attention to the timeless, from an emphasis on the oral to an emphasis on the written, from attention to the particular to the pursuit of the universal.[7]

The calculation of relations and the search for order represented the highest expression of our rationality. The ability to use what one learned about nature in order to harness it to our will was another. Rationality during the Enlightenment was closer in spirit to the proportions of the Parthenon than to the expressive contours of the Sistine ceiling. This search for order, this desire for efficiency, this need to control and predict were then and are today dominant values. They are values that pervaded the industrial revolution, and they are values that reside tacitly beneath current efforts at school reform. Current educational policy expressed in President Bush's $26 billion educational reform agenda is an effort to create order, to tidy up a complex system, to harness nature, so to speak, so that our intentions can be efficiently realized.

There is, of course, virtue in having intentions and the ability to realize them. What is troublesome is the push towards uniformity – uniformity in aims, uniformity in content, uniformity in assessment, uniformity in expectation. Of course, for technocrats uniformity is a blessing; it gets rid of complications – or so it is believed. Statistics can be a comfort; they abstract the particular out of existence. For example, we comfort ourselves in the belief that we are able to describe just what every 4th grader should know and be able to do by the time they leave the 4th grade. To do this we reify an image of an average 4th grader. Of course, very few policymakers have ever visited Ms Purtle's 4th grade classroom, where they might encounter redheaded Mickey Malone. Mickey is no statistic. As I said, particulars like Mickey Malone complicate life, but they also enrich it.

The point of my remarks thus far is to identify the roots of the increasingly technicized cognitive culture in which we operate. This culture is so ubiquitous we hardly see it. And it is so powerful that even when we do recognize it, too few of us say anything. What President Bush has said about our students also applies to us: when the bandwagon starts rolling, we too don't want to be left behind.

As you can tell, I am not thrilled with the array of values and assumptions that drive our pursuit of improved schools. I am not sure we can tinker towards Utopia and get there. Nor do I believe we can mount a revolution. What we can do is to generate other visions of education, other values to guide its realization, other assumptions on which a more generous conception of the practice of schooling can be built. That is, although I do not think revolution is an option, ideas that inspire new visions, values, and especially new practices are. It is one such vision, one that cuts across the grain, that I wish to explore with you today.

The contours of this new vision were influenced by the ideas of Sir Herbert Read, an English art historian, poet, and pacifist working during the middle of the last century.[8] He argued, and I concur, that the aim of education ought to be conceived of as the preparation of artists. By the term "artist," neither he nor I mean necessarily painters and dancers, poets and playwrights. We mean individuals who have developed the ideas, the sensibilities, the skills, and the imagination to create work that is well proportioned, skillfully executed, and imaginative, regardless of the domain in which an individual works. The highest accolade we can confer upon someone is to say that he or she is an artist, whether as a carpenter or a surgeon, a cook or an engineer, a physicist or a teacher. The fine arts have no monopoly on the artistic.

I further want to argue that the distinctive forms of thinking needed to create artistically crafted work are relevant not only to what students do, they are relevant to virtually all aspects of what we do, from the design of curricula, to the practice of teaching, to the features of the environment in which students and teachers live.

What are these distinctive forms of thinking, these artistically rooted qualitative forms of intelligence? Let me describe six of them for you and the way they might play out in school.

Consider first the task of working on a painting, a poem, a musical score. That task requires, perhaps above all else, the ability to compose qualitative relationships that satisfy some purpose. That is, what a composer composes are relationships among a virtually infinite number of possible sound patterns. A painter has a similar task. The medium and sensory modality differ, but the business of composing relationships remains. To succeed the artist needs to see, that is, to experience the qualitative relationships that emerge in his or her work and to make judgments about them.

Making judgments about how qualities are to be organized does not depend upon fealty to some formula; there is nothing in the artistic treatment of a composition like the making and matching activity in learning to spell or learning to use algorithms to prove basic arithmetic operations. In spelling and in arithmetic, there are correct answers, answers whose correctness can be proven. In the arts, judgments are made in the absence of rule. Of course, there are styles of work that do serve as models for work in the various arts, but what constitutes the right qualitative relationships for any particular work is idiosyncratic to the particular work. The temperature of a color might be a tad too warm, the edge of a shape might be a bit too sharp, the percussion might need to be a little more dynamic. What the arts teach is that attention to such matters, matters. The arts teach students to act and to judge in the absence of rule, to rely on feel, to pay attention to nuance, to act and appraise the consequences of one's choices, and to revise and then to make other choices. Getting these relationships right requires what Nelson Goodman calls "rightness of fit."[9] Artists and all who work with the composition of qualities try to achieve a "rightness of fit."

Given the absence of a formula or an algorithm, how are judgments about rightness made? I believe they depend upon somatic knowledge, the sense of closure that the good gestalt engenders in embodied experience; the composition *feels* right. Work in the arts cultivates the modes of thinking and feeling that I have described; one cannot succeed in the arts without such cognitive abilities. Such forms of thought integrate feeling and thinking in ways that make them inseparable. One knows one is right because one feels the relationships. One modifies one's work and feels the results. The sensibilities come into play and in the process become refined. Another way of putting it is that as we learn in and through the arts, we become more qualitatively intelligent.

Learning to pay attention to the way in which form is configured is a mode of thought that can be applied to all things made, theoretical or practical. How a story is composed in the context of the language arts, how a historian composes her argument, how a scientific theory is constructed, all of these forms of human creation profit from attention to the way the elements that constitute them are configured. We need to help students learn to ask not only what someone is *saying*, but how someone has *constructed* an argument, a musical score, or a visual image. Curriculum activities can be designed that call attention to such matters, activities that refine perception in each of the fields we teach. This will require activities that slow down perception rather than speed it up.

Much of our perception, perhaps most of it, is highly focal. We tend to look for particular things in our perceptual field. The virtue of such a mode of attention is that it enables us to find what we are looking for. The potential vice of such perception is that it impedes our awareness of relationships. The up and back movement of the visitor to the art gallery when looking at a painting is an example of an effort to secure both focal awareness and attention to configuration. Teachers perform similar activities. One of the important tasks of teaching is to be able to focus on the individual while attending to the larger classroom patterns of which the individual is a part. To complicate matters, these patterns change over time. The good teacher, like the good short-order cook, has to pay attention to several operations simultaneously, and they do.

A second lesson that education can learn from the arts pertains to the formulation of aims. In Western models of rational decision making, the formulation of aims, goals, objectives, or standards is a critical act; virtually all else that follows depends upon the belief that one must have clearly defined ends. Once ends are conceptualized, means are formulated, then implemented, and then outcomes are evaluated. If there is a discrepancy between aspiration and accomplishment, new means are formulated. The cycle continues until ends and outcomes are isomorphic. Ends are held constant and always are believed to precede means.

But is this true? In the arts it certainly is not. In the arts, ends may follow means. One may act and the act may itself suggest ends, ends that did not precede the act, but follow it. In this process ends shift; the work yields clues that one pursues. In a sense, one surrenders to what the work in process suggests. This process of shifting aims while doing the work at hand is what Dewey called "flexible purposing."[10] Flexible purposing is opportunistic; it capitalizes on the emergent features appearing within a field of relationships. It is not rigidly attached to predefined aims when the possibility of better ones emerges. The kind of thinking that flexible purposing requires thrives best in an environment in which the rigid adherence to a plan is not a necessity. As experienced teachers well know, the surest road to hell in a classroom is to stick to the lesson plan no matter what.

The pursuit, or at least the exploitation, of surprise in an age of accountability is paradoxical. As I indicated earlier, we place a much greater emphasis on prediction and control than on exploration and discovery. Our inclination to control and predict is, at a practical level, understandable, but it also exacts a price; we tend to do the things we know how to predict and control. Opening oneself to the uncertain is not a pervasive quality of our current educational environment. I believe that it needs to be among the values we cherish. Uncertainty needs to have its proper place in the kinds of schools we create.

How can the pursuit of surprise be promoted in a classroom? What kind of classroom culture is needed? How can we help our students view their work as temporary experimental accomplishments, tentative resting places subject to further change? How can we help them work at the edge of incompetence? These are some of the questions that this aim suggests we ask.

A third lesson the arts can teach education is that form and content are most often inextricable. How something is said is part and parcel of what is said. The message is in the form–content relationship, a relationship that is most vivid in the arts. To recognize the relationship of form and content in the arts is not to deny that for some operations in some fields form and content can be separated. I think of beginning arithmetic, say the addition of two numbers such as $4 + 4$. The sum of the numerals $4 + 4$ can be expressed in literally an infinite number of ways: 8, eight, //// ////, VIII, $300,000 - 299,992$, and so forth. In all of these examples, the arithmetic conclusion, 8, is the same regardless of the form used to represent it. But for most of what we do, form–content relations do matter. *How* history is written matters; *how* one speaks to a child matters; *what* a classroom looks like matters; *how* one tells a story matters. Getting it right means creating a form whose content is right for some purpose. The architecture of a school can look and feel like a factory or like a home. If we want children to feel like factory workers, our schools should look and feel like factories. Form and content matter, and in such cases are inseparable.

Indeed, the discovery that form and content are inseparable is one of the lessons the arts teach most profoundly. Change the cadence in a line of poetry and you change the poem's meaning. The creation of expressive and satisfying relationships is what artistically guided work celebrates.

In the arts there is no substitutability among elements (because there are no separate elements); in math there is. The absence of substitutability promotes attention to the particular. Developing an awareness of the particular is especially important for those of us who teach since the distinctive character of how we teach is a pervasive aspect of what we teach. The current reform movement would do well to pay more attention to the messages its policies send to students since those messages may undermine deeper educational values. The values about which I speak include the promotion of self-initiated learning, the pursuit of alternative possibilities, and the anticipation of intrinsic satisfactions secured through the use of the mind. Do we really believe that publishing league tables in the newspaper displaying school performance is a good way to understand what schools teach, or that the relentless focus on raising test scores is a good way to ensure quality education? The form we use to display data shapes its meaning.

Closely related to the form–content relationship is a fourth lesson the arts can teach education. It is this: Not everything knowable can be articulated in propositional form. The limits of our cognition are not defined by the limits of our language. We have a long philosophic tradition in the West that promotes the view that knowing anything requires some formulation of what we know in words; we need to have warrants for our assertions. But is it really the case that what we cannot assert we cannot know? Not according to Michael Polanyi, who speaks of tacit knowledge and says, "We know more than we can tell."[11] And Dewey tells us that while science states meaning, the arts express meaning. Meaning is not limited to what is assertable. Dewey goes on to say that the aesthetic cannot be separated from the intellectual, and for the intellectual to be complete it must bear the stamp of the aesthetic. Having a nose for telling questions and a feel for incisive answers are not empty metaphors.

These ideas not only expand our conception of the ways in which we know; they expand our conception of mind. They point to the cognitive frontiers that our teaching might explore. How can we help students recognize the ways in which we express and recover meaning, not only in the arts but in the sciences as well? How can we introduce them to the art of *doing* science? After all, the practice of any practice, including science, can be an art.

It's clear to virtually everyone that we appeal to expressive form to say what literal language can never say. We build shrines to express our gratitude to the heroes of 9/11 because somehow we find our words inadequate. We appeal to poetry when we bury and when we marry. We situate our most profound religious practices within compositions we have choreographed. What does our need for such practices say to us about the sources of our understanding and what do they mean for how we educate? At a time when we seem to want to package performance into standardized measurable skill sets, questions such as these seem to me to be especially important. The more we feel the pressure to standardize, the more we need to remind ourselves of what we should not try to standardize.

A fifth lesson we can learn from the arts about the practice of education pertains to the relationship between thinking and the material with which we and our students work. In the arts, it is plain that in order for a work to be created, we must think within the constraints and affordances of the medium we elect to use. The flute makes certain qualities possible that the bass fiddle will never produce, and vice versa. Painting with watercolor makes certain visual qualities possible that cannot be created with oil paint. The artist's task is to exploit the possibilities of the medium in order to realize aims he or she values. Each material imposes its own distinctive demands, and to use it well we have to learn to think within it.

Where are the parallels when we teach and when students learn in the social studies, in the sciences, in the language arts? How must language and image be treated to say what we want to say? How must a medium be treated for the medium to mediate? How do we help students get smart with the media they are invited to use, and what are the cognitive demands that different media make upon those who use them? Carving a sculpture out of a piece of wood is clearly a different cognitive task than building a sculpture out of plasticine clay. The former is a subtractive task, the latter an additive one. Getting smart in any domain requires at the very least learning to think within a medium. What are the varieties of media we help children get smart about? What do we neglect?

It seems to me that the computer has a particularly promising role to play in providing students with opportunities to learn how to think in new ways. Assuming the programs can be developed, and it is my impression that many already have been, operations are performable on the computer that cannot be executed through any other medium. New possibilities for matters of representation can stimulate our imaginative capacities and can generate forms of experience that would otherwise not exist. Indeed, the history of art itself is, in large measure, a history studded with the effects of new technologies. This has been at no time more visible than during the twentieth century. Artists have learned to think within materials such as neon tubing and plastic, day-glow color and corfam steel, materials that make forms possible that Leonardo da Vinci himself could not have conceived of. Each new material offers us new affordances and constraints, and in the process develops the ways in which we think. There is a lesson to be learned here for the ways in which we design curricula and the sorts of materials we make it possible for students to work with.

Decisions we make about such matters have a great deal to do with the kinds of minds we develop in school. Minds, unlike brains, are not entirely given at birth; minds are also forms of cultural achievement. The kinds of minds we develop are profoundly influenced by the opportunities to learn that the school provides. And this is the point of my remarks about what education might learn from the arts. The kinds of thinking I have described, and it is only a sample, represent the kind of thinking I believe schools should promote. The promotion of such thinking requires not only a shift in perspective regarding our educational aims; it represents a shift in the kind of tasks we invite students to undertake, the kind of thinking we ask them to do, and the kind of criteria we apply to appraise both their work and ours. Artistry, in other words, can be fostered by how we design the environments we inhabit. The lessons the arts teach are not only for our students; they are for us as well.

Winston Churchill once said that first we design our buildings and then our buildings design us. To paraphrase Churchill, we can say, first we design our curriculum, then our curriculum designs us. What I think many of us want is not only a form of educational practice whose features, so to speak, "design us," but a form of educational practice that enables students to learn how to design themselves. Thus it might be said that at its best, education is a process of learning how to become the architect of our own education. It is a process that does not terminate until we do.

Finally, we come to motives for engagement. In the arts, motives tend to be secured from the aesthetic satisfactions that the work itself makes possible. A part of these satisfactions is related to the challenge that the work presents. Materials resist the maker; they have to be crafted, and this requires an intense focus on the modulation of forms as they emerge in a material being processed. This focus is often so intense that all sense of time is lost. The work and the worker become one. At times it is the tactile quality of the medium that matters – its feel, the giving and resisting quality of the clay. At other times it is the changing relationships among fields of color. The arts, in a sense, are supermarkets for the senses. But the arts are far more than supermarkets for sensory gourmets. In the arts there is an idea which the work embodies. For the impressionists the idea was light; for the surrealists it was the unconscious; for the cubists it was time and space; for the American regionalists of the 1930s it was the ordinary lives of ordinary people that was celebrated. These interests provided direction to the work, but the quality of the work was always appraised by what it did within experience.

The arts are, in the end, a special form of experience; but if there is any point I wish to emphasize it is that the experience the arts makes possible is not restricted to what we call the fine arts. The sense of vitality and the surge of emotion we feel when touched by one of the arts can also be secured in the ideas we explore with students, in the challenges we encounter in doing critical inquiry, and in the appetite for learning we stimulate. In the long run, these are the satisfactions that matter most because they are the only ones that ensure, if it can be ensured at all, that what we teach students will want to pursue voluntarily after the artificial incentives so ubiquitous in our schools are long forgotten. It is in this sense especially that the arts can serve as a model for education.

The agenda I have proposed gives rise to more than a few questions. One is whether a conception of education that uses art as its regulative ideal is realistic.

Is it asking for too much? My answer is that ideals are always out of reach. It is no different for education's ideals. The arts provide the kind of ideal that I believe American education needs now more than ever. I say now more than ever because our lives increasingly require the ability to deal with conflicting messages, to make judgments in the absence of rule, to cope with ambiguity, and to frame imaginative solutions to the problems we face. Our world is not one that submits to single correct answers to questions or clear-cut solutions to problems; consider what's going on in the Middle East. We need to be able not only to envision fresh options; we need to have feel for the situations in which they appear. In a word, the forms of thinking the arts stimulate and develop are far more appropriate for the real world we live in than the tidy right-angled boxes we employ in our schools in the name of school improvement.

This brings us to the final portion of my remarks. Thus far I have tried to describe my concerns about our current efforts to use highly rationalized standardized procedures to reform education and to describe their historical roots. I then advanced the notion that genuine change depends upon a vision of education that is fundamentally different from the one that guides today's efforts at school reform. I proposed that education might well consider thinking about the aim of education as the preparation of artists, and I proceeded to describe the modes of thinking the arts evoke, develop, and refine. These forms of thinking, as I indicated earlier, relate to relationships that when acted upon require judgment in the absence of rule; they encourage students and teachers to be flexibly purposive (it's OK for aims to shift in process); they recognize the unity of form and content; they require one to think within the affordances and constraints of the medium one elects to use; and they emphasize the importance of aesthetic satisfactions as motives for work. In addition, I alluded to some of the locations in the context of schooling in which those forms of thinking might be developed.

In describing some of the forms of thinking the arts occasion, of necessity I had to fragment what is a seamless, unified process. I want, therefore, to emphasize here that I am not talking about the implementation of isolated curriculum activities, but rather the creation of a new culture of schooling that has as much to do with the cultivation of dispositions as with the acquisition of skills.

At the risk of propagating dualisms, but in the service of emphasis, I am talking about a culture of schooling in which more importance is placed on exploration than on discovery, more value is assigned to surprise than to control, more attention is devoted to what is distinctive than to what is standard, more interest is related to what is metaphorical than to what is literal. It is an educational culture that has a greater focus on becoming than on being, places more value on the imaginative than on the factual, assigns greater priority to valuing than to measuring, and regards the quality of the journey as more educationally significant than the speed at which the destination is reached. I am talking about a new vision of what education might become and what schools are for.

I want to bring my remarks to a close by reminding all of us here that visions, no matter how grand, need to be acted upon to become real. Ideas, clearly, are important. Without them change has no rudder. But change also needs wind and a sail to catch it. Without them there is no movement. Frankly, this may be the most challenging aspect of the proposal I have made. The public's perception of the purpose of education supports the current paradigm. We need to sail against the tide.

Our destination is to change the social vision of what schools can be. It will not be an easy journey, but when the seas seem too treacherous to travel and the stars too distant to touch, we should remember Robert Browning's observation that "a man's reach should exceed his grasp or what's a heaven for?"[12]

Browning gives us a moral message, one generated by the imagination and expressed through the poetic. And as Dewey said in the closing pages of *Art as Experience*, "Imagination is the chief instrument of the good." Dewey went on to say that "[a]rt has been the means of keeping alive the sense of purposes that outrun evidence and of meanings that transcend indurated habit."[13]

Imagination is no mere ornament; nor is art. Together they can liberate us from our indurated habits. They might help us restore decent purpose to our efforts and help us create the kind of schools our children deserve and our culture needs. Those aspirations, my friends, are stars worth stretching for.

## Notes

\*   Professor Eisner delivered this paper as the John Dewey Lecture of 2002 at a session of the John Dewey Society at the annual meeting of the American Educational Research Association, New Orleans, LA, on April 25, 2002.

1   Edwin Boring, *A History of Experimental Psychology*, 3rd edn (New York: Appleton Century Crofts, 1957).

2   Edward L. Thorndike, "The Contribution of Psychology to Education," *Journal of Educational Psychology*, 1 (1910), 6, 8.

3   For a lucid story of research in education see Ellen Lagemann, *An Elusive Science: The Troubling History of Educational Research* (Chicago, IL: University of Chicago Press, 2000).

4   Raymond Callahan, *Education and the Cult of Efficiency* (Chicago, IL: University of Chicago Press, 1962).

5   Ibid.

6   Stephen Toulmin, *Cosmopolis: The Hidden Agenda of Modernity* (New York: Free Press, 1990).

7   Ibid.

8   Herbert Read, *Education Through Art* (London: Pantheon, 1944).

9   Nelson Goodman, *Ways of World-making* (Indianapolis, IN: Hacket Publishing, 1978).

10   John Dewey, *Experience and Education* (New York: Macmillan and Co., 1938).

11   Michael Polanyi, *The Tacit Dimension* (London: Routledge and Kegan Paul, 1967).

12   Robert Browning, "Andrea del Sarto," in *The Norton Anthology of Poetry*, Alexander W. Allison, Margaret Ferguson, Mary Jo Salter, and Jon Stallworthy (eds) (New York: Norton, 1983).

13   John Dewey, *Art as Experience* (New York: Minton, Balch & Co., 1934), p. 348.

# INDEX